THE CLASSICS
OF **WESTERN
SPIRITUALITY**

THE CLASSICS OF WESTERN SPIRITUALITY
A Library of the Great Spiritual Masters

President and Publisher
Mark-David Janus, CSP

EDITORIAL BOARD

THE EMERGENCE OF
EVANGELICAL SPIRITUALITY

The Age of Edwards, Newton, and Whitefield

Edited and with an Introduction by
Tom Schwanda

Foreword by Mark A. Noll

Paulist Press
New York / Mahwah, NJ

Cover image: Jeff Folger / Vistaphotography

Cover and caseside design by Sharyn Banks
Book design by Lynn Else

Library of Congress Cataloging-in-Publication Data

The emergence of evangelical spirituality : the age of Edwards, Newton, and Whitefield / edited and with an introduction by Tom Schwanda ; foreword by Mark A. Noll.
        pages cm. — (The classics of Western spirituality)
    Includes bibliographical references and index.
    ISBN 978-0-8091-0621-9 (hardcover : alk. paper) — ISBN 978-1-58768-525-5 (ebook)
        1. Evangelicalism—History—18th century. 2. Evangelicalism—History—Sources. 3. Evangelicalism—Great Britain—History—18th century. 4. Evangelicalism—United States—History—18th century. 5. Church history—Sources. 6. Great Britain—Church history—18th century. 7. United States—Church history—18th century. I. Schwanda, Tom, 1950-, editor.
    BR1640.A25E44 2016
    270.09171'241—dc23

                                                                                    2015017595

ISBN 978-0-8091-0621-9 (hardcover)
ISBN 978-1-58768-525-5 (e-book)

Published by Paulist Press
997 Macarthur Boulevard
Mahwah, New Jersey 07430

www.paulistpress.com

Printed and bound in the
United States of America

CONTENTS

CONTENTS

CONTENTS

CONTENTS

CONTENTS

ABOUT THE CONTRIBUTOR

Tom Schwanda is associate professor of Christian Formation and Ministry at Wheaton College in Illinois. He teaches both undergraduate and graduate classes on the history of Christian spirituality and spiritual theology. He earned his Doctor of Ministry in Christian spirituality from Fuller Theological Seminary and his PhD in historical theology from Durham University, England. His research interests include seventeenth- and eighteenth-century spirituality. Tom is the author of *Soul Recreation: The Contemplative-Mystical Piety of Puritanism*, as well as numerous articles and book chapters on Puritanism, German Pietism, and early evangelicalism, in particular essays that examine the spirituality of George Whitefield, John Cennick, William Cowper, and the larger contemplative spirituality of early evangelicals.

FOREWORD

The Classics of Western Spirituality series has already brought a great deal of attention to Protestant spiritual writing, including the Pietist and evangelical traditions of the seventeenth and eighteenth centuries. Earlier volumes have provided well-edited selections for the Methodist founders John and Charles Wesley and for German Pietists, beginning with the initiators Philip Jakob Spener and August Hermann Francke, and including several important figures in the eighteenth century. To that general strand of Western Protestantism, Tom Schwanda has now added a wide-ranging sampling from individuals from the eighteenth-century Atlantic-wide British empire who, if they could not always see eye to eye among themselves, stood together as the recognized pioneers of a distinct form of modern spirituality.

The evangelicals featured in this volume were heirs of the Puritans, who had done much to intensify Christian life in England and the American colonies, while also destabilizing British politics and planting seeds of public moral seriousness in the new world. They also reflected the influence of continental Pietists, who had championed individual heart religion against efforts by European confessional regimes to enforce uniformity of religious belief and social practice. In addition, they expanded upon High Church Anglican movements that had promoted the small-group devotional practices and altruistic public services that later Methodists brought to a much wider population. Evangelical spirituality bore the marks of these earlier movements—as well as trajectories of influence stretching back through the Reformation to the classical trinitarianism of Western Christendom. It became distinctive, however, when a modern concentration on the responsibilities, capacities, duties, and choices of the individual believer was added to this inheritance. Personal engagement—what evangelicals often called "true religion," of necessity appropriated individually—provided the baseline for their movement.

It is, therefore, no surprise that the evangelicals' best-known figures have always been those who concentrated most powerfully on the necessity of a personal faith: George Whitefield, the grand itinerant renowned and beloved (while also notorious and disdained) for passionate preaching of the new birth; Jonathan Edwards, a brilliant theologian and philosopher but known best for a sermon designed to frighten listeners into the kingdom of God; John Wesley, a tireless encourager of personal "holiness unto the Lord"; and Charles Wesley, the troubadour of grace who wanted individuals to sing "Love divine, all loves excelling" as their personal story.

As the selections in this volume demonstrate, however, evangelical spirituality reached much further than obsession with conversion and inward-focused holiness. While evangelicals were never less than committed to evangelism and self-directed spiritual growth, their commitments also extended well beyond this signature emphasis. The selections that follow reveal a broad interest in communal spiritual practice, patient concern for the spiritual needs of others, some attention to ingredients of formal ecclesiology like the Lord's Supper, and considerable application to social service.

The book nicely illustrates this broad range of evangelical spiritual concerns through a remarkable range of literary genres. Evangelicals, of course, produced a torrent of sermons, doctrinal treatises, and admonitory tracts. Their deepest spiritual interests, however, are shown even more clearly in diaries, devotional manuals, poetry, letters, and especially hymnody. Eighteenth-century evangelicalism was always most characteristic when believers joined their voices in song. It is therefore especially fitting that the following pages contain a generous sampling of evangelical hymns, the most enduring contribution of this movement to world Christianity as a whole. Because Charles Wesley's hymns are represented in his own volume, there is more space here for full renditions of well-known hymns that are now sung in abbreviated or edited form: William Cowper's "God moves in a mysterious way"; Augustus Toplady's "Rock of ages cleft for me"; John Newton's "Amazing grace how sweet the sound"; and Isaac Watts's "When I survey the wond'rous cross," "Am I a soldier of the cross?" and "Jesus shall reign where e'er the sun." Yet, the hymns from figures less well-known—John Cennick, Joseph Hart, Anne Steele, Ann Griffiths—communicate just as well the deepest spiritual resources of the movement.

Mention of the English Baptist Anne Steele and the Welsh Anglican Ann Griffiths also points to the substantial contribution of women to early evangelicalism. As with most other religious traditions, evangelicalism was always a majority female movement, even as men took center stage in public. In this book, representative selections from women reflect the social breadth, as well as the spiritual depth, of the movement as a whole. The autocratic Selina Countess of Huntingdon, the dignified Mary Fletcher (a Methodist who functioned within the Church of England), and the social improver Hannah More appear alongside the African American poet Phillis Wheatley, the energetic English Methodist Hester Ann Rogers, and two friends from Newport, Rhode Island, who were among their city's most influential and also well-respected citizens, Susanna Anthony and Sarah Osborn. The inclusion in this book of selections from the former slaves Richard Allen and Olaudah Equiano, as well as the Native American Samson Occom, indicates the breakthroughs that revivalistic evangelicalism created for racial minorities.

The book begins with a focus on "New Life in Christ," where the standard themes of evangelical conversion predominate. The following sections—on the Holy Spirit, Scripture, spiritual practices, love for God, and love for neighbor—represent the natural outgrowth of a converted life for evangelicals. Tom Schwanda's judicious editing makes it possible for modern readers to discover how deep and wide a spirituality of the new birth could actually extend.

—Mark A. Noll, Francis A. McAnaney Professor of
History at the University of Notre Dame,
is the author of *The Rise of Evangelicalism:
The Age of Edwards, Whitefield and the Wesleys.*

ACKNOWLEDGMENTS

The publication of a book involves many individuals. Bernard McGinn first saw value in this volume and encouraged me to revise and develop the proposal for submission. Nancy de Flon, my editor at Paulist Press, believed in this book at the earliest stages and has been a constant source of encouragement. Her wise editing has strengthened the quality of this book. I am most grateful for them and for the staff at Paulist Press that have produced this volume.

I have benefited from conversations with many scholars in the research and writing of this book, in particular, Cynthia Aalders, Gareth Atkins, Craig Atwood, David Bebbington, Keith Beebe, Joel Beeke, James Bradley, John Coffey, Peter Forsaith, Charles Hambrick-Stowe, Geordan Hammond, Joseph Harrod, Michael Haykin, Bruce Hindmarsh, Mark Hutchinson, E. Wyn James, David Ceri Jones, Thomas Kidd, Timothy Larsen, Roy Ledbetter, Stephen Marini, Peter Morden, Mark Noll, Brandon O'Brien, Ian Randall, Alan Rathe, Garth Rosell, Lester Ruth, Alec Ryrie, Michael Sciretti, Ken Stewart, Kyle Strobel, Douglas Sweeney, Arthur Thomas, John Tyson, JoAnn Ford Watson, David Wilson, John Witvliet, and Jonathan Yeager. I especially acknowledge Craig Atwood, David Bebbington, John Coffey, Michael Haykin, Geordan Hammond, Bruce Hindmarsh, Thomas Kidd, E. Wyn James, Peter Morden, and Douglas Sweeney, who provided specific guidance on the selection of texts or other resources and offered encouragement throughout the publication of this volume. Mark Noll is part of this group, and I express my deep appreciation to him for his foreword to this book.

I also gratefully acknowledge the guidance of Paul Peucker and Lorraine Parsons, archivists at the Moravian Church Archives, Bethlehem, PA, and Moravian Church House, London, respectively. Additionally, my visits to the British Library, Calvin College Hekman library, Cambridge University libraries, The John Rylands

University Library, the Newberry Library, Puritan Reformed Theological Seminary library, and Wheaton College library have provided me with access to the necessary texts for my research. In particular, I wish to thank Nancy Falciani-White of the Wheaton College library and Laura Ladwig at the Puritan Reformed Theological Seminary. Laura graciously made available the outstanding collection of primary and secondary sources for evangelical spirituality and provided valuable research assistance. The Library Company of Philadelphia graciously gave permission for the Richard Allen selection. During my sabbatical visit to England, I presented various portions of my research at Durham University, Nazarene Theological College, Manchester, and Spurgeon's College. Thank you to each of these institutions and, in particular, to Alec Ryrie, Geordan Hammond, and Peter Morden, respectively.

I also acknowledge the support of my dean, Jill Peláez Baumgaertner, and appreciate the financial assistance for travel and sabbatical opportunity that enabled my visits to the various libraries and archives for this project. I have been fortunate to have capable college research assistants who have provided invaluable aid in this project: Hannah McGinnis, Anastasia Brown, Ashley Davila, Joy O'Reagan, Samuel Lee, and Brandon Michael Burdette—many thanks to each of you. Special thanks also to Kathleen Cruse, my department coordinator, for her assistance in preparing the texts for this book.

Most of all, I am grateful to my wife, Grace, for her support, encouragement, and patience during the time required to produce this book and especially for her assistance in proofreading and editing the manuscript.

This book is dedicated to our grandchildren: Hailey, Brooklyn, Pierce, and Aniston. May you experience the fullness of evangelical spirituality!

ABBREVIATIONS

ANB   *American Biographical Dictionary.* New York: Oxford University Press, 1999.

BDE   Timothy Larsen, ed. *Biographical Dictionary of Evangelicals.* Downers Grove, IL: InterVarsity Press, 2003.

BDEB   Donald M. Lewis, ed. *The Blackwell Dictionary of Evangelical Biography 1730–1860.* Oxford: Blackwell, 1995.

Newton, *Works*   John Newton, *Letters and Sermons.* Edinburgh: Murray & Cochrane, 1798.

Noll, *Evangelicalism*   Mark A. Noll, *Rise of Evangelicalism: The Age of Edwards, Whitefield and the Wesleys.* Downers Grove, IL: InterVarsity Press, 2003

ODNB   *Oxford Dictionary of National Biography*

INTRODUCTION

Early evangelicalism is a transatlantic story. George Whitefield is the most prominent example; born in Britain, he crossed the Atlantic Ocean thirteen times and died in Massachusetts. Count Zinzendorf and August Spangenberg visited Moravian settlements in the Colonies as well. Beyond that, Francis Asbury, Sarah Osborn, Gilbert Tennent, and John Witherspoon were born in Great Britain or Ireland but lived and exercised their ministries in America. Samson Occom and Phillis Wheatley crossed "the pond" in the other direction, preaching and seeking to expand their audience among British listeners and readers.

The eighteenth century was a time of great transition.[1] It was into this period that evangelicalism emerged. But what is evangelicalism? Following the sixteenth-century Protestant Reformation, the term became a synonym for Protestants. With the passage of time, however, it took on greater precision. Today's standard and most frequently cited definition for *evangelicalism* is from David Bebbington's classic, *Evangelicalism in Modern Britain*. He asserts that the four primary descriptors are conversionism, activism, biblicism, and crucicentrism.[2]

Conversionism means that eighteenth-century evangelicals took sin seriously. They stressed the importance of spiritual rebirth through preaching the gospel. Justification by faith through God's grace was the sole means for becoming "awakened" (a popular term among evangelicals). Conversionism also stresses assurance of salvation. *Activism* reflects the energetic response of all believers to the gospel. Out of gratitude, the converted person would seek to be a witness to the gospel. Such witness included evangelism, missions, addressing the socials ills of slavery, or compassion for the poor. *Biblicism* stresses the importance of Scripture. This was evident not only in sermons but also in personal and group reading of the Bible.

1

The development of printing expanded the distribution of the Bible to those unfamiliar with the gospel of Jesus Christ. In particular, the devotional reading of the Bible was emphasized as personal application was encouraged. Undergirding all of this is *crucicentrism*, or the foundational emphasis of the cross. Jesus died for the sins of the world so that they might have the abundant life. The imagery of the blood and wounds of the Lamb of God figured prominently in sermons and hymns alike.

While some scholars have challenged Bebbington, his definition continues to be the most widely accepted framework for exploring evangelicalism.[3] Space prevents a more detailed examination of this debate; for this, the reader is referred to other sources.[4] Bebbington responds to his critics by acknowledging the antecedent continuities of Puritanism and Pietism but maintains that they were fashioned in fuller expressions in the 1740s than in previous generations.[5]

HISTORICAL ANTECEDENTS TO EARLY EVANGELICALISM

Scholars typically identify three main historical antecedents to eighteenth-century evangelicalism.[6] First, early evangelicalism was deeply indebted to Puritanism, which has often been understood as a devotional reformation to continue the unfinished business of the Protestant Reformation. Luther, Zwingli, and Calvin sought to reform the church theologically, ecclesiastically, and in some ways liturgically. While public spirituality was addressed, the themes of personal devotion lagged behind. Puritans on both sides of the Atlantic preached against the growing formalism of the church, emphasized the necessity of grace, published a wide spectrum of devotional manuals by Lewis Bayly, Henry Scudder, and Robert Bolton to encourage godliness, and stressed the critical nature of experimental piety or personal experience. Many of their writings focused on a spirituality of the heart and challenged all believers to the necessity of personal faith in Jesus Christ.

Second, continental Pietism under Philip Jakob Spener's leadership stressed renewal amid the dead orthodoxy of the German

Lutheran Church. His *Pia Desideria* (Heartfelt Desires, 1675) encouraged laity and clergy alike to gather in conventicles to study the Bible. Practical preaching that guided daily living was also emphasized, as was better training of pastors. Count Zinzendorf welcomed refuges to his Herrnhut estate; this created the context for the origin of the Moravian Church. The English Revival, as Reginald Ward reminds us, was born in central Europe:[7] the Moravian Fetter Lane Society strongly influenced many of the British and Welsh leaders of evangelicalism. The Protestant missionary movement was also greatly indebted to the Moravians. Dutch Pietism or *Nadere Reformatie* (the Dutch "further" reformation) was especially influential with the arrival of Theodore Frelinghuysen in the middle colonies and his influence on and friendship with Gilbert Tennent and others.

High Church Anglicanism was a third significant influence on evangelicalism. At times, this is difficult to detect due to the increasing antagonism between the early evangelical leaders and the Anglican Church. But the primary agenda to retrieve the primitive Christianity of the early church, which High Church Anglicans believed was the purest expression of Christianity, was formative for evangelicals. This desire motivated them to reclaim the practices of frequent communion, personal morality, and catechism of children. Societies, mostly of young men, were established to promote personal piety and serve the poor and needy. The Oxford Holy Club, which significantly shaped the Wesleys, George Whitefield, and other future evangelical leaders, is representative of this emphasis.

Some scholars include two additional antecedents to early evangelicalism. The significance of Scots-Irish Presbyterianism is best witnessed through the sacramental occasions or Holy Fairs that created a pattern of revivalism before the 1740s. Irish-born Gilbert Tennent, who devoted his ministry to the mid-Atlantic states, dramatically illustrates this. Leigh Eric Schmidt traces the history of this chapter of spirituality in his study of the celebration of the Lord's Supper.[8] Tennent's sacramental sermons, which he preached in America, reveal the continuity with his past. This pattern would later resurface during the Cambuslang Revival in Scotland.

A fifth influence, and the one that is often dismissed, is the Welsh Revival. Decades before the conversion of Howell Harris, popular Anglican preacher Griffith Jones created an association of schools that taught people the basics of reading Scripture, catechism, and the prayer book in Welsh. By the time of his death in 1761, Jones had established 3,325 schools throughout Wales.[9] Jones's itinerant preaching also formed religious societies that would continue to exert a crucial role in the cultivation and preservation of renewed spiritual life.

The formation and development of evangelical spirituality was never static, and one could readily discover variations across the broad landscape of the eighteenth century. Ian Randall wisely observes that "evangelical spirituality…has never been entirely uniform in the way it has been expressed."[10] Within this unity and diversity of evangelical spirituality, it is essential to realize that many evangelicals read directly from Roman Catholic devotional writers, including Thomas à Kempis, Miguel de Molinos, Madame Guyon, Br. Lawrence, and Francis de Sales. Further, their reading of Puritan and Pietistic texts were often influenced by a broader awareness of Western Catholic devotional writings.

THEMATIC CATEGORIES OF EVANGELICAL SPIRITUALITY

The following categories are not intended to replace Bebbington's four-point description of evangelicalism; rather, they are employed as a convenient means for describing the nature and content of early evangelical spirituality for this book. I have combined Bebbington's cruicentrism and conversion into one category and added three additional ones, since this best reflects the texts that I have selected. This book is thematically organized to reveal the narrative shape of evangelical spirituality. Not surprisingly, there is overlap in some categories. Evangelicals always emphasized new life in Christ as the beginning of the Christian journey. While one might debate the ordering of the remaining categories, the Holy Spirit's role was essential in inspiring the Bible and guiding readers in the proper use of it. The last three themes loosely reflect the experience of a new believer who grows in the grace and truth of God; in general, they depict the imagery of a pilgrim walking in union and communion with God.[11]

New Life in Christ. The first step toward conversion is an awareness of the bondage to sin and a person's total inability to save him- or herself. One experiences freedom from sin through God's grace displayed on the cross by justification through faith. The blood of Jesus, the Lamb of God, became a significant focus in sermons and hymns. This spiritual rebirth was frequently called the "awakening."

The Holy Spirit. No one could adequately engage the Bible for reading, preaching, and teaching without depending upon the Holy Spirit. In exploring the dynamics of sanctification, the individual believer recognizes the experimental nature of the pilgrimage, which is seldom linear and often includes periods of doubt, spiritual dryness, stagnancy, and the challenge of affliction.

Scripture. While Scripture has always played a significant role in Christian spirituality, eighteenth-century evangelicals emphasized the devotional reading of Scripture. They benefited from the advancement of printing and low-cost publishing and the increase in literacy to increase the number of people able to read the Bible personally. The role of Scripture was deeply related to the reality and guidance of the Holy Spirit.

Spiritual Practices. Personal and public spiritual disciplines were a means not of gaining God's favor but of cooperating with God's grace. Unlike many contemporary evangelicals, those of the eighteenth century typically emphasized the Lord's Supper. They also employed the rich devotional language of the Song of Songs that was common in the medieval Western Catholic tradition.

Love for God. Once a person experiences union with God, there is typically a desire for a deeper communion with God. Spiritual marriage began with conversion, though usually it was employed to speak of the growing intimacy with and love for God. The bridal language of enjoyment of God was also common. Contemplation and seeking the fullness of God in heaven are common themes in these writings.

Love for Neighbor. This reflects Bebbington's category of activism. The Christian faith was a living faith that witnessed to the gospel. Compassion and justice addressed those in bondage to sin and the social evils of the day. This included the abolition of slavery, charity to the poor, and widespread missionary efforts to all corners of the globe, as well as loving one's spouse with the love of Christ. The index will guide readers in discovering that these six categories are not isolated themes but dynamically weave in and out of one another to create the fabric of evangelical spirituality.

EARLY EVANGELICAL UNDERSTANDING OF SPIRITUALITY

While the term *spirituality* does not appear in Scripture, the Apostle Paul frequently employs the words *Spirit* (for example, in Rom 8:9–11, 26–27) and *spiritual* (for example, in 1 Cor 2:13; 3:1). The *Oxford English Dictionary* first records the usage of *spirituality* in English in the early sixteenth century.[12] Nathan Bailey's prominent eighteenth-century *Universal Etymological English Dictionary* defined *spirituality* as "spiritualness, devotion." The meaning for *spiritual* was "devout, pious, religious." Thomas Sheridan is more succinct, simply stating that *spirituality* means "pure acts of the soul."[13] George Whitefield employed the term in one of his letters, but his usage does not expand its understanding.[14] John Newton is more helpful and declares in one letter "that while too many seem content with a half profession, a name to live, an outward attachment to ordinances," he desires "that we may have our loins girded, and our lamps burning, and by our simplicity and spirituality constrain those who know us to acknowledge that we have been with Jesus, have sat at his feet, and drank of his Spirit."[15] Later in that same century, Francis Asbury regularly utilized the word to express the inner life, though many of his entries tend to be terse and lacking description. Yet at times, he passionately cries out, "O for more spirituality! More purity of Heart! Lord, form me by the power of divine grace, according to all thy righteous will, that my soul may enjoy thee in glory for ever." Soon after, Asbury echoes the same plea: "My soul longs for more spirituality, and to be totally dedicated to God."[16]

Evangelicals were not limited to this single term in expressing the nature and dynamics of the spiritual life. Through a careful reading of the texts, the semantic range for spirituality can be cataloged into three categories: authenticity, lived experience, and intimacy.

One of the hallmarks of early evangelicals was the critical importance of conversion. Since the new birth in Jesus Christ was a stark
contrast with much of the existing church life on both sides of the
Atlantic, evangelicals often employed the adjective *true* or *real* before
religion, godliness, or piety. This language had a polemical twist to it
since it was a rebuke of the pretenders of the Christian faith or those
who merely professed the words without demonstrating the reality
of a personal faith in Jesus Christ. The full title of Joseph Bellamy's
best-known work, *True Religion Delineated* (1750), provides a vivid
reinforcement of this principle: *True Religion Delineated; or,
Experimental Religion, as Distinguished from Formality on the One
Hand, and Enthusiasm on the Other, Set in Scripture and Rational
Light.* That clearly marks the parameters of evangelical spirituality.
While formality that often springs from dead orthodoxy was to be
avoided, there was an equal danger from enthusiasm or fanaticism
that often centered on the Quakers. Joseph Bellamy provides this
further summary: "So that now, in a few words, we may here see,
wherein true religion does consist, as it stands distinguished from all
the false religion in the world. The godly man...is thereby influenced
to love him [i.e., God] supremely, live to him ultimately, and delight
in him superlatively."[17]

Jonathan Edwards examined this issue of whether a so-called
professing Christian could be admitted to the "Christian church." He
proclaimed, "The religion that Christ taught consisted mainly in
true piety of heart and life....But if men profess only the doctrines of
religion and the outward services, and leave out what is spiritual, the
thing that they profess is not the religion of Jesus Christ."[18] Edwards
wrote his *Religious Affections* to assist Christians in discerning
between an authentic work of God's grace and what was counterfeit.
He instructs his readers, "True religion is evermore a powerful thing;
and the power of it appears, in the first place, in the inward exercises
of it in the heart, where is the principal and original seat of it. Hence
true religion is called the power of godliness, in distinction from the
eternal appearances of it." One who has experienced this authentic
spiritual vitality seeks to deepen this vitality. Edwards writes, "So
holy desire, exercised in longings, hungerings and thirstings after
God and holiness, is often mentioned in Scripture as an important
part of true religion. (Isa 26:8; Ps 27:4; 42:1–2; 63:1–2; 84:1–2; etc.)."[19]

Mary Fletcher, when speaking of obedience, asserts, "And this simple recollecting ourselves in the presence of God, receiving every occurrence as from him; and offering up every action to him, is the spirit and life of true religion."[20] Wilberforce also challenges his readers to cultivate a real piety that confirms itself by compassionate actions.[21] While some might not recognize benevolence as a synonym for spirituality, it was definitely a fruit of it. This term was particularly common in Edwards and his disciples, Joseph Bellamy and Samuel Hopkins. Hopkins speaks for this New England trio when he articulates the meaning of *spirituality* as "the expression of true disinterested benevolence, or that love by which we are formed after the likeness of God, and he dwells in us, and we in him."[22]

Early evangelicals understood that spirituality was a lived experience that required both an inward knowledge of the presence of the triune God and the experimental or practical application of it in daily life. Newton wrote a friend regarding growth in maturity and observes, "We may grow wise apace in opinions, by books and men; but vital, experimental knowledge can only be received from the Holy Spirit, the great instructor and comforter of his people."[23] He penned a letter to a minister and asserted that wisdom "does not consist in forming a bundle of rules and maxims, but in a spiritual taste and discernment, derived from an experimental knowledge of the truth, and of the heart of man, as described in the word of God."[24] While many evangelicals read William Law's *Serious Call to a Devout and Holy Life*, they later recognized its deficiency. Whitefield devoted a full work to defining the nature of Christian devotion. His goal was to revise Law's *Serious Call* and remove that which was "not truly Evangelical" and to illustrate "the subject more fully from the Holy Scriptures."[25] Whitefield provides a summary statement affirming that "Christian devotion is nothing less than a life wholly devoted unto God." He responds to critics that if a person seeks to live such a life it would restrain their enjoyment and innocent pleasures of life and "render our lives dull, uneasy, and melancholy." Whitefield refutes that distortion, affirming that "true devotion fills our lives with the greatest peace and happiness that can be enjoyed in this world."[26] Edwards further demonstrates the nature of experimental religion from his classic *Religious Affections*: "And not only does the most important and distinguishing part of Christian experience lie in spiritual practice; but such is the nature of that sort of exercises of grace wherein spiritual practices consists, that nothing is so properly called by the name of experimental religion."[27]

Evangelicals often utilized the imagery of walking with God as a means of describing spirituality. Anne Dutton devoted a full work to this topic. She begins by confessing her inadequacy in addressing it but quickly presses on to illustrate walking with God through a number of vivid images. She asserts, "Conversation-holiness is another way in which God and his people walk together." More expansive is her understanding that walking with God is a "free communion and mutual fellowship." This "consists in a free opening of hearts, and a mutual delight in each others company." And even more: "Their communion must needs be exceeding sweet; and their mutual love-delight in each other very intense."[28] Similarly, Whitefield wrote a sermon on "Walking with God," in which, after affirming the necessity of the Holy Spirit's indwelling, he claims, "And this is what is particularly meant in the words of our text. 'And Enoch walked with God' (Gen 5:24). He kept up and maintained a holy, settled, habitual, though undoubtedly not altogether uninterrupted communion and fellowship with God, in and through Christ Jesus." He continues, "Walking with God implies, our making progress or advances in the divine life." Significantly, Whitefield recognizes that walking with God was not a solo activity and those who desire to walk with God should keep company with others and participate in Christian societies and other fellowship meetings.[29] Count Zinzendorf used a variation on this theme as one of his favorite expressions for spirituality when he spoke of "walking with the Savior" (*Umgang mit dem Heiland*).[30]

Significantly, evangelical spirituality reflected a deep experiential intimacy with the triune God. Fletcher employs the erotic language of the Song of Songs to encourage a person to enjoy God and have "blessed intercourse, and keep up a delightful communion with Christ."[31] Hester Ann Rogers declares her relationship as one of "increasing intercourse and communion with my God."[32] Asbury, in recording his victory over spiritual combat and temptations and the increased joy of God's presence, claims, "Satan has been thrusting at me, but by grace I am still kept; and my soul is employed in holy and heavenly exercises, with constant and delightful communion with

God. Oh! How I long to find every power of soul and body one continual sacrifice to God!"[33] Asbury also develops the imagery of nearness to God when he confesses his delight and enjoyment in the "sacred nearness to God."[34] While all of these descriptions come from Wesleyan Methodists, Calvinist Methodists were no stranger to the same heightened delight in God. Anne Dutton used similar language earlier in time, assuring her reader that walking with God consists in the "highest communion and sweetest intercourse with God."[35] Later, Newton summarized the expansive nature of this experience by declaring, "The communion we speak of comprises a mutual intercourse and communication in love, in counsels, and in interests."[36]

Sarah Osborn describes the soaring delight one can experience in their communion with God: "Thus I continued from day to day, in such ecstasies of joy, thirsting for full sanctification, and more intimate communion with God...earnestly begging that God would find out some way for me, that I might be made instrumental in advancing his kingdom and interest in the world."[37] Edwards also confesses his desire for a "holy communion with God."[38] Anne Dutton, confessing her own intimacy to a minister, employs trinitarian language:

> I have sweet communion with all the three persons in love...and sometimes, distinct communion with each of the divine persons, in those displays of grace, which more peculiarly belong to each of them respectively, in the great work of my salvation. And this communion which I have with God, is an inward efficacious, soul-transforming thing.[39]

While the diversity of these words is broad, they express the core principle that spirituality was a lived reality in which the person experienced God. Significantly, inward knowledge was to be expressed outwardly through acts of love and service. This was possible only through the Holy Spirit. Therefore, the spiritual life was to be engaged with the same intensity with which a person would approach any other dimension of life.

UNIQUENESS OF
LETTER WRITING AND HYMNS

Devotional manuals that had nourished seventeenth-century Puritanism and Pietism largely receded into the background with a new emphasis on letter writing and hymns. David Hempton claims, "If one wanted to search for the essence of Evangelical spirituality in the eighteenth century, the ubiquitous letter, which can stand as a metaphor for sending and receiving, and experience and telling, is probably as good a place as any to start."[40] Evangelicals took full advantage of the letter to send and receive news of what God was doing in their own particular location with colleagues and friends across regional and even transatlantic boundaries.

The sheer volume of epistles written by key evangelical leaders is one measure of their significance. Unfortunately, there is not as accurate information as one would think, since many letters are still unpublished and scattered across archives in manuscript form. This is particularly true for George Whitefield. David Ceri Jones, who is currently collecting and transcribing Whitefield's letters, estimates that the transatlantic revivalist produced at least 2,200 letters.[41] More detailed data reveals that Howell Harris, the Welsh revivalist, wrote about three thousand letters.[42] While there is no tabulation of John Newton's correspondence, he confessed in the 1790s that due to the growing demands from those who requested his counsel, he was always behind in responding to fifty to sixty letters.[43] The Baptist Anne Dutton's tombstone states that she wrote an amazing twenty-five volumes of letters.[44] Unlike John Wesley, who typically wrote short epistles, many of Dutton's are at least two or three pages in length or longer. Dutton was also in regular correspondence with Whitefield, and he frequently directed people to write to her since he was so far behind in his own correspondence.[45]

Dutton is an interesting illustration from a different angle. Originally, her letters were not as well known since they were penned anonymously or simply with her initials, A. D. This discloses the importance of letter writing as one arena in which women could participate publicly.[46] Dutton responded to critics who challenged the appropriateness of women writing in public by publishing *A Letter to Such of the Servants of Christ Who May Have Any Scruples about the Lawfulness of Printing Anything Written by a Woman* in 1743. She insists that she is not violating the biblical injunction preventing women from what she terms "Publick Authoritative Teaching" because letters and books are not read publicly.[47] She further asserts that all Christians are expected to edify others and that she is merely following the example of Priscilla in the Book of Acts (18:26). Dutton encourages her critics to imagine, when they receive a letter from her, that she had physically come to visit them. While Howell Harris exchanged many letters with Dutton and affirmed both her writing ability and the appropriateness of engaging in public discourse, he did warn her that "it would be a struggle to obtain an audience for her writing."[48]

The significance of letter writing was also evident in the "letter days" of the Moravians and later the Wesleyan and Calvinist Methodists. The Moravians began this practice in 1728 while in Germany and it was replicated in 1739 in London. These gatherings included the reading of domestic and transatlantic news of progress in advancing the gospel and prayers and singing. The entire meeting would last several hours.[49] Such networks reduced the gap between widely diverse geographical and denominational traditions and brought a greater awareness of the expansion and challenges of the emerging evangelical movement. Another measure of the importance of letter writing during this period was that the recipient paid the postage, not the sender, thus challenging writers to pen something worthy of the cost.[50] Due to the importance of epistolary correspondence, numerous letter-writing manuals existed to guide people in learning the proper methods and principles for constructing a good letter.

Central to the exchange of information was the familiar letter, a specific form of epistolary correspondence based on mutual interests and affections. The classical definition for this genre was a "mutual conversation between absent friends."[51] Bruce Hindmarsh, who has made an extensive study of the familiar letter within evangelical spirituality, observes that it revealed the "writer's own character" and required "both spontaneity and discipline, substance and personality [and] created a courteous context for discussing the spiritual life."[52] The familiar letter would provide an ideal genre for cultivating friendship. This correspondence could be between close friends. Sarah Osborn and Susanna Anthony, two colonial New England women, provide one window into this world. Their letters, written with the expectation that no one else would read them, reveal the depth of their soul in all of its struggles and delights. These familiar letters often focused on spiritual experiences, whether of personal reading of Scripture and prayer or listening to sermons or participating in the Lord's Supper. In the process, they expose the struggle to overcome sin, aridity, suffering, and illness.[53]

Many other letters were directed to ministers seeking spiritual counsel or reporting on their conversion.[54] While written in private, it was common for these epistles later to be published for the encouragement of other readers, thus demonstrating the dynamic merger of the personal and more broadly public worlds. One medium that assisted in this dissemination was the variety of weekly magazines that included letters as well as reports on the progress of the gospel in other regions. Frequently, letters would request wisdom for dealing with a wide range of spiritual or personal issues. Newton is representative of the detailed and sensitive responses to queries from writers. One scholar has remarked about Newton, "He was the St. Francis de Sales of the Evangelical movement, the great spiritual director of souls through the post. 'It is the Lord's will,' [Newton] said, 'that I should do most by my letters.'"[55] Letters were also used to engage in theological debates and polemical wrangling.[56] This could range from the vitriolic attacks between John Wesley and Augustus Toplady regarding predestination and free will to George Whitefield's scathing *Expostulatory Letter* (1753) rehearsing the errors of the Moravians, which drew a spirited response not only from Count Zinzendorf but from Peter Böhler and James Hutton as well.

HYMNBOOKS

Hymns also created opportunities to explore and experience the message of the gospel. Hymns are poetic texts that can capture the imaginations of those who sing them. But they are more; texts when united with tunes create a deeper experience then if the poetry was simply read on its own. The Moravians provide one illuminating contrast of how these texts could vary in length. Count Zinzendorf composed many hymns of a single stanza, but he also composed perhaps the longest hymn of evangelicalism, his 162-stanza adaption of the Augsburg Confession. Most hymns tended to be four to eight stanzas in length, although it was not uncommon for some to extend beyond fourteen. When longer hymns were published in hymnals, the number of their stanzas was often reduced to make them more manageable. When that has been done in this volume, the stanzas are assigned their original numbers to provide some indication of the lengths of the hymns that were sung in the eighteenth century. Most hymns in this collection are not numbered, indicating that they appear in their original format.

Early evangelical singing emerged from two divergent streams. The Moravian contribution developed from its German Pietistic heritage that originated from Martin Luther, who initially favored the composition of original hymn texts. The Calvinist tradition, descended from John Calvin, sang the Psalms exclusively. Isaac Watts, raised within this Reformed context, first experimented with paraphrasing the Psalms before he followed the Lutheran practice of composing new texts. Jonathan Edwards, who had been formed by the tradition of psalm singing, gladly embraced the innovation of new hymn texts.[57] The merger of these streams provided the foundation for Philip Doddridge, Charles Wesley, and John Cennick, among later writers, to create the great treasury of evangelical hymnody. While British hymn writing became established relatively early in the eighteenth century, it took the Americans almost another century to develop the same quantity of hymn writers.

Evangelical hymns served two purposes: to instruct and to inspire.[58] Hymns taught the content of the gospel. By singing these musical compositions, people were formed by the doctrine contained in those words. The imagery and figurative language of these texts assisted in the communication of its message. This metaphoric vocabulary increased its retention and stimulated the formation of a Christian identity and memory. John Witvliet correctly observes, "When it comes to matters of spirituality and faith, we are what we sing."[59] Newton frequently catechized children by having them memorize hymn texts, which thus developed a more vivid memory of those themes.[60] Newton also used hymns to illustrate his sermons, and Zinzendorf employed them for instruction and for reinforcing themes within Moravian worship.

Singing hymns also provided an experiential means of response. The union of text and tune evokes the affections and inspires the possibility of a deepened experience around the content of that hymn. Witvliet affirms that singing these melodies "interpret those words and give them affective shape."[61] Singing could therefore challenge the person to examine their faith and consider whether they could acknowledge and affirm those truths. In cases where the theology or commitment extended beyond the point of the person's present faith, it could create questions regarding the ability to affirm those words. Or the themes could affirm and strengthen the person with new resolve and equip them to continue in their faith. Additionally, hymn singing could prepare the heart and mind for preaching or other aspects of worship. Space does not permit for the more expansive consideration of what happens when people sing, the interaction between the personal and public world, and how one can interpret the meaning of hymns.[62]

While hymns covered a diverse range of themes, many centered on salvation in Jesus Christ. Readers will notice that of the six topical sections that comprise this book, there are more hymns in the "New Life in Christ" section than in any other. Stephen Marini validates this disproportionality, observing that the majority of evangelical hymns addressed the themes of "the economy of grace, the morphology of conversion, and the saint's life."[63] Classification of hymns can be difficult due to the breadth of topics in even a single hymn, but the large distribution of hymns in the new life in Christ category is representative of this critical foundation of evangelicalism. Marini's analysis provides a valuable means for comparison of the most frequent themes in early evangelical hymns.[64] Despite the fact that Wesleyan and Calvinist Methodists and Moravians often engaged in serious theological division, it was not uncommon for their hymnbooks to include texts from the other two streams of evangelicalism. George Whitefield's *A Collection of Hymns for Social Worship* (1753) for use at his London Tabernacle includes many hymns of Charles Wesley and John Cennick, to cite just two examples.[65]

Mark Noll summarizes the significance of hymnody thusly: "Nothing was more central to the evangelical revival than the singing of new hymns written in praise of the goodness, mercy, and grace of God." Further, he observes that hymn singing "provided one of the few bridges between classes and races" and also provided an opportunity for women "for the public expression of their faith."[66] Evangelical British women such as Anne Dutton, Anne Steele, and Ann Griffiths were all to contribute to the growing corpus of hymn writing. Hymn singing indeed became one of the gifts of evangelical spirituality that increasingly extended across diverse theological and denominational boundaries.

SELECTION OF TEXTS

The initial selection of texts for this volume was inspired by Mark Noll's "100 Primary Sources of the Era."[67] While many of the specific works listed were not related to spirituality, I was often able to substitute another text from the same author that was. Since the Classics of Western Spirituality series contains a volume devoted to the Wesleys, they were not included here; to compensate for this, numerous Methodists were added.[68] Beyond that, I intentionally selected a balance of gender, ethnic, and theological backgrounds and an equal distribution of representative texts within each of the six topical categories. Further, I sought to include the full range of devotional genres; among them are sermons, letters, hymns, theological treatises, missionary appeals, and liturgical writings from both sides of the Atlantic. Some readers who are familiar with this literature might question the inclusion of some persons or the absence of others or their texts. It was a difficult challenge to decide whom to include, and a large number of my initial selections were deleted due to space restrictions. In reality, this volume is not intended to be an exhaustive catalog but, rather, representative of the most descriptive samples of eighteenth-century evangelical spiritual writing. The texts vary in length, and shorter documents such as letters often are their original length. Longer texts have been reduced for readability for contemporary readers but are sufficient to provide an overview of the main themes. These selections within each category are arranged chronologically according to date of publication, even though many were written earlier. Additionally, I have typically used the first edition of the texts unless later publications were revised and expanded.

My desire is that the biographical introductions and primary texts will be a valuable guide for both students and interested readers to acquaint them with early evangelical spirituality. Secondary sources have been provided for each author to enlarge the reader's understanding of the person's life and context. For some of the writers, the abundance of publications prompted the need to discern the best sources. Typically, I have listed two books or articles for each person, but for those of greater significance or where three strong resources existed, I included them all. Whenever it was possible to add an accurate source specifically written on the author's spirituality, it was included. Other individuals have not received the research that they deserve and the selection of reference titles was more difficult. A general bibliography at the back of this volume will suggest additional sources for further research.

To improve readability, I have gently edited the texts by reducing the common run-on sentences and the frequent capitalization of nouns and italics and have standardized spelling to follow American practices for consistency's sake. Where necessary, I have corrected spelling and updated biblical references, though I have retained the original quotations of Scripture.

THE AUTHORS IN
THIS VOLUME

Thomas Adam[1] (1701–1784) was a British Anglican minister and author whose early ministry was marked by formalism. His reading of William Law created a protracted period of spiritual anxiety until he experienced an evangelical conversion. Adam was widely respected as a spiritual director and insightful devotional writer. His writings influenced William Romaine and Samuel Taylor Coleridge.

Richard Allen[2] (1760–1831), an African American minister born into slavery, purchased his freedom after his owner's conversion under Methodist preaching. He developed a close friendship with Francis Asbury. Early discrimination in Philadelphia motivated the creation of an exclusively African American congregation; hence, Allen founded and served as first bishop of the African Methodist Episcopal (AME) Church. Allen's ministry stressed the necessity of personal conversion, sincere piety, community activism, and social justice.

Henry Alline[3] (1748–1784) was a North American evangelist and hymn writer, born in Rhode Island but resettled in Nova Scotia with his family when he was twelve. Shortly after his dramatic conversion, he began an evangelistic ministry. Known as the "George Whitefield of Nova Scotia," Alline emphasized deep conversion and rejection of external formalism with his passionate preaching. He wrote more than five hundred hymns and some controversial works of theology, and left a lasting legacy in the Maritime Provinces.

Susanna Anthony[4] (1726–1791), an American Congregational lay leader in Newport, Rhode Island, was a key member of Sarah Osborn's religious society (see further). She struggled with periods of melancholy throughout her life. Recognized as an exemplar of noteworthy piety, Anthony intentionally remained single to dedicate herself more fully to prayer.

Francis Asbury[5] (1745–1816) was a British-born Methodist preacher and bishop. Though he lacked formal theological education, his leadership guided the growth of Methodism from a few hundred when he arrived in America in 1771 to over two hundred thousand at his death. His superb administrative skills and ability to relate to ordinary people overshadowed his weak preaching. Known for his intense piety and frugality, Asbury never owned more than he could carry on his horse. One biographer calculates that he preached over 250,000 sermons and slept in 10,000 homes during his forty-five year itinerancy.

Isaac Backus[6] (1724–1806), an American Baptist minister and champion of religious liberty, made over nine hundred itinerant preaching missions throughout much of the Colonies while serving one congregation in Massachusetts his entire life. His early resistance to taxation to support the established Congregational Church promoted religious freedom and separation of church and state. Backus's emphasis on freedom to follow duty rather than neglect responsibility finds expression in his tract on family prayer.

Joseph Bellamy[7] (1719–1790) was an American Congregational minister and theologian. His major work, *True Religion Delineated*, sought a middle ground refuting the critics of the Great Awakening, on the one hand, and those who took it to excess, on the other. Along with Samuel Hopkins, Bellamy was a major interpreter of Jonathan Edwards's "New Divinity" theology for the next generation. He devoted his entire ministry to one church in Connecticut and trained many ministers at the theological boarding school held at his house.

William Carey[8] (1761–1834) was a British Baptist minister and missionary to India whose *Enquiry into the Obligation* challenged Christians to communicate the gospel worldwide. This prompted the formation of the Baptist Missionary Society (1792). Carey devoted forty years of service in India. Skilled in both biblical and Indian languages, he translated the Bible into Bengali and numerous other dialects. Carey's legacy of translation encouraged the flourishing of Bengali culture and fostered indigenous mission activity.

John Cennick[9] (1718–1755) was a British evangelist and hymn writer who experienced conversion after a deep spiritual struggle. His itinerant ministry began when the designated preacher was late in arrival. During his brief life, Cennick served with the Wesleys, George Whitefield, and eventually Count Zinzendorf and the Moravians. His changing loyalty reflected both his and others' refinement of theological convictions. Cennick was an exceptional evangelist and prolific hymn writer who produced one of the early hymnals of the revival.

William Cowper[10] (1731–1800), a British hymn writer and poet, struggled with severe depression much of his life and attempted suicide several times. He served as a pastoral assistant to John Newton and contributed sixty-seven hymns, mostly written in 1771–72, to Newton's *Olney Hymns* (1779). In his later years, Cowper produced some of his finest poetry.

Samuel Davies[11] (1723–1761) was an American Presbyterian minister, hymn writer, educator, and passionate preacher of the gospel. His form of revival Calvinism developed seven new Presbyterian churches and numerous preaching stations in Virginia. An advocate for religious toleration and civil rights, especially in educating American slaves, Davies succeeded Jonathan Edwards as president at the College of New Jersey (now Princeton University).

Philip Doddridge[12] (1702–1751) was a British Independent minister, educator, and author who, in addition to his expertise in theology, was a proficient mathematician. His influential dissenting academy trained many men for ministry. Doddridge's *Rise and Progress of Religion in the Soul* (1745) was inspired by and dedicated to his mentor Isaac Watts and was also instrumental in the conversion of William Wilberforce and others. His moderate Calvinism was expressed in his many hymns and in his interest in evangelism and missions.

Anne Dutton[13] (1692–1765), a British Baptist writer, authored numerous theological treatises on a wide range of topics and corresponded regularly with recipients on both sides of the Atlantic. Dutton favored Calvinist theology and was attracted to George Whitefield while she engaged in polemical skirmishes with John

Wesley and the Moravians. She became a role model for other women in ministry.

Jonathan Edwards[14] (1703–1758), American Congregational minister, theologian, and prolific author, is often known by a sermon that is not characteristic of his preaching, "Sinners in the Hands of an Angry God." Seeking to integrate both the intellect and affections into his Calvinist theology, he drew deeply from Puritan sources. Edwards's revivalist ministry situated him as a key leader of the Great Awakening. After being dismissed from his Northampton, Massachusetts, congregation in 1751 due to his insistence that conversion should precede communion, he spent most of his final years as a missionary among the Native Americans in eastern Massachusetts.

Olaudah Equiano[15] (c.1745–1797) was an African sailor and abolitionist, also known as Gustavus Vassa after the sixteenth-century Swedish king. Until he purchased his freedom in 1766, he was sold and resold repeatedly into slavery. Transatlantic journeys took him throughout the American Colonies, the Caribbean, England, and beyond. The Church of England rejected Equiano's desire to return to Africa as a missionary. His best-selling spiritual autobiography, *The Interesting Narrative of the Life of Olaudah Equiano* (1789), broadened his abolitionist efforts.

John Fletcher[16] (1729–1785), a British Anglican minister and author, was born in Switzerland and settled in England in 1750. His entire ministry to one parish revealed a deep love for the poor. In 1781, he married Mary Bosanquet. John Wesley repeatedly invited Fletcher to succeed him, and although he refused, he still supported Wesley's Methodist movement. Irenic in spirit, he emphasized unity and toleration with the Calvinists, to whom he acknowledged a debt in his theological formation. Fletcher's disciplined piety and purity of character inspired many.

Mary [née Bosanquet] Fletcher[17] (1739–1815), a British Methodist lay leader and preacher, was one of the most significant female leaders during her time. She formed a community in her home (for which she wrote monastic-like vows) that provided for the needs of children and adults. John Wesley was impressed with her preaching, although her ministry exceeded his permission. In 1781, she married John Fletcher and partnered in ministry with him until his death, after which she continued to lead Methodist societies and exhort and expound Scripture.

Andrew Fuller[18] (1754–1818) was an English Baptist minister and theologian whose early doctrinal struggles were resolved by a renewed dedication to search the Scriptures for the truth. Fuller affirmed human freedom without denying God's sovereignty and identified with the evangelical Calvinism of Jonathan Edwards. He served as secretary and influential leader of the Baptist Missionary Society. Princeton and Yale attempted to grant him honorary doctorates in recognition of his leadership, but he refused these honors.

Ann Griffiths[19] (1776–1805), a Welsh hymn writer, received little formal education but was deeply influenced by the Bible—in particular the Song of Songs—and the *Book of Common Prayer* in the formation of her poetry. While her literary corpus contains only thirty hymns and eight letters, her influence has been felt widely in Wales and beyond. Desire for intimacy with God figures prominently in her hymns.

Howell Harris[20] (1714–1773) was a Revivalist and early leader of Welsh Calvinist Methodism. Gifted as a vibrant preacher and capable administrator, he organized many religious societies to foster spiritual growth. His erratic personality and often harsh discipline of others isolated him temporarily from the leadership of Welsh Methodism. During the early years of the Evangelical Awakening, Harris divided his time between Wales and London, often in an attempt to reconcile the divisions between Wesleyan and Calvinist Methodism and the Moravians.

Joseph Hart[21] (1712–1768) was a British Independent minister and hymn writer. Originally a teacher of ancient languages, he experienced severe spiritual turmoil until 1757, when he was converted by a sermon on Revelation 3:10 at the London Fetter Lane Moravian Chapel. Hart became a popular preacher and wrote 220 hymns, many of which reflect his Calvinist theology.

Selina Hastings, Countess of Huntingdon[22] (1707–1791), was a Calvinist Methodist lay leader. Initially attracted to John Wesley, she later appointed George Whitefield as her personal chaplain. Her highly ambitious, domineering, and inflexible leadership created frequent conflict with others. Hastings used her personal wealth to establish numerous chapels (e.g., "Connexion") in the major spa centers of England to reach the wealthy with the evangelical message.

Samuel Hopkins[23] (1721–1803), an American Congregationalist minister and theologian influenced by Jonathan Edwards, became, along with Joseph Bellamy, a leader of the "New Divinity Movement" that stressed consistent Calvinism. His crowning achievement, the *System of Doctrine* (1793), asserted the priority of Scripture amid the challenges of Enlightenment thinking. A preacher at the First Congregational Church in Newport, Rhode Island, a thriving slave-trading port, Hopkins became an influential abolitionist; he declared slavery to be America's worst sin.

Devereux Jarratt[24] (1733–1801), American Episcopal minister and evangelist, was converted by Presbyterians but sought ordination in the Episcopal Church in hopes of sparking greater evangelical fervor in his childhood denomination. Mostly self-taught, Jarratt was recognized as one of the leading Anglican Evangelicals in America. He cooperated with the Methodists and his preaching played a significant role in the Virginia revival of 1776.

Sarah Jones[25] (1753–1794), an American Methodist from Virginia, was known for her intensely disciplined piety that created frequent experiences of ecstatic rapture. She became a Methodist over the strong objections of her husband, who eventually was converted by her faith. Jones's vast correspondence included American Methodist leader Francis Asbury, who preached her funeral. Her epithet "Mother of Israel" reflects her notable leadership within Methodism.[26]

William McCulloch[27] (1691–1771) was a Church of Scotland minister. Though not an eloquent preacher, his sermons on regeneration prepared the way for the Cambuslang Revival of 1742 that centered on the preparation for and celebration of the Lord's Supper. McCulloch recorded the conversion narratives from the communion weekends held during this revival. He corresponded with Jonathan Edwards. He also encouraged the use of prayer societies and foreign missions.

Hannah More[28] (1745–1833), a British author and educational and moral crusader known by her enemies as "the bishop in petticoats," sought to awaken the upper class to their moral responsibilities. Her correspondence with John Newton and friendship with William Wilberforce contributed to her shared efforts toward abolition. With her sister, More developed charity schools to teach poor children how to read the Bible and the catechism.

John Newton[29] (1725–1807) was a British Anglican minister and hymn writer. His early life included years as a slave trader, which ended due to ill health. The morality of slavery was still hotly debated at this time. Eventually becoming the most prominent Evangelical Anglican in England, Newton regretted his involvement in the slave trade and encouraged William Wilberforce in his abolitionist efforts. He befriended William Cowper and together they published the *Olney Hymns* (1779). In his correspondence, Newton provided spiritual direction to numerous people.

Samson Occom[30] (1723–1792), a Native American Presbyterian minister, attended the Indian Charity School for training Native American missionaries in Connecticut and later preached over three hundred sermons in England to raise funds for the institution. He felt betrayed when the school moved to New Hampshire as Dartmouth College and rejected its original focus on Native Americans in favor of elite white men. Known as the "Pious Mohegan," while Occom was the most famous Native American evangelist of his time, he also ministered to whites.

Sarah Osborn[31] (1714–1796) was born in Britain and immigrated as a child with her family to New England, settling in Newport, Rhode Island. She formed a religious society that met weekly for decades, the members of which devoted themselves to mutual encouragement, prayers for ministers, and the advancement of Christ's kingdom throughout the world. A close personal friend of Susanna Anthony, she taught school to support her family.

Samuel Pearce[32] (1766–1799), a British Baptist minister and promoter of missions, was one of the founding members of the Baptist Missionary Society in 1792. Known as a passionate and effective communicator, he expanded his local church ministry by evangelistic preaching in the surrounding villages. His request to join William Carey in India was denied because his leadership was more necessary at home. Pearce's life was marked by a deep personal spirituality and affectionate love for his wife.

Hester Ann Rogers[33] (1756–1794) was a British Methodist laywoman widely known for her holiness. Like Sarah Jones, she, too, was a "Mother of Israel" and her spiritual writings influenced many on both sides of the Atlantic. Her husband, James Rogers, declared her responsible for two thousand conversions in Dublin. When she was twenty-five, John Wesley appointed her a class leader, and she later cared for him on his deathbed.

William Romaine[34] (1714–1795), a British Anglican minister and popular London preacher, was converted to evangelicalism a decade after his ordination. A proficient Hebrew scholar, Romaine favored metrical psalmody over the hymns of the Evangelical Awakening. Calvinist in his theology, he maintained a friendship with John Wesley. John Newton eulogized him as the most popular evangelical since George Whitefield.

Thomas Scott[35] (1747–1821) was a British Anglican minister and biblical commentator. John Newton was instrumental in guiding him to an evangelical faith. Scott's best-selling *Commentary on the Whole Bible*, first published in 174 weekly installments, earned him the epithet "the commentator." His writings influenced many into the nineteenth century, including John Henry Newman.

Augustus Gottlieb Spangenberg[36] (1704–1792), a German Moravian leader, bishop, and transatlantic missionary, led the first Moravian journey to the American colonies (Georgia). He later established the Moravian community in Bethlehem, Pennsylvania, as well as missionary efforts with Native Americans. Spangenberg's organizational and financial wisdom prepared for and guided the Moravian presence in Britain. He became Zinzendorf's successor following the Count's death, providing stable leadership and repositioning the Moravian Church for the future.

Anne Steele[37] (1716–1778) was a British Baptist hymn writer who often wrote under the name *Theodosia*. Recognized as the first major woman hymn writer, she was influenced by Isaac Watts and, in turn, inspired many future female authors. While many accounts of her life continue to circulate inaccuracies about specific tragedies, Steele did experience much suffering that created hymns of both lament and affliction as well as praise and confidence in God's power to transform life.

Gilbert Tennent[38] (1703–1764), an American Presbyterian minister and revivalist, was born in Ireland, immigrated to the American colonies in 1718, and was educated at his father's ministerial training school in Pennsylvania, known as the "Log College." Tennent's most famous sermon, *The Danger of an Unconverted Ministry* (1740), harshly attacked fellow ministers who lacked proof of conversion and a vibrant piety. His later theological disagreements with Count Zinzendorf produced greater humility, reversed his severe stance, and eventually reconciled him with his earlier critics.

Augustus Toplady[39] (1740–1778), a British Anglican minister and hymn writer, frequently engaged in bitter controversy with John Wesley and his followers over free will and predestination. Toplady was equally critical of any expressions of theological orthodoxy devoid of spiritual warmth. During the months before he died from tuberculosis, Toplady experienced deep enjoyment and almost constant communion with Christ.

Henry Venn[40] (1725–1797) was a British Anglican minister and writer who embraced both the Church of England liturgy and its church order with a vibrant evangelical piety and preaching. His devotional classic, *The Complete Duty of Man*, reflects a moderate Calvinism. Venn was deeply ascetical in his personal practices. Through correspondence and counseling, he guided many younger evangelicals preparing for ministry, including Charles Simeon, who became the central leader of evangelicals in the next generation.

Thomas Walsh[41] (1730–1759) was an Irish Methodist itinerant and biblical scholar. His revivalist preaching often generated fierce opposition. John Wesley esteemed him the best Hebraist he knew and asserted that with six men of Walsh's dedication, he could transform the country. Walsh's brief life was marked by zeal, excessive work without adequate rest, and daily pain, likely from tuberculosis.

Isaac Watts[42] (1674–1748) was a British Independent minister and a prolific author and hymn writer. Shaped by Puritan roots, he received a classical education in rhetoric and languages. Watts wrote his first poem at the age of seven and later published major works on education, philosophy, theology, and poetry. Known as the "Father of English Hymnody," he served as a critical bridge from exclusive metrical psalmody to original compositions that shaped evangelical hymns. Watts believed that hymns should address and be understood by all classes of people.

Phillis Wheatley[43] (1753–1784) was an African American poet who wrote her first poem at thirteen and published the first book by an African American writer. Sold into slavery at the age of seven, she learned to read and write with the guidance of her Boston family. Well-known for her popular elegies, which comprised over a third of her writings, Wheatley also corresponded with Samson Occom, Richard Allen, and Countess Huntingdon.

George Whitefield[44] (1714–1770) was a British Anglican minister who traveled seven times to North America to conduct preaching tours and rightly earned the title of transatlantic revivalist. Throughout much of his life, Whitefield was the center of controversy. Early theological disputes over predestination created two forms of Methodism: the Calvinist Methodism of Whitefield and the Arminian Methodism of the Wesleys. Although he was one of the most significant leaders of the Great Awakening and English Revival, Whitefield had little interest in organization and instead devoted himself to preaching the gospel of the new birth in Christ.

William Wilberforce[45] (1759–1833) was a British member of Parliament and an abolitionist, first elected to Parliament in 1780. Philip Doddridge's *Rise and Progress of Religion in the Soul* contributed to his conversion, and John Newton provided both spiritual and political counsel. Wilberforce championed the efforts that eventually abolished the slave trade in 1807. More broadly, he desired a "reformation of manners" in all areas of life. His popular *A Practical View of the Prevailing Religious System of Professed Christians* (1797) refuted external formalism and stressed the reality of a vital Christianity.

William Williams[46] (1717–1791), often called *Pantycelyn* (the name of the farm where he spent most of his life), was a prolific Welsh author, preacher, and leader of the Welsh Evangelical Revival. Acknowledged as the "Father of Welsh Hymnody," he composed hymns that employed rich biblical imagery, often focused on the theme of pilgrimage. Also significant was his book on the Welsh experience meetings, written to guide others into deeper Christian maturity.

John Witherspoon[47] (1723–1794), a Presbyterian minister, led the Popular (or evangelical) party of the Church of Scotland. In 1768, he became president of the College of New Jersey (later Princeton University) with the hope of unifying the conflicted American Presbyterians. He was the only minister to sign the Declaration of Independence. Witherspoon's blending of piety and politics is evidenced in his famous fast day sermon at the start of the Revolutionary War.

Nicholas Ludwig, Count von Zinzendorf[48] (1700–1760), was a German Pietist and leader of the Moravian Church. His offer of his estate to the persecuted refugees of the Bohemian Brethren, who were the spiritual descendants of John Hus (ca.1372–1415), inspired the reestablishment of the *Unitas Fratrum* or Moravian Church. Zinzendorf's foundational christological theology emphasized his devotion to the Side Wound of Jesus, which he believed was the birthplace of the Christian Church, a theme that appears frequently in the two thousand hymns he penned. He was a master at organization and spiritual nurture, and exerted an early influence on John Wesley.

1

NEW LIFE IN CHRIST

INTRODUCTION

The reality of the human condition confronts people with the tragedy of pain and brokenness. Early evangelicals took sin seriously and understood its disastrous effects, the way it splintered relationships with both God and humanity. The vivid language employed in describing sin—including some of the terms used throughout the texts of this section: *worm of dust, lost, blind, wretched, pitiful,* and *starving*—expresses the depth of this awareness. Evangelicals recognized that sin created doubt, fear, and numerous expressions of spiritual turmoil. Sin could also convince a person that they could never escape this prison because they were unworthy. Fortunately, these eighteenth-century believers were also cognizant of God's grace and the promise of new life in Christ. Regardless of a person's experience, God was rich in mercy and assured them that there was a better way of living. God's outstretched arms of welcome always extended the invitation to come and be healed, restored, and forgiven. This was possible because Jesus Christ, the Lamb of God, shed his blood on the cross to save all those who would believe and follow him (John 1:29). The importance of Christ's blood even inspired the fascination of some with the side wound of Jesus, which they emphasized. For early evangelicals, this was truly "amazing grace" that redeemed and created assurance of peace and comfort to troubled souls. The proper response to Jesus' invitation was sincere repentance that exchanged the sinner's old life for one that sought, through self-denial, to follow Jesus daily. These twin themes of the cross and conversion became the message that was preached and communicated by ministers and laypeople alike. The result of being spiritually awakened challenged all who practiced a formalistic or "Pharisee-like faith," especially ministers who had not experienced the spiritual rebirth.

It is often difficult to classify spiritual texts because of their richness and depth and the fact that they may address topics from more than one thematic category in this book. To assist readers, the index at the back of this book will provide cross-references when specific readings relate to one of the other five themes.

THE TEXTS

Isaac Watts, "Crucifixion to the World by the Cross of Christ, Gal. 6:14"[1]

When I survey the wondrous cross
Where the young Prince of Glory dy'd,
My richest gain I count but loss,
And pour contempt on all my pride.

Forbid it, Lord, that I should boast
Save in the death of Christ my God;
All the vain things that charm me most,
I sacrifice them to his blood.

See from his head, his hands, his feet,
Sorrow and love flow mingled down;
Did e're such love and sorrow meet?
Or thorns compose so rich a crown?

His dying crimson like a robe
Spread o'er his body on the tree,
Then am I dead to all the globe,
And all the globe is dead to me.

Were the whole realm of nature mine,
That were a present far too small;
Love so amazing, so divine
Demands my soul, my life, my all.

Gilbert Tennent, *The Danger of an Unconverted Ministry*, Preached at Nottingham, in Pennsylvania, March 8, 1740[2]

> And Jesus, when he came out, saw much people, and was moved with compassion toward them, because they were as sheep not having a shepherd. (Mark 6:34)

As a faithful ministry is a great ornament, a blessing, and comfort to the church of God, even the feet of such messengers are beautiful, so on the contrary, an ungodly ministry is a great curse and judgment; these caterpillars labor to devour every green thing.

There is nothing that may more justly call forth our saddest sorrows and make all our powers and passions mourn in the most doleful accents, the most incessant, insatiable, and deploring agonies, than the melancholy case of such who have no faithful ministry! This truth is set before our minds in a strong light, in the words that I have chosen now to insist upon, in which we have an account of our Lord's grief, with the causes of it. We are informed that our dear Redeemer was moved with compassion toward them. The original word signifies the strongest and most vehement pity, issuing from the innermost bowels [i.e., affections].

But what was the cause of this great and compassionate commotion in the heart of Christ? It was because he saw much people as sheep having no shepherd. Why, had the people then no teachers? O yes! They had heaps of Pharisee teachers that came out, no doubt after they had been at the feet of Gamaliel the usual time, and according to the acts, canons, and traditions of the Jewish church. But notwithstanding of the great crowds of these orthodox, letter-learned and regular Pharisees, our Lord laments the unhappy case of that great number of people who, in the days of his flesh, had no better guides because that those were as good as none (in many respects) in our Savior's judgment. For all them, the people were as sheep without a shepherd.

From the words of our text, the following proposition offers itself to our consideration: that the case of such is much to be pitied who have no other but Pharisee shepherds or unconverted teachers. In discoursing upon this subject, I would

1. enquire into the characters of the old Pharisee teachers;
2. show why the case of such people, who have no better, should be pitied; and
3. show how pity should be expressed upon this mournful occasion!

First I am to enquire into the characters of the old Pharisee teachers. Now, I think the most notorious branches of their character were these: pride, policy, malice, ignorance, covetousness, and bigotry to human inventions in religious matters. The old Pharisees were very proud and conceited; they loved the uppermost seats in the synagogues and to be called rabbi, rabbi....They looked upon others that differed from them and the common people with an air of disdain, and especially any who had a respect for Jesus and his doctrine, and disliked them....

Although some of the old Pharisee shepherds had a very fair and strict outside, yet were they ignorant of the new birth; witness Rabbi Nicodemus, who talked like a fool about it....Ay, if they had but a little of the learning then in fashion, and a fair outside, they were presently put into the priest's office, though they had no experience of the new birth. O sad!...

And what a mighty respect had they for the Sabbath day? In so much that Christ and his disciples must be charged with the breach thereof, for doing works of mercy and necessity. Ah the rottenness of those hypocrites! It was not so much respect to the Sabbath as malice against Christ; that was the occasion of the charge; they wanted some plausible pretense to offer against him in order to blacken his character.

And what a great love had they in pretense to those pious prophets who were dead before they were born? While in the meantime they were persecuting the Prince of Prophets! Hear how the King of the church speaks to them upon this head, Matthew 23:29–33: "Woe unto you, Scribes and Pharisees, hypocrites; because ye build the tombs of the prophets, and garnish the sepulchers of the righteous; and say, If we had been in the days of our fathers, we would not have been partakers with them in the blood of the prophets. Ye serpents, ye generation of vipers, how can ye escape the damnation of Hell?"

The second general head of discourse is to show why such people, who have no better than the old Pharisee teachers, are to be pitied.

1. Natural men have no call of God to the ministerial work under the gospel dispensation. Isn't it a principal part of the ordinary call of God to the ministerial work to aim at the glory of God and, in subordination thereto, the good of souls, as their chief marks in their undertaking that work? And can any natural man on earth do this? No! no!…Now, are not all unconverted men wicked men? Does not the Lord Jesus inform us, (John 10:1) that "he who entereth not by the Door into the sheep-fold, but climbeth up some other way, the same is a thief and a robber?" In the ninth verse Christ tells us that "He is the Door; and that if any man enter in by him, he shall be saved, by him," i.e., by faith in him, says [Matthew] Henry.* Hence we read of a door of faith being opened to the Gentiles (Acts 14:27). It confirms this gloss, that salvation is annexed to the entrance before mentioned. Remarkable is that saying of our Savior, Matthew 4:19: "Follow me, and I will make you fishers of men." See, our Lord will not make men ministers until they follow him. Men that do not follow Christ may fish faithfully for a good name and for worldly self but not for the conversion of sinners to God. Is it reasonable to suppose that they will be earnestly concerned for others' salvation when they slight their own? Our Lord reproved Nicodemus for taking upon him the office of instructing others, while he himself was a stranger to the new birth (John 3:10)….For how can these men be faithful that have no faith?…

2. The ministry of natural men is uncomfortable to gracious souls….

Natural men, not having true love to Christ and the souls of their fellow creatures, hence their discourses are cold and sapless, and as it were freeze between their lips! And not being sent of God, they want that divine authority with which the faithful ambassadors of Christ are clothed, who herein resemble their blessed Master, of whom it is said that "he taught as one having authority, and not as the scribes" (Matt 7:29).

---

*Matthew Henry authored the popular *Complete Commentary on the Bible* (1708–1710).

And Pharisee teachers, having no experience of a special work of the Holy Ghost upon their own souls, are therefore neither inclined to nor fitted for discoursing frequently, clearly, and pathetically upon such important subjects. The application of their discourses is either short or indistinct and general. They difference not the precious from the vile, and divide not to every person his portion, according to the apostolic direction to Timothy. No! They carelessly offer a common mess to their people and leave it to them to divide it among themselves as they see fit. This is indeed their general practice, which is bad enough; but sometimes they do worse, by misapplying the word, through ignorance, or anger....

And natural men, wanting the experience of those spiritual difficulties which pious souls are exposed to in this vale of tears, they know not how to speak a word to the weary in season. Their prayers are also cold; little childlike love to God, or pity to poor perishing souls, runs through their veins. Their conversation has nothing of the savor of Christ, neither is it perfumed with the spices of heaven.... Poor Christians are stunted and starved who are put to feed on such bare pastures and such dry nurses, as the Rev. Mr. Hildersham* justly calls them. It's only when the wise virgins sleep that they can bear with those dead dogs that can't bark; but when the Lord revives his people, they can't but abhor them! O! It is ready to break their very hearts with grief, to see how lukewarm those Pharisee teachers are in their public discourses while sinners are sinking into damnation, in multitudes! But

3. The ministry of natural men is for the most part unprofitable, which is confirmed by a threefold evidence of Scripture, reason, and experience. Such as the Lord sends not, he himself assures us, shall not profit the people at all (Jer 23:32)....And right reason will inform us how unfit instruments they are to negotiate that work they pretend to. Is a blind man fit to be a guide in a very dangerous way? Is a dead man fit to bring others to life?...Isn't an unconverted minister like a man who would learn others to swim before he has learned it himself, and so is drowned in the act and dies like a fool?

I may add that sad experience verifies what has been now observed concerning the unprofitableness of the ministry of uncon-

---

*Arthur Hildersham (1563–1632) was a well-known English Puritan preacher.

verted men. Look into the congregations of unconverted ministers and see what a sad security reigns there, not a soul convinced that can be heard of, for many years together; and yet the ministers are easy, for they say they do their duty! Ay, a small matter will satisfy us in the want of that which we have no great desire after. But when persons have their eyes opened and their hearts set upon the work of God, they are not so soon satisfied....

4. The ministry of natural men is dangerous, both in respect of the doctrines and practice of piety. The doctrines of original sin, justification by faith alone, and the other points of Calvinism are very cross to the grain of unrenewed nature. And though men, by the influence of a good education and hopes of preferment, may have the edge of their natural enmity against them blunted, yet it's far from being broken or removed; it's only the saving grace of God that can give us a true relish for those nature-humbling doctrines and so effectually secure us from being infected by the contrary. Is not the carnality of the ministry one great cause of the general spread of Arminianism, Socinianism, Arianism, and Deism, at this day through the world?

And alas! What poor guides are natural ministers to those who are under spiritual trouble? They either slight such distress altogether and call it melancholy, or madness, or dab those that are under it with untempered mortar. Our Lord assures us that the salt which has lost its savor is good for nothing....Pharisee teachers will with the utmost hate oppose the very work of God's Spirit upon the souls of people, and labor by all means to blacken it, as well as the instruments which the Almighty improves to promote the same, if it comes near their borders, and interferes with their credit or interest. Thus did the Pharisees deal with our Savior....

Third general head was to show how pity should be expressed upon this mournful occasion! My brethren, we should mourn over those that are destitute of faithful ministers and sympathize with them. Our bowels [i.e. affections] should be moved with the most compassionate tenderness over those dear fainting souls that are "as sheep having no shepherd," and that after the example of our blessed Lord!

Dear sirs! We should also most earnestly pray for them, that the compassionate Savior may preserve them, by his mighty power, through faith unto salvation; support their sinking spirits under the melancholy uneasinesses of a dead ministry; sanctify and sweeten to them the dry morsels they get under such blind men, when they have none better to repair to.

And more especially, my brethren, we should pray to the Lord of the harvest to send forth faithful laborers into his harvest, seeing that the harvest truly is plenteous, but the laborers are few….And indeed, my brethren, we should join our endeavors to our prayers. The most likely method to stock the church with a faithful ministry, in the present situation of things, the public academies being so much corrupted and abused generally, is to encourage private schools, or seminaries of learning, which are under the care of skillful and experienced Christians, in which those only should be admitted who, upon strict examination, have, in the judgment of a reasonable charity, the plain evidences of experimental religion. Pious and experienced youths who have a good natural capacity and great desires after the ministerial work from good motives might be sought for and found up and down the country and put to private schools of the prophets, especially in such places where the public ones are not….

5. If the ministry of natural men be as it has been represented, then it is both lawful and expedient to go from them to hear godly persons; yes, it's so far from being sinful to do this that one who lives under a pious minister of lesser gifts, after having honestly endeavored to get benefit by his ministry, and yet gets little or none but does find real benefit and more benefit elsewhere, I say he may lawfully go, and that frequently, where he gets most good to his precious soul, after regular application to the pastor where he lives, for his consent, and proposing the reasons thereof, when this is done in the spirit of love and meekness, without contempt of any, as also without rash anger, or vain curiosity….

If the great ends of hearing may be attained as well and better by hearing of another minister than our own, then I see not why we should be under a fatal necessity of hearing him, I mean our parish minister, perpetually, or generally….Well then, and may not these ends be obtained out of our parish line? Faith is said to come by hearing (Rom 10). But the Apostle doesn't add, your parish minister. Isn't the same word preached out of our parish? And is there any restriction in the promises of blessing the word to those only who keep within their parish line ordinarily? If there be, I have not yet met with it; yes,

I can affirm that so far as knowledge can be had in such cases, I have known persons to get saving good to their souls by hearing over their parish line; and this makes me earnest in defense of it.

John Cennick, "Children of the heav'nly King"[3]

1. Children of the heav'nly King,
As ye journey sweetly sing:
Sing your Savior's worthy praise!
Glorious in his works and ways!

2. We are trav'lling home to God,
In the Way, the fathers trod:
They are happy now; and we
soon their happiness shall see!

3. Glory be to Jesu's Name!
Glory be to Christ the Lamb!
Thro' thy blood were we redeem'd,
When we justly were condemn'd.

4. O ye banish'd seed be glad!
Christ our Advocate is made:
Us to save our flesh assumes,
Brother to our soul becomes.

5. Shout ye little flock! and blest,
You on Jesu's throne shall rest:
There your seat is now prepar'd,
There your kingdom and reward!

7. Fear not, brethren! joyful stand,
On the borders of your land:
Jesus Christ your Father's Son,
Bids you undismay'd go on.

8. Lord, obediently we go,
Gladly leaving all below:

Only Thou our Leader be,
And we still will follow Thee.

Nicholas Ludwig Zinzendorf and others, *The Pleurodie* (Formerly *Te Pleura*)[4]

Praise the election by grace
In the holy mark in the side!
O dear Lamb, be blessed
For the opening of your side!
All angels and the heavenly host
Who gaze at that with love,
But soon must veil their faces
Before the ruby light.
The church alone, Jesus' bride,
Because from there it was dug out and built,
Looks directly into the sunlight
With uncovered face.

Pax tibi, Gloria,
Cultus, memoria,
Tu pallor faucium!
Ave, Cor saucium!

That is:
Peace to you and glory,
Worship and remembrance,
You, face so pale!
Hail, broken heart!

1. Go deep within, my heart, the riven side,
Deep, deep, I say, deep within!
In its proper time, Jesus' faithfulness brings
What is earthly to the Spirit's house.

2. The one who in a dream looks in,
Does not want to awaken again.
In short, the magnet of the holy side
Attracts far beyond heaven and earth.

3. When the Lamb of God appears visibly,
And the world cries for caves in the cliffs;
Then will place of the spear-piercing
Be the medal that honors him.

    The living blood from the side
    Cries out, Cries out, Mercy!

4. Prince Isaiah saw the wound
Through the view-point of the old covenant:
Behold, and see the cleft in the rock
And in that cleft, the tomb's fountain,
Through which you chosen people
Are dug out and hewn.

5. John, Jesus' close comrade,
Saw how he was opened.
(When he was pacing in his room
And beginning his Gospel;
It thundered, said Seribent [his secretary]:
But as he came to the writing
About the holy pierced side;
What must it have been to him then?)

6. Jesus Christ showed the rest
Who he was through this wound,
And Thomas, whom the Lord commanded,
Felt in the side and the nail marks.

7. Which moved him so much
That he paid the first homage.
Now the feeling congregation calls out:
Honor to the holy pierced side! Amen.

8. Although we honor all the wounds alike
And feed upon the entire corpse;
Still we concentrate on the breast our
Thanks, shame, pain, joy, love, and desire.

9. When the new work of God originated,
So that the wife embraces her husband; (Jer 31:22; Rev 1:13)
The God's suffering sheep gave birth
To his beloved She in sleep.

10. We are poor little children,
Who have nothing in ourselves but sin,
But whom Jesus wound-bloom
Has broken through to holiness.

11. In order flesh of his flesh and bone
And spirit or his spirit to be;
That each to the womb
Gives his special devotion.

12. And at the end of all distress
One says to his beloved God:
What right my body has to the earth,
Is because it was formed in this womb.

13. That I have a poor soul, indeed,
More naturally to the side hole,
Out of which my Creator bore me anew,
When Jesus was crucified.

14. Daily, sings your Christendom,
Lamb! and wishes itself to be in the side.
The Vine and the branches
Belong in one another in there.

15. That the church shares in God's nature,
Is ascribed only from there.
The point of religion
Remains, at least, in that aeon.

16. The one whom creatures never see,
To him one holds the liturgy there.
The inexpressible things that Paul saw,
One finds there all together.

17. To where God the worthy Holy Spirit
Points so diligently,
There the assembly of Christians
Account it for their own proper place.

18. What wonder, that at this time
The evening red shines of bright?
The brethren's church at this time
Is a brother to the holy side, the bloody side.

Joseph Hart, "Come, and Welcome, to Jesus Christ"[5]

Come, ye sinners, poor and wretched,
   Weak and wounded, sick and sore.
Jesus ready stands to save you,
   Full of pity join'd with pow'r.
He is able, he is able, he is able;
   He is willing: doubt no more.

Ho! Ye needy; come, and welcome;
   God's free bounty glorify.
True belief, and true repentance,
   Ev'ry grace that brings us nigh,
Without money, without money, without money,
   Come to Jesus Christ, and buy.

Let not conscience make you linger;
   Nor of fitness fondly dream.
All the fitness he requireth
   Is, to feel your need of Him:
This he gives you, this he gives you, this he gives you;
   'Tis the Spirit's rising beam.

Come, ye weary, heavy laden,
   Bruis'd and mangled by the fall;
If you tarry, till you're better,
   You will never come at all.

Not the righteous, not the righteous, not the righteous;
   Sinners Jesus came to call.

View him grov'ling in the garden;
   Lo! your Maker prostrate lies.
On the bloody tree behold him:
   Hear him cry, before he dies;
It is finish'd; it is finish'd; it is finish'd.
   Sinner, will not this suffice?

Lo! The incarnate God, ascended,
   Pleads the merit of his blood.
Venture on him, venture wholly;
   Let no other trust intrude.
None but Jesus, none but Jesus, none but Jesus,
   Can do helpless sinners good.

Saints and angels, join'd in concert,
   Sing the praises of the Lamb;
While the blissful seats of heaven
   Sweetly echo with his name.
Hallelujah! Hallelujah! Hallelujah!
   Sinners here may sing the same.

Mary Fletcher, *Jesus, Altogether Lovely*[6]

Be of one mind, live in peace, and the God of love and peace shall be with you. (2 Cor 13:2)

Hoxton, March 10, 1763.

My dear sisters,

Since the time my heavenly father has been pleased to discover to me [that] it was his will to call me from you to another place, this thought has often occurred to my mind: "Have I discharged my duty faithfully toward them? Have I strove to discern their every danger, and to warn them of it, as

44

if it were my own soul? And have I from time to time, not failed to declare unto them whatever has appeared to me a more excellent way?" I as I looked back, I found I was dissatisfied, and many things arose in my mind, as necessary to be spoken, before I could be content to part with you. Again, I thought, though I should speak them now, yet after a little time I shall feel a desire of repeating them. This consideration induced me to write a few lines to each of you, that I may be clear of your blood.

My desire and prayer to God for you is that you may every moment behold Jesus as altogether lovely! The infinite consequence this is of to your soul has often been the subject of our conversation. That there is but one way of beholding him now, and that this way is by faith, we all know; but how to keep this eye of the soul always clear and unsullied, like the finest glass free from every speck and flaw, is the point we want to be instructed in. Let us therefore simply draw near to him who will give us wisdom liberally, because we need it; and who while we serve him in uprightness, will not lay folly to our charge.

Our grand enemy, well knowing that nothing can hurt the soul while its eye is simply fixed on Jesus, makes his continual attack here; sometimes by pleasing, sometimes by painful objects which he is always presenting to the mind, hoping to turn away its eye from him who alone is lovely; and because this roaring lion is always watching for our destruction, and every object round us tends to the same end, our Lord hath strictly commanded all who would follow him, first, to take up their cross daily, and secondly, to deny themselves.

It is by a life of self-denial alone that the eye of our faith can be kept clear. I was not a little blest the other day with the words of a good man, expressing his desire of being devoted to God in a solemn observance of chastity, poverty, and obedience. The words struck me much and appeared to contain the whole of a Christian life. The Lord was pleased to apply them close to my soul; and I will endeavor simply to relate what then occurred on each head....

1. On chastity. "Blessed are the pure in heart, for they shall see God." Their eye being unclouded does behold the invisible in everything. Heaven above and earth beneath, all to them is full of God. Their understanding being no longer darkened with any pollution of flesh or spirit, they continually, as a clear mirror, reflect the glorious image of him whom, beholding, they are constrained to cry out, "My beloved is fairer than ten thousand, and altogether lovely." And while we are speaking of chastity in its first sense (I mean with reference to Jesus and the soul), we shall easily discern that every deviation from him is a degree of spiritual adultery. Is he the God of our body and not of our soul? Does he require us to keep our garments unspotted and does he not require purity in the inward parts? Surely he does; "for without holiness of heart, no man shall see the Lord." And however fair and beautiful our outward life may appear, unless our heart is kept unpolluted, Jesus will not come and make his abode with us. Now what outward sin does to the body, thoughts do to the soul; and as a wife, treacherously departing from her husband, divorces herself from him according to the law of God, so the soul, embracing any imagination or idea contrary to the purity of her heavenly bridegroom, dissolves the union subsisting between them. And yet, so strange is the infatuation under which we labor that many who would start at outward sin will nevertheless very quietly submit to be carried away for minutes (nay, perhaps hours) with such thoughts as grievously retard their progress in holiness.

Reflecting with sorrow on this a few nights ago, it was in a lively manner impressed upon my mind that we should consider our souls as the image of God and our bodies as temples of the Lord, both pure and consecrated to his service and our hearts as an altar, on which the love of Jesus as a pure flame should continually burn, and that the fuel we are to cast into this fire is every earthly object that presents itself, whether to the eye, the ear, or any other of our senses, casting them in as soon as perceived, feeling the force of that expression, "All the vain things that charm me most, I sacrifice to Jesu's love!" And it would not be long before our tender-hearted Lord would answer, a sacrifice well pleasing in my sight.

A second sense in which I would consider the above expression some, I know, may take offense at. But it is not my business to please. I am only to do all I can for your soul, simply committing it to that God whose I am, and whom I desire in all things to obey. I hereby apply myself to those whose desire it is to care only how they may please the Lord and, for that reason, make it their cry day and night that they may be preserved from every snare and singly live to Jesus....

My business with you is only to guard you against those snares which Satan will assuredly lay for your feet. The first and, indeed, the most dangerous snare he can throw in your way is any kind or degree of intimacy with single men. Indeed I would wish you to be very sparing in your conversation with any man, but more especially with those that are single. All familiarity with these ought to be avoided, even with the most devout....The second stratagem of Satan will be to overcloud your light and lead you to dwell, in your mind, on the advantages you might meet with in another way of life; and if once he can get you so far, he will soon draw a curtain over those delightful views, stop those sweet breathings of your soul after Jesus which once you enjoyed in the days of your simplicity, when your soul was stranger to any other language....

To avoid this, you must stand all the day long on your watch tower, fixing it in your mind: "I have given myself wholly unto you; and will know no other love than thine," and every thought to contrary, however innocent in its appearance, however reasonable or profitable, must be cast into that fire of Jesu's love burning on your heart! What to another woman may be innocent, to you would be pollution; that which to a free woman might be even commendable, to her that is bound to a husband would be a degree of adultery. Leave not then your heavenly Bridegroom; do not for one moment, not even in thought but lean your feeble soul continually on him who even in this life is "able to keep you from falling" and to preserve "you faultless in the presence of his glory with exceeding joy."...

2. On poverty. We may consider this first with regard to outward things, and secondly the temper of the soul. And here we have eminently the example of our blessed Lord, who became poor for us; and while the whole earth was his, and all the fullness of it, was nevertheless himself as a banished man, not having where to lay his head. And if the Spirit of our Lord is in us, we shall willingly embrace, for his sake, what he embraced for ours. I do not here mean that we are always bound at once to dispose of all we have in this world, in order to become a Christian. By no means: we should in many cases, by so doing, put it out of our power to act in that sphere of life God has called us to. But I mean that we should so possess, as if we possessed not; remembering that nothing of what we possess is properly our own, but only delivered over to us for a little time, that as faithful stewards we may dispose of every farthing for his poor family, a part of which we are; and therefore have with them an equal right to all that is necessary, for that place God has fixed us in....

But is this poverty in temporal things all which God requires? Surely, no, it is the poor in spirit our Lord has pronounced blessed and declares that theirs is the kingdom of heaven. But that we may the more closely apply it to ourselves, let us first consider what this poverty of spirit does not, secondly what it does consist in; and thirdly, what are the fruits we may expect from it?

First, it does not consist in lowly words, in saying, God has done nothing for us, when we know he has wrought many and great deliverances; or, in at all denying what he has done for our souls.

Secondly, it does not consist in so becoming all things to all people, as to hurt our own souls, to countenance sin, or to be backward in testifying our Savior openly.

But it consists in the true knowledge of ourselves, from the light of God shining on our hearts, by faith. And this knowledge is the ground and foundation of all religion....They know their God is a consuming fire; and they glory in having him so casting themselves, as it were, upon it, and rejoicing that all which will not bear this refining flame should be consumed; determined to drink deep into that spirit of humility, which alone can abide the day of his coming, or stand when he appears.

But what are the fruits we may expect to see from this poverty of spirit? It will show itself in various ways; but in none more than these four: unwearied patience, constant gentleness, entire resignation and a perfect willingness to be accounted nothing in the esteem of other persons....

3. On obedience. To you who have kept the faith, it will not be grievous to say, study obedience as the rule of your life. Obedience to God and to people, for his sake. But what is the obedience we owe to God? Absolute and entire, in small as well as great things, and because it is in little things we are most apt to offend, I will speak most particularly of these. This obedience requires us always to have a ready mind, simply determined to follow the light of God, whatever it may cost us; and when we have laid ourselves out and think to do some great thing for God and our neighbor, to be equally willing, the end we proposed should be either answered or frustrated. So likewise when we have proposed to spend a day in such or such a manner and the providence of God prevents, we should remember, "The hairs of my head are all numbered." And none has any power against a child of God, but what is given him from above. Therefore submit to it, as the order of that God who has declared that in his sight "obedience is better than sacrifice; and to hearken than the fat of rams." In short, we should see God in everything, and make it our sole business inwardly to listen to that still small voice which none but silent souls can hear; and outwardly, to meet him in the order of his providence, remembering we are all his own, and "lying before him as soft wax, ready to be formed into any shape he pleases." And this simple recollecting ourselves in the presence of God, receiving every

occurrence as from him, and offering up every action to him, is the spirit and life of true religion....

Next let us consider what it is to obey other people for the Lord's sake, and whom we are so to obey. First, this obedience does not consist merely in affection: "I will do what such a one orders, because I love him, or because he hath done me much good, and therefore I find great pleasure in obeying him." This is often idolatry rather than obedience.

Secondly, neither does it consist in obeying such or such a person "because he is very spiritual, and perhaps nearer the heart of Christ than most others." This is as if I was to throw away the laws of my own king in order to follow those of another, because I believe him to be a better man.

Indeed, I cannot conceive that obedience which God requires us to pay to another to be anything less than a willing and ready submission to the directions or desires of those who are in authority over us, as far as the light of God in our souls does not contradict, and that purely and entirely out of love to God, forgetting the creature and only bearing in our minds, "It is God we obey in him." But one artifice of Satan which we have great need to guard against is that we are often apt to imagine the light of God contradicts when it really does not. And the very thing we fancy we may not comply with would many times be of more use to us than any other, for indeed, what self-denial can so unite our souls to God as an entire renunciation of our own will and a continual giving it up to that of another?...

I again repeat, the earnest desire of my soul for you is that you may abide in the faith and endure to the end. That you may covet to walk in the most excellent way, and be found continually standing on your guard and watching unto prayer. Then will the eternal God be your refuge, and underneath you the everlasting arms. He will set your sins far from you and cause you to dwell in purity of heart and in safety. You shall be a people saved of the Lord, who shall himself become your guide and your exceeding great reward.

Samson Occom, An Extract of a Sermon, Preached August 17, 1766[7]

And it repented the LORD that he had made man on the earth, and it grieved him at his heart. (Gen 6:6)

Such is the infinite mercy and goodness of God that he puts his people into various ways for their own good, and he never gives them a blow unless he gives them timely warning, and if you will not repent, you may expect that the blow of the Lord will fall on you. "And God saw that the wickedness of man was great in the earth; whatsoever pleased them in the ways of wickedness they practiced"; and then followed the words of my text, "And it repented the LORD that he had made man on the earth, and it grieved him at his heart." What solemn words these are! I think they would move the heathens; I think they would make them shed tears; it grieved him at his heart, and this shows us how disagreeable and odious sin is in the sight of God.

In further discoursing on these words, first, I shall show what sin is. You have had the word of God open to you all your days wherein sin is discovered; yet I shall at this time inform you what sin is. First, it is a transgression of the law of God, it is that which is contrary to him, it is that which would destroy every thing that belongs to God. When God sent forth his Son, how did sinners rise up against him, they followed him, and at last they killed him. It began first between two brothers, I mean Cain and Abel; and Cain rose up and slew his brother, Abel. It is what God hates, and he cannot away with it, since God is so holy, so good, and so just, and sin is so bad, so filthy. It is abominable to him, and the Spirit of God is grieved with the sin of humanity; and it grieved him in his passage through this world, when he beheld Jerusalem, that great city, he wept over it, because they had given themselves over to all manner of wickedness. And sin grieves the people of God—witness the psalmist, who says that fountains of tears flowed from his eyes; and one of the prophets, I think it is Jeremiah, wished to have a place in the wilderness, there to weep out his life for the sins of his people.

Secondly, I come to show what destruction sin has made among the sons of humanity. And for this we need not look far from the Bible; all the confusion that is among humanity is occasioned by sin; it is disagreeable to God. To conclude, he is our Benefactor, he is our God, he is our Redeemer; and if we allow this, how can we in our hearts sin against him, and how comes it to pass that we go quite contrary to what we read in the word of God? Have not we reason to think that the Lord is angry with us, that he is grieved at his heart? And as we have occasioned this, let us be sorry for our own sins and repent of them. Let us live as become rational creatures, as accountable beings that must answer for every thought, word, and action at the great tribunal. Let us examine, for the time to come, how it stands between God and our souls, to the end that we may be received to the fruition of God's glory.

Samson Occom, An Extract of a Sermon, Preached September 7, 1766[8]

My sheep hear my voice, and I know them, and they follow me. (John 10:27)

We find that the word of God is good; it is represented by him many ways. There must be a number that the Lord owns as his sheep, and some that do not belong to his flock. In further discoursing on these words:

I shall [first] show who are those that the Lord calls his sheep; it must certainly be those that have repented and are converted to him. My sheep hear my voice. It is the work of the Spirit to show humanity their lost and undone state. Persons are overwhelmed with sin, but God opens a way of salvation through Jesus Christ. And when they come to comply with this voice, then it is delightful, it is charming. The whole Bible was a sealed book to them till the Spirit revealed it, but now they know what it is, they understand the Scriptures so as to receive them; it is sweet to their taste. Then they see the sinfulness of their nature. They then wish to be in a solitary place, there to weep out their lives with the prophet Jeremiah.

Secondly, by being favored with God's voice we may soon discover his people. Christians rejoice in each other.

Thirdly, how is it, that the Lord Jesus Christ knows his sheep? This is no difficulty. God knows all things; he knows his sheep by their peculiar marks; they have that of holiness upon them. The Lord Jesus Christ supports his sheep in all their distresses and difficulties that they meet with in this world, and he will stand by them and deliver them out of all their troubles; and at last he will give them a crown of life. He hears all their prayers that they offer up to him. He remembers them, so as to give them at last, according to his promise, a great and glorious reward. He will be their Comforter and Guide through this vale of tears and will acknowledge them in that upper world before all his holy angels. They have nothing to do but to keep his statutes and ordinances, and he will preserve them.

To conclude, first, have we ever heard his voice? Are we his sheep? Have we found a way of salvation through Jesus Christ? Did we comply with it? This makes me remember a poor Indian [*sic*] woman that some years ago was converted. As soon as she knew this book to be the book of God, she said that it was as thunder and lightning unto her soul, and every word that she read was against her; but a little while after, she said it was all sweet, it was pleasant to her taste, and all for her good; I want to be a true Christian, one that devotes himself up to God, entirely depending on him.

Secondly, do we hear the voice of the Lord from time to time? Do we find him speaking to us? Do we find sweet communion with him? If we do, happy are we! Then we have nothing to do but to follow the Lamb where ever he goes; and if there are any in this assembly that have not heard his voice, he knows you, he is acquainted with all your secret thoughts, and you must give an account of them at his bar. You who have despised his mercy will then be placed on his left hand. And how can you stand? How can you bear to hear that sentence pronounced on you, "Depart from me, ye cursed, into everlasting fire, prepared for the Devil and his angels." Oh! don't be contented with the outward forms of religion, but endeavor to be real Christians, that we all may meet together in heaven.

Samuel Davies, "The Glories of God in Pardoning Sinners," Micah 7:18[9]

Great God of wonders! All thy ways
Are matchless, godlike, and divine.
But the fair glories of thy grace

More godlike and unrivall'd shine:
Who is a pard'ning God like thee?
Or who has grace so rich and free?

Crimes of such horror to forgive,
Such guilty daring worms to spare,
This is thy grand prerogative,
And none shall in the honor share.
Who is a pard'ning God like thee?
Or who has grace so rich and free?

Angels and men resign your claim
To pity, mercy, love and grace;
These glories crown Jehovah's name
With an incomparable blaze.
Who is a pard'ning God like thee?
Or who has grace so rich and free?

In wonder lost, with trembling joy,
We take the pardon of our God,
Pardon for crimes of deepest die,
A pardon bought with Jesus' blood.
Who is a pard'ning God like thee?
Or who has grace so rich and free?

O may this strange, this matchless grace,
This godlike miracle of love
Fill the wide earth with grateful praise,
And all th' angelic hosts above!
Who is a pard'ning God like thee?
Or who has grace so rich and free?

Augustus Toplady, "Rock of ages" (A Prayer, Living and Dying)[10]

Rock of ages, cleft for me,
Let me hide myself in Thee!
Let the water and the blood,

From thy riven side which flow'd,
Be of sin the double cure;
Cleanse me from its guilt and pow'r.

Not the labors of my hands
Can fulfill thy law's demands:
Could my zeal no respite know,
Could my tears forever flow,
All for sin could not atone:
Thou must save, and Thou alone.

Nothing in my hand I bring;
Simple to thy cross I cling;
Naked, come to Thee for dress;
Helpless, look to Thee for grace;
Foul, I to the Fountain fly:
Wash me, Savior, or I die!

While I draw this fleeting breath—
When my eye-strings break in death—
When I soar to worlds unknown—
See Thee on thy judgement-throne—
Rock of ages, cleft for me,
Let me hide myself in Thee!

John Newton, "Faith's Review and Expectation" (1 Chr 17:16–17)[11]

Amazing grace! (how sweet the sound)
   That saved a wretch like me!
I once was lost, but now am found,
   Was blind, but now I see.

'Twas grace that taught my heart to fear,
   And grace my fears relieved;
How precious did that grace appear,
   The hour I first believed!

Through many dangers, toils and snares,
    I have already come;
'Tis grace has brought me safe thus far,
    And grace will lead me home.

The Lord has promised good to me,
    His word my hope secures;
He will my shield and portion be,
    As long as life endures.

Yes, when this flesh and heart shall fail,
    And mortal life shall cease,
I shall possess, within the veil,
    A life of joy and peace.

The earth shall soon dissolve like snow,
    The sun forbear to shine;
But God, who called me here below,
    Will be for ever mine.

Anne Steele, "Longing Souls Invited to the Gospel Feast, Luke 14:22"[12]

Ye wretched, hungry, starving poor,
    Behold a royal feast!
Where mercy spreads her bounteous store,
    For every humble guest.

See, Jesus stands with open arms;
    He calls, he bids you come:
Guilt holds you back, and fear alarms;
    But see, there yet is room.

Room in the Savior's bleeding heart:
    There love and pity meet;
Nor will he bid the soul depart,
    That trembles at his feet.

In him, the Father reconcil'd
  Invites your souls to come;
The rebel shall be call'd a child,
  And kindly welcom'd home.

O come, and with his children taste
  The blessings of his love;
While hope attends the sweet repast,
  Of nobler joys above.

There, with united heart and voice,
  Before th' eternal throne,
Ten thousand thousand souls rejoice,
  In ecstasies unknown.

And yet ten thousand thousand more,
  Are welcome still to come:
Ye longing souls, the grace adore;
  Approach, there yet is room.

Henry Alline, ["My Conversion"][13]

Thus I continued until the 26th of March, 1775, and there being no preaching in the town, that day I spent, yes all the day, in reading, praying and meditating, sometimes in the house, and sometimes walking in the fields, but found no relief from any quarter. As I was about sunset wandering about in the fields lamenting my miserable, lost and undone condition, and almost ready to sink under my burden, I thought I was in such a miserable case as never any person was before, and did not see any prospect of ever obtaining any relief. O the thought of continuing in such a dark vault and distressing storm as I was in, how could I bear it, or what must I do! O why did God make me to be thus miserable, and leave me (as I thought he had) to perish in this condition, being a stranger to myself, to God and to all happiness? I returned to the house under as much distress as I could hardly bear, and when I got to the door, just as I was stepping off the threshold, the following impressions came into my mind like a powerful, but small still voice. You have been seeking, praying, reforming, laboring, reading, hearing and meditating, and what have you done by it toward your salvation? Are you any nearer to conversion now than when you first began? Are you any more prepared for heaven, or fitter to appear before the impartial bar of God, than when you first began to seek?

It brought such conviction on me, and that immediately to my mind, that I was obliged to say that I did not think I was one step nearer than at first, nor any more happy or prepared than years ago, but as much condemned, as much exposed, and as miserable as before. Then were again in an instant impressed on my mind these words: Should you live as much longer as you have, and seek as much, pray as much, do as much and reform as much; as you have done nothing now, you will have done nothing then, and then what will you be the better? My soul cried out within me, no, no. I shall never be better, if I live ten or twenty years longer. O what shall I do, what shall I say, or where shall I flee? I am undone; and if there be not some way found out that I am a stranger to and never stepped one step in, I am gone forever. O mercy, mercy, Lord have mercy on me, or I am undone to all eternity. And now I began to be stripped and saw that I had done nothing, and never could do any thing. I had often thought that this was not right, and that was not right; I went wrong this way and that way; did not keep my watch this time or that time; which was the reason that I had not been converted; but if I had done so and so, and had not gone astray here and there, I should have found mercy before now, and I intend to keep a better watch, seek more earnestly, and seek more humbly, love, etc., and then I shall find mercy. But O these hopes and the ways I had so often and so long practiced all failed me, and I saw that I could neither extricate myself out of my lost, undone condition, nor recommend myself to God by any thing I had done or ever could do if I were to live a thousand years. And I appeared further from conversion than ever; for under some agreeable frames, when I felt my passions moved, I would hope that I was nearer conversion; but now even all those agreeable frames were gone, and I found that I could neither love, pray, praise nor repent. But my heart felt hard, my will stubborn, my soul dry and barren, starving for want of one crumb of bread, all my wisdom and human prudence seemed to be gone, and I was as ignorant as a beast; and my original sin and fountain of corruption appeared ten thousand times greater and worse than all my actual sins. I cried out within myself, O Lord God, I am lost, and if you O Lord do not find out some new way I know nothing of, I shall never be saved, for the ways and methods I have prescribed to myself have all failed me, and I am willing they should fail. O Lord, have mercy, O Lord, have mercy.

These discoveries continued until I went into the house and sat down, which was but a short time, though I saw more than I could express or had seen for some time. After I sat down, being all in con- fusion like a drowning man that was just giving up to sink, I had nothing now to depend on but on some invisible and unknown God to whom I was continually groaning with groans unutterable. I have nothing now to support me or help me; what must I do? Or where shall I go? Will God have mercy on me, or must I sink forever? Being almost in an agony, I turned very suddenly round in my chair, and seeing part of an old Bible laying in one of the chairs, I caught hold of it in great haste and, opening it without any premeditation, cast my eyes on the 38th Psalm, which was the first time I ever saw the word of God. It took hold of me with such power that it seemed to go through my whole soul and read therein every thought of my heart, and raised my whole soul with groans and earnest cries to God, so that it seemed as if God was praying in, with, and for me. This so affected me that I could not refrain from tears and was obliged to close the book, but still continued praying in the same words; for it seemed as if I could repeat them almost as well without the book as with it. After I had sat thus for some time, repeating over and praying in that psalm, I again opened the Bible without any design to turn to any particular place; I cast my eyes on the 40th Psalm; the three first verses, being different from the rest, came with power and energy to my heart, but did not still take hold of it as any evidence of my being converted, but things appeared new, and I could not tell what to make of it....At that instant of time when I gave up all to him to do with me as he pleased, and was willing that God should reign in me and rule over me at his pleasure, redeeming love broke into my soul with repeated Scriptures with such power that my whole soul seemed to be melted down with love. The bur- den of guilt and condemnation was gone, darkness was expelled, my heart humbled and filled with gratitude, and my will turned of choice after the infinite God, whom I saw I had rebelled against and been deserting from all my days. Attracted by the love and beauty I saw in his divine perfections, my whole soul was inexpressibly ravished with the blessed Redeemer; not with what I expected to enjoy after death or in heaven, but with what I now enjoyed in my soul; for my whole soul seemed filled with the divine being. My whole soul that was a few minutes ago groaning under mountains of death, wading through storms of sorrow, racked with distressing fears, and crying to an unknown God for help, was now filled with immortal love, soaring on the wings of faith, freed from the chains of death and darkness, and crying out, my Lord and my God; you are my rock and my fortress, my shield and my high tower, my life, my joy, my present and my everlasting portion.

O the astonishing wonders of his grace, and the boundless ocean of redeeming love! Millions and millions of praises belong to his name. O how shall I make the least return! O what a wretch have I been to stand it out against such love! I have long and often wondered that God did not have mercy on me and convert me; but now I saw it was my own fault, and wondered why he waited so long upon such a miserable rejecter of his grace....But O free grace, free grace! O how infinitely condescending was the Ancient of Days to become an infant of a span long to redeem perishing and immortal souls! He deserves their praises forever; and my soul longs to praise him, for he is my prophet, my priest and my king; and this is my beloved, and this is my friend, O daughters of Jerusalem. O the infinite condescension of God to a worm of the dust! For though my whole soul was filled with love, and ravished with a divine ecstasy beyond any doubts or fears or thought of being then deceived, for I enjoyed a heaven on earth, and it seemed as if I were wrapped up in God, and that he had done ten thousand times more for me than ever I could expect, or had ever thought of. Yet he still stooped to the weakness of my desires and requests, made as before observed on the 13th of February; though I had no thoughts of it then, until it was given me. Looking up, I thought I saw that same light, though it appeared different, and as soon as I saw it, the design was opened to me according to his promise, and I was obliged to cry out, enough, enough, O blessed God; the work of conversion, the change and the manifestations of it are no more disputable than that light which I see, or any thing that ever I saw. I will not say I saw either of those lights with my bodily eyes, though I thought then I did, but that is no odds to me, for it was as evident to me as any thing I ever saw with my bodily eyes, and answered the end it was sent for. O how the condescension melted me, and thought I could hardly bear that God should stoop so low to such an unworthy wretch, crying out still, enough, enough, O my God, I believe, I believe; at the same time I was ravished with his love, and saying, go on, go on blessed God in love and mercy to me, and although I do not deserve you, yet I cannot live without you, and I long to drink deeper and deeper in your love. O what secret pleasure I enjoyed! Happiness and food that the world knows nothing of, substantial food and settled joy. O I would rather be a doorkeeper in the house of my God than to dwell in the tents of wickedness, crowned with all the dignities of this lower world, surrounded with all the enjoyments of time and the most exalted pleasures of sense.

In the midst of all my joys, in less than half an hour after my soul was set at liberty, the Lord discovered to me my labor in the ministry and call to preach the gospel. I cried out, amen, Lord I'll go, I'll go, send me, send me and although many (to support the ministry of antichrist) will pretend there is no such thing as a man's knowing in these days he is called to preach any other way than his going to the seats of learning to be prepared for the ministry and then authorized by men, yet, blessed be God, there is a knowledge of these things which an unconverted man knows nothing of. For my own part it was so clear to me that I had not the least doubt but I should preach the gospel; although to all appearances in the sight of man there was none appeared more unlikely, for my capacity in the world was low, being obliged to labor daily with my hands to get a living; my father's estate was not very large, and my parents being almost past labor, I had the whole care of these temporal concerns. As for learning, it was true I had read and studied more than was common for one in my station, but my education was but small; what I had of human literature I had acquired of myself without schooling, excepting what I obtained before I was eleven years of age, for I never went to school after I came to Nova Scotia; so that if learning only would make ministers of Christ, as the world vainly imagine, I had it not; but blessed be God, I trust I had that to go with me which was better than all the wisdom and learning; neither had I the least doubt, when I was near to God, of being not qualified, though after that, when I got in the dark, I had but said with all my soul, I'll go, I'll go; send me, send me with the glad tidings of salvation and messages of peace to all people; yes, my whole soul thirsted to go; and at that time found nothing of the fear of others or the storms and trials of a frowning world in the way. Although before I had any liberty for my soul from the 40th Psalm, those words, as before observed, were spoken to me: "Many shall see it, and fear, and shall trust in the Lord." O that ever God should make me instrumental in bringing one soul to the knowledge of a Savior! O Lord, send me with meekness and humility.

Richard Allen, Excerpt from His *Life, Experiences, etc.*[14]

I was born in the year of our Lord 1760, on February 14th, a slave to Benjamin Chew of Philadelphia. My mother and father and four children of us were sold into Delaware State, near Dover, and I was a child and lived with him until I was upward of twenty years of age, during which time I was awakened and brought to see myself poor, wretched and undone, and without the mercy of God must be lost. Shortly after I obtained mercy through the blood of Christ, and was constrained to exhort my old companions to seek the Lord. I went rejoicing for several days and was happy in the Lord, in conversing with many old experienced Christians. I was brought under doubts and was tempted to believe I was deceived, and was constrained to seek the Lord afresh. I went with my head bowed down for many days. My sins were a heavy burden. I was tempted to believe there was no mercy for me. I cried to the Lord both night and day. One night I thought hell would be my portion. I cried unto him who delights to hear the prayers of a poor sinner; and all of a sudden my dungeon shook, my chains flew off, and glory to God, I cried. My soul was filled. I cried, enough for me, the Savior died. Now my confidence was strengthened that the Lord, for Christ's sake, had heard my prayers and pardoned all my sins. I was constrained to go from house to house, exhorting my old companions and telling to all around what a dear Savior I had found. I joined the Methodist society and met in class at Benjamin Wells's, in the forest, Delaware State. John Gray was the class leader. I met in his class for several years.

My master was an unconverted man, and all the family; but he was what the world called a good master. He was more like a father to his slaves than any thing else. He was a very tender, humane man. My mother and father lived with him for many years. He was brought into difficulty, not being able to pay for us, and mother having several children after he had bought us, he sold my mother and three children. My mother sought the Lord and found favor with him and became a very pious woman. There were three children of us [that] remained with our old master. My oldest brother embraced religion, and my sister. Our neighbors, seeing that our master indulged us with the privilege of attending meeting once in two weeks, said that Stokeley's negroes would soon ruin him; and so my brother and myself held a council together that we would attend more faithfully to our master's business, so that it should not be said that religion made us worse servants, we would work night and day to get our crops forward, so that they should be disappointed. We frequently went to meeting on every other Thursday; but if we were likely to be backward with our crops we would refrain from going to meeting. When our master found we were making no provision to go to meeting, he would frequently ask us if it was not our meeting day, and if we were not going. We would frequently tell him, "No, sir, we would rather stay at home and get our work done." He would tell us, "Boys, I would rather you would go to your meeting; if I am not good myself, I like to see you striving yourselves to be good." Our reply would be, "Thank you, sir; but we would rather stay and get our crops forward." So we always continued to keep our crops more forward than our neighbors; and we would attend public preaching once in two weeks and class meeting once a week. At length our master said he was convinced that religion made slaves better and not worse, and often boasted of his slaves for their honesty and industry. Some time after I asked him if I might ask the preachers to come and preach at his house. He being old and infirm, my master and mistress cheerfully agreed for me to ask some of the Methodist preachers to come and preach at his house. I asked him for a note. He replied, if my word was not sufficient, he should send no note. I accordingly asked the preacher. He seemed somewhat backward at first, as my master did not send a written request; but the class leader (John Gray) observed that my word was sufficient; so he preached at my old master's house on the next Wednesday. Preaching continued for some months; at length Freeborn Garrison preached from these words: "Thou art weighed in the balance, and art found wanting." In pointing out and weighing the different characters, and among the rest weighed the slaveholders, my master believed himself to be one of that number, and after that he could not be satisfied to hold slaves, believing it to be wrong. And after that he proposed to me and my brother buying our times, to pay him sixty pounds gold and silver, or two thousand dollars continental money, which we complied with in the year 17—.

We left our master's house, and I may truly say it was like leaving our father's house; for he was a kind, affectionate, and tender-hearted master, and told us to make his house our home when we were out of a place or sick. While living with him we had family prayer in the kitchen, to which he frequently would come out himself at time of prayer, and my mistress with him. At length he invited us from the kitchen to the parlor to hold family prayer, which we attended to. We had our stated times to hold our prayer meetings and give exhortations at in the neighborhood.

I had it often impressed upon my mind that I should one day enjoy my freedom; for slavery is a bitter pill, notwithstanding we had a good master. But when we would think that our day's work was never done, we often thought that after our master's death we were liable to be sold to the highest bidder, as he was much in debt; and thus my troubles were increased, and I was often brought to weep between the porch and the altar. But I have had reason to bless my dear Lord that a door was opened unexpectedly for me to buy my time and enjoy my liberty. When I left my master's house I knew not what to do, not being used to hard work, what business I should follow to pay my master and get my living. I went to cutting of cordwood. The first day my hands were so blistered and sore that it was with difficulty I could open or shut them. I kneeled down upon my knees and prayed that the Lord would open some way for me to get my living. In a few days my hands recovered and became accustomed to cutting of wood and other hardships, so I soon became able to cut my cord and a half and two cords a day. After I was done cutting, I was employed in a brickyard by one Robert Register at fifty dollars a month, continental money. After I was done with the brick-yard I went to days' work, but did not forget to serve my dear Lord. I used off times to pray sitting, standing, or lying; and while my hands were employed to earn my bread, my heart was devoted to my dear Redeemer. Sometimes I would awake from my sleep preaching and praying. I was after this employed in driving of wagon in time of the continental war, in drawing salt from Rehobar, Sussex county, in Delaware. I had my regular stops and preaching places on the road. I enjoyed many happy seasons in meditation and prayer while in this employment.

After peace was proclaimed I then traveled extensively, striving to preach the gospel. My lot was cast in Wilmington. Shortly after, I was taken sick with the fall fever and then the pleurisy. September the 3d, 1783, I left my native place. After leaving Wilmington, I went into New Jersey and there traveled and strove to preach the gospel until the spring of 1784. I then became acquainted with Benjamin Abbot, that great and good apostle. He was one of the greatest men that ever I was acquainted with. He seldom preached but what there were souls added to his labor. He was a man of as great faith as any that ever I saw. The Lord was with him, and blessed his labors abun-dantly. He was as a friend and father to me. I was sorry when I had to leave West Jersey, knowing I had to leave a father. I was employed in cutting of wood for Captain Cruenkleton, although I preached the gospel at nights and on Sundays. My dear Lord was with me and blessed my labors, glory to God, and gave me souls for my hire. I then visited East Jersey and labored for my dear Lord, and became acquainted with Joseph Budd and made my home with him, near the new mills, a family, I trust, who loved and served the Lord. I labored some time there but, being much afflicted in body with the inflam-matory rheumatism, was not so successful as in some other places. I went from there to Jonathan Bunn's, near Bennington, East Jersey. There I labored in that neighborhood for some time. I found him and his family kind and affectionate, and he and his dear wife were a father and mother of Israel. In the year 1784 I left East Jersey, and labored in Pennsylvania. I walked until my feet became so sore and blistered the first day that I scarcely could bear them to the ground. I found the people very humane and kind in Pennsylvania. I having but little money, I stopped at Caesar Water's, at Radnor township, twelve miles from Philadelphia. I found him and his wife very kind and affectionate to me. In the evening they asked me if I would come and take tea with them, but after sitting awhile, my feet became so sore and painful that I could scarcely be able to put them to the floor. I told them that I would accept of their kind invitation, but my feet pained me so that I could not come to the table. They brought the table to me. Never was I more kindly received by strangers that I had never before seen than by them. She bathed my feet with warm water and bran; the next morning my feet were better and free from pain. They asked me if I would preach for them. I preached for them the next evening. We had a glorious meeting. They invited me to stay till Sabbath day and preach for them. I agreed to do so and preached on Sabbath day to a large congregation of different persuasions, and my dear Lord was with me, and I believe there were many souls cut to the heart and were added to the ministry. They insisted on me to stay longer with them. I stayed and labored in Radnor several weeks. Many souls were awakened and cried aloud to the Lord to have mercy upon them. I was frequently called upon by many inquiring what they should do to be saved. I appointed them to prayer and supplication at the throne of grace, and to make use of all manner of prayer, and pointed them to the invitation of our Lord and Savior Jesus Christ, who has said, "Come unto me, all ye that are weary and heavy laden, and I will give you rest." Glory be to God! and now I know he was a God at hand and left not afar off. I preached my farewell sermon and left these dear people. It was a time of visitation from above. Many were the slain of the Lord. Seldom did I ever experience such a time of mourning and lamentation among a people. There were but few colored people in the neighborhood, the most of my congregation was white. Some said, this man must be a man of God; I never heard such preaching before.

Selina Hastings, Letter to Mr. Cadogan, May 15, 1780[15]

My dear sir, I feel much indebted to my excellent friend Mrs. Talbot for the honor of a letter from you which should have met my earliest and best acknowledgments, had not business of a peculiar nature and many pressing engagements prevented me from using my pen. Well, my dear sir, to God let us render all the glory! And I lift my heart in prayer to him on your behalf that he may make you a burning and shining light! Having experienced the life and power of godliness in your own soul be careful to approve yourself as the minister of God, as the ambassador of the Lord of life. You ask my advice as to the general tone of your pulpit addresses. Alas! Sir, who is sufficient for these things? At the foot of the Savior's cross let us seek those rays of light which will infallibly guide us into all truth. There may you and I be ever found in deepest humility and prostration of soul before God, renouncing all dependence on an arm of flesh, and seeking the illuminating influences of his Spirit. In contemplating the glories of redemption, that wonderful scheme which was planned in the councils of heaven, what finite mind is not lost and absorbed! What a proof of the power of divine grace does our own experience furnish! Each of us may say with Paul, "For this cause I obtained mercy, that in me first Jesus Christ might shew forth all long-suffering, for a pattern to them which should hereafter believe in him to life everlasting." You say you have counted the cost and expect hatred and opposition. Hatred to Christ and his gospel is natural to the apostate person that many will treat your message with disdain. But be not discouraged in the faithful discharge of your high and honorable calling, and exclaim with sorrow, "Who hath believed our report, and to whom is the arm of the Lord revealed?" I refer you to that focus of the promises of our divine Immanuel, "I will never leave thee nor forsake thee." Earth and hell have united to frustrate the designs of God, but their united force has been as dust before the wind, when the omnipotence of Jehovah is exerted to carry into effect the councils and decrees of eternity.

Viewing the awful state of millions, without God and without hope in this world, cry aloud and spare not. My dear sir, has the gospel come to us in power, in the Holy Ghost, and in much assurance? Have we not prayed a thousand times, "Thy kingdom come"? O, then, let us remember the state of the multitudes immersed in sensuality, wretchedness, and accumulated vice, and erect the standard of evangelical truth among them, disperse the seed of heaven in every direction, and the dews of heaven will descend upon it; labor to win souls to Christ, and "become all things to all men, if by any means you may save some." Let Christ be preached—only preached—the glorious gospel of God our Savior must be the sum and substance of all your preaching. The sinners' only hope, the sinners' only friend, his blood and righteousness their only plea, this must be a prominent feature in all your addresses to your listeners, and the success which has ever attended the preaching of these soul-saving truths evinces it the only instrument for the conversion of sinners.

Your embassy is an embassy of love. Before Peter was sent forth, his affection and sincerity were decided in the presence of witnesses. Put the inquiry to your own heart, "Lovest thou me?" and may God the Holy Ghost enable you to respond with scrupulous sincerity; for in this question is involved the grand security of your ultimate success here and your final happiness in a world to come. Touched with the feelings of human misery, and tenderly solicitous for the fallen, guilty condition of all, you must display his surpassing love and proclaim aloud the divine efficacy of that blood which he sweat in Gethsemane and shed on Calvary for sinners, that it may, by the power of his Spirit, be sprinkled upon every heart as the only antidote to cleanse and purify from sin and iniquity, and render every recipient zealous of good works. You know not the trials that are before you. Stand prepared for every event; and with Christian courage persevere through the waters and through the fires of persecution. Be wise as serpents. With a firm step resist every allurement to draw you aside. They of your own household, your brethren after the flesh, will exert all their influence to shake your confidence in the word and promises of God. No weapon formed against you shall prosper; continue, therefore, "grounded and settled in the faith, and be not moved away from the hope of the gospel." It is satisfactory to know "that your labors will not be in vain in the Lord." Your "doctrine shall drop as the rain—your speech shall distill as the dew, as the small rain upon the tender herb, and as the showers upon the grass." The word of the Lord "shall have free course and be glorified: it shall not return unto him void."

And now, my dear sir, I have to ask your forgiveness for this tedious letter. But my days are few and numbered and I may never see your face till we meet at the right hand of the throne of God. My prayers will ever attend you that you may be steadfast, unmovable, and always abounding in the work of that divine and gracious Master who has called you to labor in his vineyard. I now surrender you into the everlasting arms of him who is "able to keep you from falling, and to present you faultless before the throne of his glory with exceeding joy." "The Lord bless you, and keep you. The Lord make his face to shine upon you, and be gracious unto you. The Lord lift the light of his countenance upon you, and give you peace" here, and never-ending happiness in his kingdom of glory hereafter. But how feeble the benediction of a worm redeemed from earth and hell! Hear the voice of your great High Priest, our exalted Prince and Savior: "All power is given to me in heaven and on earth, and, lo, I am with you always!"

Present my cordial love and affection to dear Mrs. Talbot. Entreat her to pray for me, that my faith fail not. In the midst of weakness and discouragement, may my soul be stayed in God's faithful word and patiently serve the Lord, till he shall see fit to remove my vile and sinful being to serve him as he would amidst the "spirits of the just made perfect." But all my crosses and losses I account as nothing, so that I may be the poor yet honored instrument of communicating the unsearchable riches of Christ to perishing sinners. And "unto me, who am less than the least of all saints" has this grace, this singular honor, been conferred for more than forty years. What condescending mercy to dust and ashes! Lord, what am I that I should be made instrumental of good to others? "Not unto me! Not unto me!" to thy infinite grace and mercy be all the glory!

In the world, and yet not of it, must be your motto, my dear and reverend sir; that Jesus may continually lift up the light of his countenance upon you and give you all peace and joy in believing is the earnest prayer of your ever-affectionate friend, and servant for Christ's sake.

S. Huntingdon

2

HOLY SPIRIT

INTRODUCTION

Early evangelicals affirmed the reality of the Trinity and recognized the divinity of the Holy Spirit. Jesus' promise of the indwelling of the Holy Spirit in every believer's life was foundational. Evangelicals maintained that this gift was for every age and not just for the first century, a stance that resulted in the charge of "enthusiasm" by the opposition. Yet, while the evangelicals emphasized the importance of being inspired by God to live a vital spiritual life, they distanced themselves from the excesses of spiritual excitement, fanaticism, and special revelations, not to mention from the more radical sense of being "enthusiasts," who were subversive and political troublemakers. This lived experience of faith was named "experimental" or "heart" religion and sought the integration of head and heart. It created a division between the faithful, who attempted to live a vibrant spiritual life amid their struggles and brokenness, and the "pretenders" who manifested their spirituality only externally. While the ministry of the Holy Spirit is varied, key themes in the texts featured in this chapter include sanctification, the dynamic interaction of Scripture (i.e., the word) and Spirit in the inspiration of and proper use of the Bible, perseverance throughout the pilgrimage of life's trials of affliction, sorrow, and doubt, and guidance to attain the eternal triumph and victory over sin. Growing in holiness or conformity to the revealed will of God was stressed, with the resulting emphasis upon sorrow for sin and holy affections that would inspire deeper sanctification. In times of affliction and temptation, believers were counseled to stand firm and accept their suffering for Christ. Evangelicals were continually reminded to thirst for the Holy Spirit and to seek these manifestations of the Spirit's presence and power in their daily lives.

THE TEXTS

Isaac Watts, "Holy Fortitude"[1]

Am I a soldier of the cross,
    A follower of the Lamb?
And shall I fear to own his cause,
    Or blush to speak his Name?

Must I be carry'd to the skies
    On flow'ry beds of ease,
While others fought to win the prize,
    And sail'd thro' bloody seas?

Are there no foes for me to face?
    Must I not stem the flood?
In this vile world a friend to grace,
    To help me on to God?

Sure I must fight if I would reign:
    Increase my courage, Lord:
I'll bear the toil, endure the pain,
    Supported by thy word.

Thy saints in all this glorious war
    Shall conquer tho' they die;
They see the triumph from afar,
    And seize it with their eye.

When that illustrious day shall rise,
    And all thy armies shine
In robes of victory thro' the skies,
    The glory shall be thine.

George Whitefield, "The Indwelling of the Spirit, the Common Privilege of All Believers"[2]

Nothing has rendered the cross of Christ of less effect, nothing has been a greater stumbling block and rock of offence to weak minds, than a supposition, now current among us, that most of what is contained in the gospel of Jesus Christ was designed only for our Lord's first and immediate followers and consequently calculated for one or two hundred years. Accordingly many now read the life, sufferings, death, and resurrection of Jesus Christ in the same manner as learned men read Caesar's *Commentaries* or the conquests of Alexander: as things rather intended to afford matter for speculation than to be acted over again in and by us.

As this is true of the doctrines of the gospel in general, so it is in particular of the operations of God's Spirit upon the hearts of believers, for we no sooner mention the necessity of our receiving the Holy Ghost in these last days, as well as formerly, but we are looked upon by some as enthusiasts and mad, and by others, represented as willfully deceiving the people and undermining the established constitution of the church.

Judge you then, my brethren, whether it is not high time for the true ministers of Jesus Christ, who have been themselves made partakers of this heavenly gift, to lift up their voices like a trumpet; and if they would not have those souls perish for which the Lord Jesus has shed his precious blood, to declare with all boldness that the Holy Spirit is the common privilege and portion of all believers in all ages; and that we also, as well as the first Christians, must receive the Holy Ghost [if] ever we can be truly called the children of God.

For this reason, (and also that I might answer the design of our church in appointing the present festival) I have chosen the words of the text....

First, I shall briefly show what is meant by the word *Spirit.* Secondly, I shall show that this Spirit is the common privilege of all believers. Thirdly, I shall show the reason on which this doctrine is founded. Lastly, I shall conclude with a general exhortation to believe on Jesus Christ, whereby alone we can be qualified to receive this Spirit.

And, first, I am briefly to show what is meant by the Spirit. By the Spirit, or the Holy Ghost, is to be understood the third person in the ever-blessed Trinity, consubstantial and coeternal with the Father and the Son, proceeding from yet equal to them both. For to use the words of our church in this day's office, that which we believe of the glory of the Father, the same we believe of the Son and of the Holy Ghost, without any difference or inequality.

Thus, says St. John, in this first Epistle, "There are three that bear record in Heaven, the Father, the Word, and the Holy Ghost, and these three are one" (1 John 5:7). And our Lord when he gave his apostles commission to go and teach all the nations commands them to baptize in the name of the Holy Ghost, as well as of the Father and the Son. And St. Peter said to Ananias, "Why hath Satan filled your heart to lie to the Holy Ghost?" (Acts 5:3). And, [in] verse 4 he says, "Thou hast not lied unto men, but unto God." From all which passages it is plain that the Holy Ghost is truly and properly God, as well as the Father and the Son. This is an unspeakable mystery, but a mystery of God's revealing, and therefore to be assented to with our whole hearts. Seeing God is not a man that he should lie, nor the Son of Man that he should deceive.

I proceed, secondly, to prove, that the Holy Ghost is the common privilege of all believers. But here I would not be understood of so receiving the Holy Ghost as to enable us to work miracles or show outward signs and wonders. For I allow our adversaries that to pretend to be inspired, in this sense, is being wise above what is written. Perhaps it cannot be proved that God ever interposed in this extraordinary manner, but when some new revelation was to be established, as at the first settling of the Mosaic and gospel dispensation. And as for my own part, I cannot but suspect the Spirit of those who insist upon a repetition of such miracles at this time. For the world being now become nominally Christian, at least (though, God knows, little of the power is left among us), there need not outward miracles, but only an inward cooperation of the Holy Spirit with the word to prove that Jesus is that Messiah which was to come into the world.

Besides, it is possible for you, O listener, to have faith so as to be able to remove mountains or cast out devils; no, you might speak with the tongue of men and angels, yes, and bid the sun stand still in the midst of heaven; yet, what would all these gifts of the Spirit avail you without being made partaker of his sanctifying graces? Saul had the spirit of government for a while so as to become another man, and yet was a castaway. And many who cast out devils in Christ's name at the last will be disowned by him. If therefore you had only the gifts, but was destitute of the graces of the Holy Ghost, they would only serve to lead you with so much the more solemnity to hell.

Here then, I say, we join issue with our adversaries and will readily grant that we are not in this sense to be inspired, as were our Lord's first apostles. But unless we have eyes which see not and ears that hear not, how can they read the latter part of the text and not confess that the Holy Spirit, in another sense, is the common privilege of all believers, even to the end of the world? "This spake he of the Spirit, which they that believe on him should receive." Observe, he does not say, they that believe on him for one or two ages, but they that believe on him in general, i.e., at all times and in all places. So that unless we can prove that St. John was under a delusion when he wrote these words, we must believe that we, even we also, shall receive the Holy Ghost if we believe on the Lord Jesus with our whole hearts.

Again, our Lord, just before his bitter passion, when he was about to offer up his soul an offering for the sins of the world; when his heart was most enlarged, and he would undoubtedly demand the most excellent gift for his disciples, prays, "That they all may be one, as Thou, Father, art in me, and I in thee, that they also may be one in us. I in them, and thou in me, that they be made perfect in one"; that is, that all his true followers might be united to him by his Holy Spirit, by as real, vital, and mystical a union, as there is between Jesus Christ and the Father. I say all his true followers, for it is evident from our Lord's own words that he had us and all believers in view when he put up this prayer: "Neither pray I for these alone, but for them also which shall believe on me through their Word"; so that, unless we treat our Lord as the high priests did and count him a blasphemer, we must confess that all who believe in Jesus Christ through the word or ministration of the apostles are to be joined to Jesus Christ by being made partakers of the Holy Spirit.

There's a great noise made of late about the word *enthusiast*, and it has been cast upon the preachers of the gospel as a term of reproach. But every Christian, in the proper sense of the word, must be an enthusiast. That is, must be inspired of God, or have God in him. For who dares say he is a Christian, till he can say, "God is in me"? St. Peter tells us we have many great and previous promises that we may be made partakers of the divine nature. Our Lord prays that we may be one as the Father and he are one; and our own church, in conformity to these texts of Scripture, in her excellent communion office, tells us that those who receive the sacrament worthily "dwell in Christ, and Christ in them; that they are one with Christ, and Christ with them." And yet, Christians in general must have their names cast out as evil, and ministers in particular must be looked upon as deceivers of the people, for affirming that we must be really united to God by receiving the Holy Ghost. Be astonished, O heavens, at this!

Indeed, I will not say, our letter-learned preachers deny this doctrine in express words. But, however, they do it in effect. For they talk professedly against inward feelings, and say we may have God's Spirit without feeling it, which is in reality to deny the thing itself. And had I a mind to hinder the progress of the gospel and to establish the kingdom of darkness, I would go about telling people they might have the Spirit of God, and yet not feel it....

I am now, in the third place, to show the reasonableness of this doctrine. I say, the reasonableness of this doctrine, for however it may seem foolishness to the natural person, yet to those who have tasted of the good word of Life and have felt the power of the world to come, it will appear to be founded on the highest reason, and is capable, to those who have eyes to see, even of a demonstration, I say of a demonstration. For it stands on this self-evident supposition, that we are fallen creatures, or, to use the Scripture expression, "Have all died in Adam."...

If it be true, then, that we are all by nature a motley mixture of brute and devil, it is evident that we all must receive the Holy Ghost before we can dwell with and enjoy God. When you read how the prodigal in the Gospel was reduced to follow a condition as to eat husks with swine, and how Nebuchadnezzar was turned out to graze with oxen, I am confident you pity their unhappy state. And when you hear how Jesus Christ will say, at the last day, to all that are not born again of God, "Depart from me, ye cursed, into everlasting fire, prepared for the devil and his angels," do not your hearts shrink within you, with a secret horror? And if creatures with only our degree of goodness cannot bear even the thoughts of dwelling with beasts or devils, to whose nature we are so nearly allied, how do we imagine, God, who is infinite goodness and purity itself, can dwell with us, while we are partakers of both their natures? We might as well think to reconcile heaven and hell.

When Adam had eaten the forbidden fruit, he fled and hid himself from God. Why? Because he was naked; that is, he was alienated from the life of God, the due punishment of his disobedience. Now we are all by nature naked and void of God, as he was at that time; and consequently, till we are changed and clothed upon by a divine nature again, we must fly from God also.

Hence then appear the reasonableness of our being obliged to receive the Spirit of God. It is founded on the doctrine of original sin. And therefore you will always find that those who talk against feeling the operations of the Holy Ghost very rarely, or very slightly at least, mention our fall in Adam. No, they refer St. Paul's account of the depravity of unbelievers, only to those of old time. Whereas 'tis obvious, on the contrary, that we are all equally included under the guilt and consequences of our first parent's sin, even as others; and to use the language of our own Church Article [i.e., the Thirty-Nine Articles of the Church of England], bring into the world with us a corruption which renders us liable to God's wrath and eternal damnation....

For I was, in the last place, to exhort you all to come to Jesus Christ by faith, whereby you, even you also, shall receive the Holy Ghost. "For this spake he of the Spirit, which they that believe on him should receive." This, this is what I long to come to. Hitherto I have been preaching only the law, but behold I bring you glad tidings of great joy. If I have wounded you before, be not afraid, behold, I now bring a remedy for all your wounds. For notwithstanding you are all now sunk into the nature of the beast and devil, yet if you truly believe on Jesus Christ, you shall receive the quickening Spirit promised in the text and be restored to the glorious liberties of the sons of God. I say, if you believe on Jesus Christ. "For by faith we are saved; it is not of works, least any one should boast." And however some may say, there is a fitness required in the creature, and that we must have a righteousness of our own before we can lay hold on the righteousness of Christ; yet, if we believe the Scripture, "Salvation is the free gift of God in Christ Jesus our Lord; and whosoever believeth on him with his whole heart, though his soul be black as Hell itself, shall receive the gift of the Holy Ghost." Behold then, I stand up, and cry out in this great day of the feast, "Let every one that thirsteth come unto Jesus Christ and drink. He that believeth on him, out of his belly shall flow not only stream or rivulets, but whole rivers of living water." This I speak, my brethren, of the Spirit which they that believe on Jesus shall certainly receive. For Jesus Christ is the same yesterday, today, and forever. He is the Way, the Truth, the Resurrection, and the Life. Who ever believes on him, though he were dead, yet shall he live.

There is no respect of persons with Jesus Christ. High and low, rich and poor, one with another may come to him with an humble confidence, if they draw near by faith. From him we may all receive grace upon grace. For Jesus Christ is full of grace and truth, and ready to save to the uttermost all that by a true faith turn unto him. Indeed the poor generally receive the gospel, and God has chosen the poor in this world [as] rich in faith. But though not many mighty, not many noble are called; and though it be easier for a camel to go through the eye of a needle than for a rich man to enter into the kingdom of God, yet even to you that are rich do I now freely offer salvation by Jesus Christ, if you will renounce yourselves and come to Jesus Christ as poor sinners. I say, as poor sinners; for the poor in spirit are only so blessed as to have a right to the kingdom of God. And Jesus Christ calls none to him but those that thirst after his righteousness, and feel themselves weary and heavy laden with the burden of their sins. Jesus Christ justifies the ungodly. He came not to call the righteous, but sinners to repentance.

Do not then say you are unworthy; for this is a faithful and true saying, and worthy of all to be received, that Jesus Christ came into the world to save sinners; and if you are the chief of sinners, if you feel yourselves such, verily Jesus Christ came into the world chiefly to save you. When Joseph was called out of the prison house to Pharaoh's court, we are told that he stayed some time to prepare himself; but do you come with all your prison clothes about you; come poor, and miserable, and blind, and naked as you are, and God the Father shall receive you with open arms as he did the returning prodigal. He shall cover your nakedness with the best robe of his dear Son's righteousness, shall seal you with the signet of his Spirit, and feed you with the fatted calf, even with the comforts of the Holy Ghost. Oh let there then be joy in heaven over some of you believing. Let me not go back to my Master and say, Lord, they will not believe my report. Harden no longer your hearts, but open them wide and let the King of Glory in. Believe me, I am willing to go to prison or death for you; but I am not willing to go to heaven without you. The love of Jesus Christ constrains me to lift up my voice like a trumpet. My heart is now full. Out of the abundance of the love which I have for your precious and immortal souls my mouth now speaks. And I could now not only continue my discourse till midnight, but I could speak till I could speak no more. And why should I despair of any? No, I can despair of no one, when I consider Jesus Christ has had mercy on such a wretch as I am. However you may think of yourselves, I know that by nature I am but half a devil and half a beast. The free grace of Christ prevented [i.e., preceded] me. He saw me in my blood, he passed by me, and said unto me, live. And the same grace which was sufficient for me is sufficient for you also. Behold, the same blessed Spirit is ready to breathe on all your dry bones, if you will believe on Jesus Christ whom God has sent. Indeed you can never believe on or serve a better Master, one that is more mighty, or more willing to save. Indeed I can say the Lord Christ is gracious, his yoke is easy, his burden exceeding light. After you have served him many years, like the servants under the law, was he willing to discharge you, you would say, we love our Master, and will not go from him. Come then, my guilty brethren, come and believe on the Lord that bought you with his precious blood. Look up by faith, and see whom you have pierced. Behold him bleeding, panting, dying! Behold him with arms stretched out ready to receive you all. Cry unto him as the penitent thief did, Lord, remember us now for you in your kingdom, and he shall say to your souls, "Shortly shall you be with me in paradise." For those whom Christ justifies, them he also glorifies, even with that glory which he enjoyed with the Father before the world began. Do not say, I have bought a piece of ground, and must go see it; I have bought a yoke of oxen, and must go prove them; I have married a wife, I am engaged in an eager pursuit after the lust of the eye and the pride of life; and therefore cannot come. Do not fear having your name cast out as evil, or being accounted a fool for Christ's sake. Yet a little while, and you shall shine like the stars in the firmament forever. Only believe, and Jesus Christ shall be to you wisdom, righteousness, sanctification, and eternal redemption. Your bodies shall be fashioned like unto his glorious body, and your souls fall into all the fullness of God.

Jonathan Edwards, "An Appendix Containing Some Reflections and Observations on the Preceding Memoirs of Mr. Brainerd"[3]

We have here opportunity, as I apprehend, in a very lively instance, to see the nature of true religion and the manner of its operation when exemplified in a high degree and powerful exercise. Particularly it may be worthy to be observed:

How greatly Mr. Brainerd's religion differed from that of some pretenders to the experience of a clear work of saving conversion wrought on their hearts, who, depending and living on that, settle in a cold, careless, and carnal frame of mind and in a neglect of thorough, earnest religion, in the stated practices of it. Although his convictions and conversion were in all respects exceeding clear and very remarkable, yet how far was he from acting as though he thought he had got through his work, when once he had obtained comfort and satisfaction of his interest in Christ and title to heaven. On the contrary, that work on his heart by which he was brought to this was with him evidently but the beginning of his work, his first entering on the great business of religion and the service of God, his first setting out in his race. His obtaining rest of soul in Christ, after earnest striving to enter in at the strait gate and being violent to take the kingdom of heaven, he did not look upon as putting an end to any further occasion for striving and violence in religion; but these were continued still, and maintained constantly, through all changes, to the very end of life. His work was not finished, nor his race ended, till life was ended, agreeable to frequent Scripture representations of the Christian life. He continued pressing forward in a constant manner, forgetting the things that were behind and reaching forth toward the things that were before. His pains and earnestness in the business of religion were rather increased than diminished, after he had received comfort and satisfaction concerning the safety of his state. Those divine principles by which after this he was actuated, of love to God, longings and thirsting after holiness, seem to be more effectual to engage him to pains and activity in religion than fear of hell had been before.

And as his conversion was not the end of his work or of the course of his diligence and strivings in religion, so neither was it the end of the work of the Spirit of God on his heart, but on the contrary, the beginning of that work; the beginning of his spiritual discoveries, and holy views; the first dawning of the light which thenceforth increased more and more; the beginning of his holy affections, his sorrow for sin, his love to God, his rejoicing in Christ Jesus, his longing after holiness. And the powerful operations of the Spirit of God in these things were carried on from the day of his conversion, in a continued course, to his dying day. His religious experiences, his admiration, his joy and praise and flowing affections, did not only hold up to a considerable height for a few days, weeks, or months at first, while hope and comfort were new things with him, and then gradually dwindle and die away till they came to almost nothing, and so leave him without any sensible or remarkable experience of spiritual discoveries, or holy and divine affections, for months together; as it is with many who, after the newness of things is over, soon come to that pass that it is again with them very much as it used to be before their supposed conversion, with respect to any present views of God's glory, of Christ's excellency, or of the beauty of divine things, and with respect to any present thirsting for God, or ardent outgoings of their souls after divine objects. But only now and then they have a comfortable reflection on things they have met with in times past and are something affected with them, and so rest easy, thinking all things are well; they have had a clear work and their state is safe, and they doubt not but they shall go to heaven when they die. How far otherwise was it with Mr. Brainerd than it is with such persons! His experiences, instead of dying away, were evidently of an increasing nature. His first love and other holy affections even at the beginning were very great, but after months and years became much greater and more remarkable; and the spiritual exercises of his mind continued exceeding great (though not equally so at all times, yet usually so), without indulged remissness, and without habitual dwindling and dying away, even till his decease. They began in a time of general deadness all over the land, and were greatly increased in a time of general reviving of religion. And when religion decayed again and a general deadness returned, his experiences were still kept up in their height and his holy exercises maintained in their life and vigor, and so continued to be, in a general course, wherever he was and whatever his circumstances were, among English and Indians, in company and alone, in towns and cities, and in the howling wilderness, in sickness and in health, living and dying. This is agreeable to Scripture descriptions of true and right religion and of the Christian life. The change wrought in him at his conversion was agreeable to Scripture representations of that change which is wrought in true conversion: a great change, and an abiding change, rendering him a new man, a new creature, not only a change as to hope and comfort and an apprehension of his own good estate, and a transient change consisting in high flights of passing affection, but a change of nature, a change of the abiding habit and temper of his mind....

His religion did apparently and greatly differ from that of many high pretenders to religion who are frequently actuated by vehement emotions of mind and are carried on in a course of sudden and strong impressions and supposed high illuminations and immediate discoveries, and at the same time are persons of a virulent "zeal, not according to knowledge." His convictions preceding his conversion did not arise from any frightful impressions of his imagination, or any external images and ideas of fire and brimstone, a sword of vengeance drawn, a dark pit open, devils in terrible shapes, etc., strongly fixed in his mind. His sight of his own sinfulness did not consist in any imagination of a heap of loathsome material filthiness within him; nor did his sense of the hardness of his heart consist in any bodily feeling in his breast of something hard and heavy like a stone, nor in any imaginations whatever of such a nature.

His first discovery of God or Christ at his conversion was not any strong idea of any external glory or brightness, or majesty and beauty of countenance, or pleasant voice; nor was it any supposed immediate manifestation of God's love to him in particular; nor any imagination of Christ's smiling face, arms open, or words immediately spoken to him as by name, revealing Christ's love to him, either words of Scripture or any other. But a manifestation of God's glory, and the beauty of his nature, as supremely excellent in itself, powerfully drawing and sweetly captivating his heart; bringing him to a hearty desire to exalt God, set him on the throne, and give him supreme honor and glory, as the King and Sovereign of the universe. And also a new sense of the infinite wisdom, suitableness, and excellency of the way of salvation by Christ powerfully engaging his whole soul to embrace this way of salvation, and to delight in it....

Mr. Brainerd's religion was not selfish and mercenary: his love to God was primarily and principally for the supreme excellency of his own nature and not built on a preconceived notion that God loved him, had received him into favor, and had done great things for him or promised great things to him. So his joy was joy in God and not in himself. We see by his diary how, from time to time through the course of his life, his soul was filled with ineffable sweetness and comfort. But what was the spring of this strong and abiding consolation? Not so much the consideration of the sure grounds he had to think that his state was good, that God had delivered him from hell, and that heaven was his; or any thoughts concerning his own distinguished happy and exalted circumstances, as a high favorite of heaven; but the sweet meditations and entertaining views he had of divine things without himself; the affecting considerations and lively ideas of God's infinite glory, his unchangeable blessedness, his sovereignty and universal dominion; together with the sweet exercises of love to God, giving himself up to him, abasing himself before him, denying himself for him, depending upon him, acting for his glory, diligently serving him, and the pleasing prospects or hopes he had of a future advancement of the kingdom of Christ, etc.

It appears plainly and abundantly all along, from his conversion to his death, that the beauty, that sort of good which was the great object of the new sense of his mind, the new relish and appetite given him in conversion, and thenceforward maintained and increased in his heart, was holiness, conformity to God, living to God, and glorifying him. This was what drew his heart; this was the center of his soul; this was the ocean to which all the streams of his religious affections tended; this was the object that engaged his eager thirsting desires and earnest pursuits. He knew no true excellency or happiness but this. This was what he longed for most vehemently and constantly on earth; and this was with him the beauty and blessedness of heaven which made him so much and so often to long for that world of glory; it was to be perfectly holy and perfectly exercised in the holy employments of heaven, thus to glorify God, and enjoy him for ever.

His religious illuminations, affections, and comfort seemed, to a great degree, to be attended with evangelical humiliation, consisting in a sense of his own utter insufficiency, despicableness, and odiousness, with an answerable disposition and frame of heart. How deeply affected was he almost continually with his great defects in religion; with his vast distance from that spirituality and holy frame of mind that became him; with his ignorance, pride, deadness, unsteadiness, barrenness? He was not only affected with the remembrance of his former sinfulness before his conversion, but with the sense of his present vileness and pollution. He was not only disposed to think meanly of himself as before God, and in comparison of him, but amongst men and as compared with them. He was apt to think other saints better than he; yes, to look on himself as the meanest and least of saints; yes, very often, as the vilest and worst of humanity. And notwithstanding his great attainments in spiritual knowledge, yet we find there is scarce anything that he is more frequently affected and abased with a sense of than his ignorance.

How eminently did he appear to be of a meek and quiet spirit, resembling the lamb-like, dove-like Spirit of Jesus Christ! How full of love, meekness, quietness, forgiveness, and mercy! His love was not merely a fondness and zeal for a party, but a universal benevolence very often exercised in the most sensible and ardent love to his greatest opposers and enemies. His love and meekness were not a mere pretense and outward profession and show, but they were effectual things, manifested in expensive and painful deeds of love and kindness, and in a meek behavior; readily confessing faults under the greatest trials and humbling himself even at the feet of those from whom he supposed he had suffered most; and from time to time very frequently praying for his enemies, abhorring the thoughts of bitterness or resentment toward them....

His assurance and comfort differed greatly from a false enthusiastic confidence and joy in that it promoted and maintained mourning for sin. Holy mourning, with him, was not only the work of an hour or a day, at his first conversion; but sorrow for sin was like a wound constantly running; he was a mourner for sin all his days. He did not, after he received comfort and full satisfaction of the forgiveness of all his sins and the safety of his state, forget his past sins, the sins of his youth, committed before his conversion; but the remembrance of them, from time to time, revived in his heart with renewed grief...

His religion did not consist in unaccountable flights and vehement pangs, suddenly rising and suddenly falling, at times exalted almost to the third heavens, and then at other turns negligent, vain, carnal, and swallowed up with the world for days and weeks if not months together. His religion was not like a blazing meteor or like a flaming comet (or a wandering star, as the apostle Jude calls it, verse 13) flying through the firmament with a bright rain and then quickly going out into perfect darkness; but more like the steady lights of heaven that are constant principles of light, though sometimes hid with clouds. Nor like a land-flood, which flows far and wide with a rapid stream, bearing down all before it, and then dried up; but more like a stream fed by living springs which, though sometimes increased by showers and at other times diminished by drought, yet is a constant stream. His religious affections and joys were not like those of some who have rapture and mighty emotions from time to time in company but have very little affection in retirement and secret places. Though he was of a very sociable temper and loved the company of saints, and delighted very much in religious conversation and in social worship, yet his warmest affections, and their greatest effects on animal nature, and his sweetest joys, were in his closet devotions and solitary transactions between God and his own soul, as is very observable through his whole course, from his conversion to his death. He delighted greatly in sacred retirements and loved to get quite away from all the world, to converse with God alone, in secret duties....

And the greater and sweeter his comforts were, the more vehement were his desires after holiness. For it is to be observed that his longings were not so much after joyful discoveries of God's love and clear views of his title to future advancement and eternal honors in heaven, as after more of present holiness, greater spirituality, a heart more engaged for God, to love and exalt and depend on him, an ability better to serve him, to do more for his glory, and to do all that he did with more of a regard to Christ as his righteousness and strength, and after the enlargement and advancement of Christ's kingdom in the earth. And his desires were not idle wishes, but such as were powerful and effectual, to animate him to the earnest, eager pursuit of these things, with utmost diligence and unfainting labor and self-denial. His comforts never put an end to his seeking after God and striving to obtain his grace but, on the contrary, greatly engaged him therein.

His religion did not consist only in experience without practice. All his inward illuminations, affections and comforts seemed to have a direct tendency to practice and to issue in it. And this, not merely a practice negatively good, free from gross acts of irreligion and immorality, but a practice positively holy and Christian, in a serious, devout, humble, meek, merciful, charitable, and beneficent conversation; making the service of God and our Lord Jesus Christ the great business of life, which he was devoted to and pursued with the greatest earnestness and diligence to the end of his days, through all trials....

I am far from thinking (and so was he) that clearness of the order of experiences is, in any measure, of equal importance with the clearness of their nature. I have sufficiently declared in my discourse on *Religious Affections* (which he expressly approved of and recommended) that I do not suppose a sensible distinctness of the steps of the Spirit's operation and method of successive convictions and illuminations is a necessary requisite to persons being received in full charity, as true saints, provided the nature of the things they profess be right and their practice agreeable. Nevertheless, it is observable (which cuts off all objection from such as would be most unreasonably disposed to object and cavil in the present case) so it was, that

Mr. Brainerd's experiences were not only clear in the latter respect, but remarkably so in the former: so that there is not perhaps one instance in five hundred true converts that on this account can be paralleled with him.

William Williams, "Come, Holy Spirit, now descend"[4]

Come, Holy Spirit, now descend,
And shower from above
Upon my dry and wither'd soul
Thy everlasting love.

Reveal thy glories and thy grace,
The beauties of thy name;
Remove my sin, that heavy load
Of painful guilt and shame.

Allure my soul above the world,
Where vanities abound;
And lull'd secure upon thy breast,
May I be ever found.

Taught to be wise above the wiles
Of the malicious foe,
And trample on his secret snares
Where ever I may go.

Thou God alone canst make me strong,
Thy Word can faith convey;
When with thy strength I am endued
I'll never more dismay.

Samuel Davies, "Holiness and Felicity"[5]

This is my chief design at present, and to this my text naturally leads me. It contains these doctrines:

First, that without holiness here it is impossible for us to enjoy heavenly happiness in the future world. To see the Lord is here put for enjoying him (see Rom 8:24) and the metaphor signifies the happiness of the future state in general, and more particularly intimates that the knowledge of God will be a special ingredient there. See a parallel expression in Matthew 5:8.

Secondly, that this consideration should induce us to use the most earnest endeavors to obtain the heavenly happiness. Pursue holiness because "without it no man can see the Lord." Hence I am naturally led,

1. To explain the nature of that "holiness, without which no man shall see the Lord."
2. To show what endeavors should be used to obtain it. And,
3. To urge you to use them by the consideration of the absolute necessity of holiness.*

1. I am to explain the nature of holiness. And I shall give you a brief definition of it, and then mention some of those dispositions and practices which naturally flow from it. The most intelligible description of holiness, as it is inherent in us, may be this: "It is a conformity in heart and practice to the revealed will of God." As the Supreme Being is the standard of all perfection, his holiness in particular is the standard of ours. Then we are holy when his image is stamped upon our hearts and reflected in our lives; so the Apostle defines it: "And that you put on the new man, which after God is created in righteousness and true holiness" (Eph 4:24). "Whom he did predestinate to be conformed to the image of his Son" (Rom 8:29). Hence holiness may be defined, "A conformity to God in his moral perfections." But as we cannot have a distinct knowledge of these perfections, but as they are manifested by the revealed will of God, I choose to define holiness as above: "A conformity to his revealed will." Now his revealed will comprises both the law and the gospel: the law informs us of the duty which we as creatures owe to God as a Being of supreme excellency, as our Creator and Benefactor, and to

---

*Editor's note: Only the development of the first point is included here.

humanity as our fellow-creatures; and the gospel informs us of the duty which as sinners we owe to God as reconcilable through a Mediator. Our obedience to the former implies the whole of morality, and to the latter the whole of evangelical graces, as faith in a Mediator, repentance, etc.

From this definition of holiness it appears, on the one hand, that it is absolutely necessary to see the Lord, for unless our dispositions are conformed to him, we cannot be happy in the enjoyment of him: and on the other hand, that they who are made thus holy are prepared for the vision and fruition of his face, as they can relish the divinest pleasure. But as a concise definition of holiness may give an auditory but very imperfect idea of it, I shall expatiate upon the dispositions and practices in which it consists, or which naturally result from it, and they are such as follow.

1. A delight in God for his holiness. Self-love may prompt us to love him for his goodness to us, and so many unregenerate persons may have a selfish love to God on this account. But to love God because he is infinitely holy, because he bears an infinite detestation to all sin and will not indulge his creatures in the neglect of the least instance of holiness, but commands them to be holy as he is holy, this is a disposition connatural to a renewed soul only and argues conformity to his image. Every nature is most agreeable to itself, and a holy nature is most agreeable to a holy nature.

Here I would make a remark which may God deeply impress on your hearts, and which for that purpose I shall subjoin to each particular: that holiness in fallen humanity is supernatural, I mean, we are not born with it, we give no discoveries of it till we have experienced a great change. Thus we find it in the present case [that] we have no natural love to God because of his infinite purity and hatred to all sin; no, we would love him more, did he give us greater indulgences, and I am afraid the love of some persons is founded upon a mistake: they love him because they imagine he does not hate sin, nor them for it, so much as he really does; because they think he will bring them to heaven at last, let them live as they lived; and because they do not expect he is so inexorably just in his dealings with the sinner. It is no wonder they love such a soft, easy, passive being as this imaginary deity; but did they see the luster of that holiness of God which dazzles the celestial armies, did they but know the terrors of his justice and his implacable indignation against sin, their innate enmity would show its poison and their hearts would rise against God in all those horrible blasphemies with which awakened sinners are so frequently shocked. Such love as this is so far from being acceptable that it is the greatest affront to the Supreme Being, as, if a profligate loved you on the mistaken supposition that you were such a libertine as himself, it would rather inflame your indignation than procure your respect.

But to a regenerate mind how strong, how transporting are the charms of holiness! Such a mind joins the anthem of seraphs with the most divine complacency (Rev 4:8) and anticipates the song of glorified saints, "Who would not fear thee, O Lord, and glorify thy name, for thou only art holy?" (Rev 15:4). The perfections of God lose their luster, or sink into objects of terror or contempt, if this glorious attribute be abstracted. Without holiness power becomes tyranny, omniscience craft, justice revenge and cruelty, and even the amiable attribute of goodness loses its charms and degenerates into a blind promiscuous prodigality or foolish undiscerning fondness; but when these perfections are clothed in the beauties of holiness, how god-like, how majestic, how lovely and attractive do they appear!...

2. Holiness consists in a hearty complacence in the law of God because of its purity. The law is the transcript of the moral perfections of God, and if we love the original we shall love the copy. Accordingly it is natural to a renewed mind to love the divine law, because it is perfectly holy, because it makes no allowance for the least sin, and requires every duty that it becomes us to perform toward God (Pss 119:14; 19:7–10; Rom 7:12, compared with v. 22).

But is this our natural disposition? Is this the disposition of the generality? Do they not, on the contrary, secretly find fault with the law, because it is so strict? And their common objection against that holiness of life which it enjoins is that they cannot bear to be so precise. Hence they are always for abating the rigor of the law, for bringing it down to some imaginary standard of their own, to their present ability, to sins of practice without regard to the sinful dispositions of the heart; or to the prevailing dispositions of the heart without regard to the first workings of concupiscence, those embryos of iniquity; and if they love the law at all, as they profess to do, it is upon the supposition that it is not so strict as it really is but grants them greater indulgences (Rom 8:7).

Hence it appears that, if we are made holy at all, it must be by a supernatural change; and when that is affected, what a strange and happy alteration does the sinner perceive? With what pleasure does he resign himself a willing subject to that law to which he was once so averse? And when he fails (as alas! he does in many things) how is he humbled! He does not lay the fault upon the law as requiring impossibilities, but lays the whole fault upon himself as a corrupt sinner.

3. Holiness consists in a hearty complacence in the gospel method of salvation, because it tends to illustrate the moral perfections of the Deity and to discover the beauties of holiness. The gospel informs us of two grand pre-requisites to the salvation of fallen humanity: namely, the satisfaction of divine justice by the obedience and passion of Christ, that God might be reconciled to them consistently with his perfections. And the sanctification of sinners by the efficacy of the Holy Ghost, that they might be capable of enjoying God, and that he might maintain intimate communion with them without any stain to his holiness. These two grand articles contain the substance of the gospel, and our acquiescence in them is the substance of that evangelical obedience which it requires of us, and which is essential to holiness in a fallen creature.

Now it is evident that without either of these the moral perfections of the deity, particularly his holiness, could not be illustrated or even secured in the salvation of a sinner. Had he received an apostate race into favor who had conspired in the most unnatural rebellion against him without any satisfaction, his holiness would have been eclipsed; it would not have appeared that he had so invincible an abhorrence of sin, so zealous a regard for the vindication of his own holy law or to his veracity, which had threatened condign [i.e., fitting] punishment to offenders. But by the satisfaction of Christ his holiness is illustrated in the most conspicuous manner; now it appears that God would upon no terms save a sinner but that of adequate satisfaction, and that no other was sufficient but the suffering of his coequal Son; otherwise he would not have appointed him to sustain the character of Mediator; and now it appears that his hatred of sin is such that he would not let it pass unpunished even in his own Son, when only imputed to him. In like manner, if sinners while unholy were admitted into communion with God in heaven, it would obscure the glory of his holiness, and it would not then appear that such was the purity of his nature that he could have no fellow-ship with sin. But now it is evident that even the blood of Immanuel cannot purchase heaven to be enjoyed by a sinner while unholy, but that every one that arrives at heaven must first be sanctified. An unholy sinner can be no more saved, while such, by the gospel than by the law; but here lies the difference, that the gospel makes provision for his sanctification, which is gradually carried on here and perfected at death, before his admission into the heavenly glory.

Now it is the genius of true holiness to acquiesce in both these articles. A sanctified soul places all its dependence on the righteousness of Christ for acceptance. It would be disagreeable to it to have the least concurrence in its own justification. It is not only willing, but delights to renounce all its own righteousness and to glory in Christ alone (Phil 3:3). Free grace to such souls is a charming theme, and salvation is more acceptable because conveyed in this way....

So a holy person rejoices that the way of holiness is the appointed way to heaven. He is not forced to be holy merely by the servile consideration that he must be so or perish, and so unwillingly submits to the necessity which he cannot avoid, when in the mean-time, were it put to his choice, he would choose to reserve some sins and neglect some painful duties. So far from this, that he delights in the gospel-constitution, because it requires universal holiness, and heaven would be less agreeable were he to carry even the least sin thither [i.e., in that direction]. He thinks it no hardship that he must deny himself in his sinful pleasures, and habituate himself to so much strictness in religion; no, but he blesses the Lord for obliging him to it, and where he fails he charges himself with it and is self-abased upon the account....

4. Holiness consists in a habitual delight in all the duties of holiness toward God and humanity and an earnest desire for communion with God in them. This is the natural result of all the foregoing particulars. If we love God for his holiness, we shall delight in that service in which our conformity to him consists; if we love his law, we shall delight in that obedience which it enjoins; and if we take complacence in the evangelical method of salvation, we shall take

delight in that holiness without which we cannot enjoy it. The service of God is the element, the pleasure of an holy soul; while others delight in the riches, the honors, or the pleasures of this world, the holy soul desires one thing of the Lord, that it may behold his beauty while enquiring in his temple (Ps 27:4). Such a person delights in retired converse with heaven in meditation and prayer (Pss 139:17; 63:5–6; 73:28). He also takes pleasure in justice, benevolence, and charity toward men (Ps 112:5, 9) and in the strictest temperance and sobriety (1 Cor 9:27).

Moreover, the mere formality of performing religious duties does not satisfy a true saint unless he enjoys a divine freedom therein, receives communications of grace from heaven, and finds his graces quickened (Ps 42:1–2). This consideration also shows us that holiness in us must be supernatural, for do we naturally thus delight in the service of God? Or do you all now thus delight in it? Is it not rather weariness to you, and do you not find more pleasure in other things? Surely you must be changed, or you can have no relish for the enjoyment of heavenly happiness.

5. To constitute us saints indeed there must be universal holiness in practice. This naturally follows from the last, for as the body obeys the stronger volitions of the will, so when the heart is prevailingly disposed to the service of God the person will habitually practice it. This is generally mentioned in Scripture as the grand characteristic of real religion, without which all our pretensions are vain (1 John 3:3–10, v. 3; John 15:14). True Christians are far from being perfect in practice, yet they are prevailingly holy in all manner of conversation; they do not live habitually in any one known sin or willfully neglect any one known duty (Ps 119:6). Without this practical holiness no person shall see the Lord; and if so, how great a change must be wrought on most before they can see him, for how few are thus adorned with a life of universal holiness? Many profess the name of Christ, but how few of them depart from iniquity? But to what purpose do they call him Master and Lord while they do not the things which he commands them?

Thus I have as plainly as I could described the nature and properties of that holiness without which no person shall see the Lord, and they who are possessed of it may lift up their heads with joy, assured that God has begun a good work in them and that he will carry it on; and on the other hand, they that are destitute of it may be assured that, unless they are made new creatures, they cannot see the Lord.

William Cowper, "The Light and Glory of the Word"[6]

The Spirit breathes upon the word,
And brings the truth to sight;
Precepts and promises afford
A sanctifying light.

A glory gilds the sacred page,
Majestic like the sun
It gives a light to every age,
It gives, but borrows none.

The hand that gave it, still supplies
The gracious light and heat;
His truths upon the nations rise,
They rise, but never set.

Let everlasting thanks be thine
For such a bright display,
As makes a world of darkness shine
With beams of heav'nly day.

My soul rejoices to pursue
The steps of him I love;
Till glory breaks upon my view
In brighter worlds above.

Anne Steele, "God the Only Refuge of the Troubled Mind"[7]

Dear refuge of my weary soul,
On thee, when sorrows rise:

On thee, when waves of trouble roll,
   My fainting hope relies.

While hope revives, though prest with fears,
   And I can say, my God,
Beneath thy feet I spread my cares,
   And pour my woes abroad.

To thee, I tell each rising grief,
   For thou alone canst heal;
Thy word can bring a sweet relief
   For every pain I feel.

But oh! when gloomy doubts prevail,
   I fear to call thee mine;
The springs of comfort seem to fail,
   And all my hopes decline.

Yet, gracious God, where shall I flee?
   Thou art my only trust,
And still my soul would cleave to thee,
   Though prostrate in the dust.

Hast thou not bid me seek thy face?
   And shall I seek in vain?
And can the ear of sovereign grace
   Be deaf when I complain?

No, still the ear of sovereign grace
   Attends the mourner's prayer;
O may I ever find access,
   To breathe my sorrows there.

Thy mercy-seat is open still;
   Here let my soul retreat,
With humble hope attend thy will,
   And wait beneath thy feet.

Howell Harris, Letter 7 To Mr. T——
Pancheston Manachlog, December 10, 1740[8]

Dear Brother,

I could not let slip this opportunity without sending you my hearty wishes for your growth in knowledge of the mysteries of God's kingdom of grace in the heart; and may the Spirit of light and power always rest upon you. You have many enemies to encounter, but none so dangerous as self and unbelief, with their inseparable companions; consulting with flesh and blood, fearing others, doubting the faithfulness of the most faithful Friend, etc. O, how should we dread self-love, self-righteousness, self-will, self-confidence, and self-wisdom! All these, if not destroyed, oppose the setting up of Christ's kingdom in our souls and tempt us to deny him, and they have each of them their armor to defend themselves; carnal-reasoning, and all that are born after the flesh, with all their preaching, and conversation defend them. O my dear brother; in a teacher that is not receiving from the Spirit of God nothing is more dangerous than letter learning and head- or book-knowledge. It would be well if we knew and preached no more than we felt, and were willing to be fools till Christ makes us wise; then we should be wise indeed. Whatever you may suffer, from the blind leaders of the blind, who are a curse to the nation, let me beg you, as I long to see you shine with the faithful at last; be strong in faith and fear not. Then shall the Spirit of glory rest upon you, and you shall have strength, according to your day; I am an instance and a witness of this. My most ardent wishes and prayers are that you may be made faithful. I see, we stand in continual need of the Spirit of God to wound and heal us, to cast us down and lift us up, to show us our misery and help us to destroy sin; to work grace, and to act with grace, when wrought in us; and to make and keep us nothing, in our own eyes—nothing less than Almighty power can do this well. But a sight of forgiving love and a justifying Jesus can make us leave all our idols and love him with all our hearts and souls. How can we love him if we are not persuaded he loves us? Faith is the spring of every grace and all true obedience. And unbelief is the root, or fountainhead, of all rebellion and disobedience, and feeds every lust. I see but few convinced of the evil, or of the sin of unbelief, though it makes God a liar and denies all his glorious perfections, renders the word of God, praying, conversing, etc. of no effect, bars the heart against Christ, blinds the mind, destroys the love, estranges us from God, and feeds self-love, lust, slavish fear, love of the world, etc. And if any, but surely much of it remains in the saints, and O! how does it dishonor God, stop their growth in grace, and give Satan the advantage over them. And most think that to doubt (which is the fruit of unbelief) is to be on sure footing: whereas, all ought to be assured that they are either out of Christ or in Christ. Most think to go toward heaven by doing and not by believing; working for life, and not from life received; with Christ in the head, and self in the heart. It is in vain to press to holiness, till the root of holiness be in us which is faith; we cannot grow in sanctification when we are not in a state of justification, and then we press on, to make our calling and election sure. God commands this, and to fear is yielding to unbelief, lest a promise being made, we fall short of it. I know, dear brother, you will not misconstrue my freedom in this for love constrains. Write to, and pray for, your unworthy brother, H. H.

Howell Harris, Letter 35 To Mr. Kinsman, at Plymouth London, March 19, 1747[9]

I long to hear how you go on, trusting that our dear Savior does become more amiable in your eyes, drawing you from every thing to himself; does cause you to weep and mourn before him with godly sorrow for all sinners, and the want of conformity to him in yourselves, and others. O when shall he reign as King in the hearts of all his followers? When shall every thought, and motion within us be brought into subjection to him? Sure, this must be all our cry, as we grow more acquainted with him; we should then long to have the same mind which is in him, and desire to love, as he loves, and to behave to others, even toward the rebellious, as he has to us (even when we were nothing but enmity) with forbearance, patience, and love. Pray let us always contend for all the fruits of the Spirit, and especially faith, love, and humility, that by our fruits, all may be obliged to own we are his disciples. My cry is, and has been, that my lot may be cast among such as indeed, are without guile, and sunk deeper and deeper in true poverty of Spirit, into the loving Spirit of Jesus; and to love his redeemed ones, in him, as poor sinners, in themselves, not withstanding all infirmities that may appear to me, in them, either in judgment or practice.

My dear brother, if our Savior intends you for any further service, in his great and glorious family, let your heart be prepared for trials of all kinds: from within and without, from the world and the Church, from the prejudices, weaknesses, and corruptions of the lambs of the flock; and from the sinister views, worldly wisdom, and pharisaical tempers of carnal professors; much more from the bigotry and narrow heartedness of others that shall come among us to disturb us, and that according to their light, for conscience sake. But let not my dear brother's heart fail him, under these and a thousand other considerations, though every difficulty that shall indeed meet you. But, let it make you cry mightily, for the witness of the Holy Spirit, to see your work and place; then you will be able, in faith, to charge the Lord with all your burdens; and to expect all strength, wisdom, and inward as well as outward qualifications from him who employed you. Then you will not run away from the work, nor be worshiped by others or devil, or your own heart in it, but thankfully embrace the cross, seeing it the highest honor, and privilege to suffer trials, as well as to be active for the Lamb's bride. O my brother, a great work is begun on earth, and where it will end, God only knows; but happy those that shall be employed in it.

Tell the Society I remember them, and longing to see you all again with my love to your spouse,

I am yours, most heartily, in our dear Lord, H. H.

William Romaine, "The Eternal Triumph"[10]

This is the great lesson which the believer is learning till he comes to the end of his faith, what is promised him, and what he hopes to be at the appearing of our Lord Jesus Christ. This is the center to which all his experience tends, and while he keeps it in view, it so enlivens and animates his prospect that, come what may, he goes on his way rejoicing in hope of the glory of God. "Eye hath not seen, nor ear heard, neither have entered into the heart of man, the things which God hath prepared for them that love him. But God hath revealed them unto us by his Spirit." And by his holy inspiration he opens the eyes of the understanding, both to understand what is revealed and also to know the things that are freely given to us of God; for great as they are, endless as they are, the natural person receives not the things of the Spirit of God, neither can he know them, because they are spiritually discerned. But he that is spiritual has spiritual senses given him to exercise upon spiritual things, he is made certain of their reality, his faith gives a substance to the things hoped for and evidence to the things not seen, an hope that never makes ashamed an evidence very clear and satisfying, sometimes he can triumph in hope of the glory of God, when the Holy Spirit sheds abroad in his heart the Father's love and bestows great joy and peace in believing. But he who is thus taught of God knows only in part. An apostle knew no more. The best of our present enjoyment is only a foretaste of the heavenly banquet. But even this little is of such a nature, and has such efficacy, that when it is truly believed, it influences the whole person, while he looks not at the things which are seen, but at the things which are not seen. For the things which are seen are temporal, but the things which are not seen are eternal. They are not seen by the eye of the body, but are visible by the eye of faith; so we read, "Come, taste and see, how gracious the Lord is." By this eye of faith Moses saw him that is invisible, and this sight so affected him, and had such an influence upon his heart and life, that he lived above the world with all its temptations. This is the victory that overcame the world, even his faith. The same sight still works the same effect producing a real value for spiritual and eternal things and forming the heart to love and to practice the apostle's rule. My conversation is in heaven, from whence also I look for the Savior the Lord Jesus Christ, by whom the world is crucified unto me, and I unto the world.

In the Scripture view of our victory in Christ, there are two great points which will take in all that is revealed of our eternal triumph—namely, the complete conquest of all our enemies and the full and eternal enjoyment of all possible good. These two truths come now under our consideration; and if we can meditate upon them under the influence of the Holy Spirit and mix faith with his revelation, we shall have a good warrant to begin those praises which will never end, and to sing in harmony with all the redeemed our everlasting jubilee.

When we come to the end of our faith, even the eternal salvation of our souls, our victory is described to be a perfect deliverance from all evil, from sin and from suffering. Sin has brought all pain into the world, miseries upon the body, miseries upon the soul, spiritual wickedness, numerous hosts of woes, mighty principalities and powers, it has armed thousands, yes millions of them for our destruction, made us our own enemies by enslaving us to divers lusts and passions, making us the prey to earthly, sensual, devilish tempers and, as if there was not suffering enough in the world, filling us with many imaginary fears which occasion real suffering. At last come the wages of sin, death with its terrors and hell with its torments. O what a deliverer! What a deliverance!...

Of this blessed and complete victory over all sin, and all suffering, the prophet Isaiah had a delightful prospect, speaking of it in these words: "And the ransomed of the Lord shall return, and shall come to Zion with songs, and everlasting joy upon their heads; they shall obtain joy and gladness, and sorrow and sighing shall flee away." O give thanks unto the Lord, Jehovah, for he is good, for his mercy endures for ever: Let the redeemed of the Lord say so, whom he hath redeemed from the hand of the enemy....

The beloved John was favored with a view of the same eternal conquest which the ransomed of the Lord shall have over all their enemies, and he speaks of it thus: "And I heard a great voice out of heaven, saying, Behold the tabernacle of God is with men, and he will dwell with them, and they shall be his people, and God himself shall be with them, and be their God: And God shall wipe away all tears from their eyes, and there shall be no more curse, and there shall be no more death, neither sorrow nor crying, neither shall there be any more pain: For the former things are passed away: And he that sat upon the throne said, Behold I make all things new." This is Jesus, the King of kings, and Lord of lords, who reigns, the Lord God omnipotent for this very purpose, that this Scripture may be fulfilled to the uttermost, and to eternity. He was the Word made flesh, who tabernacled amongst us, being that most holy temple which God pitched and not man, out of whose fullness believers receive all grace, and all glory. The compassions of Jesus are like himself, infinite and endless. He loves his redeemed too well to let either sin or sorrow come near them. They might have been holy mourners in their pilgrimage when they went through the valley of Baca, but now he has wiped away their tears, all tears from their eyes. The curse that caused them he has removed. That death, the wages of which they deserved, he has changed into life. The pillars in his house which are to go out no more are thereby delivered from sorrow and crying, and from every pain; all the former things are passed away, sin is no more and pain is no more. Into the kingdom of Jesus nothing of the old person is suffered to enter, for he creates all things new. The Lord from heaven makes all his people like himself, conformed to his own image in righteousness and true holiness…and if we can read it in faith, with prayer, and with a continual dependence upon the teaching and application of the Holy Spirit, he will give us to form our hearts and lives upon the certainty of what he has revealed. For our conversation will then be in heaven, and we shall have both the knowledge, and also the experience of heavenly things, growing according to our faith….

Who can tell what the believer shall then be, when this promise shall be fulfilled? When he shall be brought as near to the Godhead, as a creature can possibly be, joined to the Lord Jesus by the Holy Spirit, an habitation of God through the Spirit, and through Jesus unto the Father, and in this holy and blessed communion, finding an eternal heaven of happiness, an exceeding great reward. When it is received in this its fullness it is a reward, but of grace, a gift of sovereign mercy, great, something worthy of the great God, like himself, exceeding great, eternally great. O, Holy Ghost, keep the hope of it lively. O make it every day more lively, till through thy blessing I come to know it as it is....

May not the believer, ought he not, to rejoice with exceeding great joy, who has this prospect before him? Who that is out of heaven can have more reason than he has? Survey it, O my soul: Take a narrow review of it. Examine over and over again the Psalmist's description of it, and see what can be added to make it absolutely perfect. If nothing can, if it be as full as God can make it, may my heart grow in holy desires after the glory that is to be revealed, and triumph in the God of my salvation.

Our Lord gives us the same description in these words, speaking to his apostles: "I appoint unto you a kingdom, as my Father hath appointed unto me (in the surest, fullest manner that it can be conveyed) that ye may eat and drink at my table in my kingdom, and sit upon thrones, judging the twelve tribes of Israel." The king of this holy land is Immanuel, God Jesus; he is the King of kings, the Lord Creator of all worlds, and the government of them all is upon his shoulders, and the names of his redeemed are written upon his heart. For them he has made abundant provision, that they may feast with him at his table and may be receiving out of his fullness every grace that can make them completely and eternally blessed. For they shall sit down with him upon his throne and shall share with him in all his royalties, blessing and adoring him in their everlasting songs of triumph. "Unto him that loved us, and washed us from our sins in his own blood, and hath made us kings and priests unto God and his Father: To him be glory and dominion for ever and ever. Amen." The apostle John calls upon us now to begin the heavenly song, and he would have us to do it with the sweetest melody in our hearts, praising our sovereign Lord, who has taken our nature into union with himself in order that by his Spirit we might be joined to him our glorified head, and might by faith partake of his holy and heavenly nature. No words can describe more fully the dignity to which by virtue of this union we shall be exalted; nay it is not to be conceived at present how great it will be. "Behold what manner of love the Father hath bestowed upon us, that we should be called the sons of God: therefore the world knoweth us not, because it knew him not:

Beloved, now are we the sons of God, and it doth not yet appear what we shall be, but we know, that when he shall appear we shall be like him; for we shall see him as he is: And every man that hath this hope in him, purifieth himself even as he is pure." O what a dignity is this: What upon earth is to be compared for one moment to it, sons of God and sons of Adam, who have borne the image of the earthly, advanced to bear the image of the heavenly? This is a glory which surpasses all understanding. It did not yet appear as it is to the beloved John; he knew as much of it as perhaps ever one did, but it was far greater than his knowledge. He knew it but in part: he was indeed sealed with the Holy Spirit of promise, who is the earnest of our inheritance until the redemption of the purchased possession. But the earnest is not the inheritance itself. It is only a pledge and a security, that at the appearing of Jesus Christ, the great God and our Savior, we shall be put into full possession. At present we have it in the promise of the God of truth, and faith in his promise begets a hope that will never make us ashamed, because it will keep us patiently waiting for the manifestation of the sons of God, when we shall come to the eternal enjoyment of all the riches, and pleasures, and honors of our sonship with Christ our glorified Head.

The apostle would lead us also to consider the fountain from whence all this blessedness springs, from the Father, what manner of love the Father hath bestowed upon us. The love expressed by this name, *Father*, has no parallel. It had no beginning, and it will have no ending. It is from everlasting to everlasting, bringing with it out of its infinite ocean all the streams of grace which make glad the city of God, and never stopping till it return with all the happy objects of his love to the same great ocean again. The apostle would have us to behold and to admire the miracles of the Father's love which he purposed and wrought out and bestowed upon us who are sinners even as others, and yet to the everlasting praise and glory of his grace chosen and called effectually, brought into the family and household of faith by the Spirit of adoption, and ennobled sons of God; what an exaltation and what a blessedness! Made the children of God, heirs of God, and joint heirs with Christ with him who is Lord of all admitted to share with him in his kingdom, his crown, his glories; according to his own prayer, "Father, I will that they also whom thou hast given me be with me, where I am, that they may behold my glory," may be with me, may be like me. O what an animating view is here for the highest rejoicing of faith and hope! Christ by taking our nature into union with himself has advanced it into the greatest dignity of which it is capable, for it is heaven to be with him, where he is in his glory; like him, conformed to that standard of all perfection in body and soul, perfectly and eternally. What a hope should this beget and cherish? Even a hope full of glory and immortality! Especially as all this honor is according to the Father's covenant purposes: for whom he did foreknow, them he also did predestinate to be conformed to the image of his son, that he might be the first-born among many brethren; moreover whom he did predestinate, them he also called, and whom he called, them he also justified, and whom he justified, them he also glorified. What shall we say to these things? Can there be greater grace shown from the God of all grace? Can there be higher honor conferred than to be so exalted from the depth of sin and misery as to be raised to the honors of sonship, even to a conformity to the Son of God? O what sentiments had that blessed one of it, when he said, "As for me, I will behold thy face in righteousness, I shall be satisfied when I awake after thy likeness; for thou wilt shew me the path of life; in thy presence is the fullness of joy, and at thy right hand there are pleasures for evermore." Conformity to Jesus brings with it this fullness of joy; and the hope of it is an active and a lively grace....

These are some of the Scripture authorities from which this conclusion may be fairly drawn: that a believer, whatever view he may take of himself, either from what he was when dead in trespasses and sins, or from what he now is, quickened by the Spirit of Christ and living by faith, yet crying out under a sense of his corruptions, O wretchedness that I am, who shall deliver me; yet he may thank God through Jesus Christ his Lord. For he is warranted, he is commanded to rejoice in the Lord always, and to triumph in the God of his salvation....

These are some of the blessed effects of looking to Jesus and living by faith upon him and his fullness. In this way there is continual matter of triumph. Let the believer look back on what he was by nature, or on what he is now in his renewed state by grace, or, looking forward to the glory that is to be revealed at the appearing of his Savior, when he shall be with him in the kingdom which cannot be moved, and shall be like him, all his members conformed to their most glorious Head and partaking of his divine riches and honors and pleasures; what upon earth can exceed such a prospect! What can administer greater happiness than to have the evidence of it kept clear and open! What can make life more comfortable and the end of our faith more desirable than such great and blessed things! Promised and given most freely in time, yes, in the fullest manner that almighty love can bestow them in eternity. For such mercies bless the Lord, O my soul; and all that is within me, bless his holy Name.

John Newton, "Divine Guidance"[11]

Dear Sir,

It is well for those who are duly sensible of their own weakness and fallibility, and of the difficulties with which they are surrounded in life, that the Lord has promised to guide his people with his eye, and to cause them to hear a word behind them, saying, "This is the way, walk ye in it," when they are in danger of turning aside either to the right hand or to the left. For this purpose, he has given us the written word to be a lamp to our feet, and encouraged us to pray for the teaching of his Holy Spirit, that we may rightly understand and apply it. It is, however, too often seen that many widely deviate from the path of duty and commit gross and perplexing mistakes while they profess a sincere desire to know the will of God, and think they have his warrant and authority. This must certainly be owing to misapplication of the rule by which they judge, since the rule itself is infallible and the promise sure. The Scripture cannot deceive us, if rightly understood; but it may, if perverted, prove the occasion of confirming us in a mistake. The Holy Spirit cannot mislead those who are under his influence; but we may suppose that we are so, when we are not. It may not be unseasonable to offer a few thoughts upon a subject of great importance to the peace of our minds and to the honor of our holy profession. Many have been deceived as to what they ought to do, or in forming a judgment before hand of events in which they are nearly concerned, by expecting direction in ways which the Lord has not warranted. I shall mention some of the principal of these, for it is not easy to enumerate them all.

Some persons, when in doubt, have opened the Bible at a venture and expected to find something to direct them in the first verse they should cast their eye upon....If people will be governed by the occurrence of a single text of Scripture, without regarding the context or duly comparing it with the general tenor of the word of God and with their own circumstances, they may commit the greatest extravagances, expect the greatest impossibilities, and contradict the plainest dictates of common sense, while they think they have the word of God on their side....Yet it is certain that matters big with important consequences have been engaged in, and the most sanguine expectations formed, upon no better warrant than dipping (as it is called) upon a text of Scripture.

A sudden strong impression of a text that seems to have some resemblance to the concern upon the mind has been accepted by many as an infallible token that they were right, and that things would go just as they would have them; or, on the other hand, if the passage bore a threatening aspect, it has filled them with fears and disquietudes which they have afterward found were groundless and unnecessary. These impressions, being more out of their power than the former method, have been more generally regarded and trusted to, but have frequently proved no less delusive. It is allowed that such impressions of a precept or a promise as humble, animate, or comfort the soul, by giving it a lively sense of the truth contained in the words [that] are both profitable and pleasant; and many of the Lord's people have been instructed and supported (especially in a time of trouble) by some seasonable word of grace applied and sealed by his Spirit with power to their hearts. But if impressions or impulses are received as a voice from heaven, directing to such particular actions as could not be proved to be duties without them, a person may be unwarily misled into great evils and gross delusions, and many have been so. There is no doubt but the enemy of our souls, if permitted, can furnish us with Scriptures in abundance in this way, and for these purposes.

Some persons judge of the nature and event of their designs by the freedom which they find in prayer. They say they commit their ways to God, seek his direction, and are favored with much enlargement of spirit; and therefore they cannot doubt but what they have in view is acceptable in the Lord's sight. I would not absolutely reject every plea of this kind, yet without other corroborating evidence, I could not admit it in proof of what it is brought for. It is not always easy to determine when we have spiritual freedom in prayer. Self is deceitful; and when our hearts are much fixed and bent upon a thing, this may put words and earnestness into our mouths. Too often we first secretly determine for ourselves and then come to ask counsel of God; in such a disposition we are ready to catch at everything that may seem to favor our darling scheme....

Upon the whole, though the Lord may give to some persons, upon some occasions, a hint or encouragement out of the common way, yet expressly to look for and seek his direction in such things as I have mentioned is unscriptural and ensnaring. I could fill many sheets with a detail of the inconveniences and evils which have followed such a dependence, within the course of my own observation. I have seen some presuming they were doing God service, while acting in contradiction to his express commands. I have known others infatuated to believe a lie, declaring themselves assured, beyond the shadow of a doubt, of things which, after all, never came to pass; and when at length disappointed, Satan has improved the occasion to make them doubt of the plainest and most important truths, and to account their whole former experience a delusion. By these things weak believers have been stumbled, cavils and offences against the gospel multiplied, and the ways of truth evil spoken of.

But how then may the Lord's guidance be expected? After what has been premised negatively, the question may be answered in a few words. In general, he guides and directs his people by affording them, in answer to prayer, the light of his Holy Spirit, which enables them to understand and to love the Scriptures. The word of God is not to be used as a lottery; nor is it designed to instruct us by shreds and scraps which, detached from their proper places, have no determinate import; but it is to furnish us with just principles, right apprehensions to regulate our judgments and affections, and thereby to influence and direct our conduct. They who study the Scriptures in an humble dependence upon divine teaching are convinced of their own weakness, are taught to make a true estimate of everything around them, are gradually formed into a spirit of submission to the will of God, discover the nature and duties of their several situations and relations in life, and the snares and temptations to which they are exposed. The word of God dwells richly in them, is a preservative from error, a light to their feet, and a spring of strength and consolation. By treasuring up the doctrines, precepts, promises, examples, and exhortations of Scripture in their minds, and daily comparing themselves with the rule by which they walk, they grow into an habitual frame of spiritual wisdom and acquire a gracious taste which enables them to judge of right and wrong with a degree of readiness and certainty, as a musical ear judges of sounds. And they are seldom mistaken, because they are influenced by the love of Christ which rules in their hearts and a regard to the glory of God, which is the great object they have in view....

I am. &c

Ann Griffiths, "Even when the soul most ardent"[12]

Even when the soul most ardent
Burns the most with living fire,
It can ne'er to the perfection
Of God's holy law aspire;
O that I might pay it honor

108

By accepting his free grace,
And in that most sweet communion,
Through the blood, might find a place.

I shall feel a mighty wonder
When that blessed hour finds birth
When my mind, that here goes wandering
After the mean toys of earth,
Finds its undistraught devotion
To his Person henceforth given,
And unshakably conforming
To the holy laws of heaven.

Devereux Jarratt, "On Affliction," Virginia, October 24, 1795[13]

My ever-dear friend,

It has so happened that your last letters to me (of July 6 and September 4) were enclosed in letters to your brother Williamson, so as he happened to be at my house on the very days on which they were received; I have therefore had an opportunity of reading not only your letter to me, but also that which was written and addressed to him by the partner of your affliction. The contents are truly affecting. I sincerely sympathize with you both and wish to comfort you but what shall I say? Topics of consolation are not wanting, they abound in the blessed word. But I find from yours that these are so familiar to your mind that, should I write a volume, I could suggest nothing but what you already know. My prayer is that the Lord may apply them to your hearts by his Spirit, and then will they be consolatory indeed. I cannot comfort you, but Jesus can and will in his own good time; be therefore encouraged to hope and expect a happy issue.

I have often preached on the subject of afflictions, but as yours arise from a source with which I cannot be so well acquainted as many others, what I say on this occasion may seem rather like speaking by rote than from the real fellow feeling. However I think I have been in circumstances so nearly resembling yours (especially when my favorite nephew died) that I hope you will discover nothing of the stoic in what I write. It would be disingenuous and impertinent in me to advise you to forget or even suspend the feelings which such a repeated stroke must excite in a tender parent's breast. Sensibility is not a crime, especially in cases where it is impossible not to feel, and where the most indulgent of all parents intended we should feel; for unless we feel our trials, how can we exercise a becoming submission under them? Your grief must be great and I join you in thanks to the Lord in preserving you from a murmuring spirit; and, I trust, amidst all the pleadings of flesh and blood, you still found, and will still continue to find, something within you which aims to say, without reserve or exception, "Not my will but thine be done." That is a sweet portion of Scripture, Hebrews 12:5, 11. It is so plain in itself, and so suitable to you that no comment will be necessary. You will here observe that he who knows our frame is pleased to allow that afflictions, for the present, are not joyous but grievous; but here is a consideration which may afford some support under them, that they are well intended, and that those who are exercised thereby shall come out of the furnace refined, more humble, more spiritual, more fruitful in righteousness. The part assigned the people of God, in affliction, is pointed out by St. James; let them pray. It is our part and duty to pray for help in time of need, and to endeavor to turn our thoughts to that fountain of consolation, and thence derive such considerations as have a suitable tendency to alleviate our grief and sorrows. The will of God concerning you and yours has been manifested by the late events, and all you can do is to look to him for strength to sustain, and grace to be still and know that he is God; that he has a right to dispose of us and ours as he pleases, and that in the exercise of this right he is certainly good and wise. I hope the Lord, the only comforter, has brought, and will still bring, such thoughts with warmth and efficacy to your mind as may be most seasonable; and, though your wound may be still painful, yet faith and prayer will not only support you now but accelerate the blessed end. There is something in grief not easily accounted for, it seems bewitching; it is painful in itself, and yet we seem loth to part with it; yes, we are prone to indulge it, and to brood over such thoughts and circumstances which are most likely to increase and prolong it. And why is it thus, unless the Lord when he afflicts, intends or designs not only that we should grieve, but also that our grief should prove medicinal and terminate with the blessing intended by it? The Lord employs afflictions for his people's good, and many advantages are derived from them; so that, perhaps, we could not well do without them.

First. Afflictions tend to quicken us in prayer. It is a pity it should be so; but experience testifies that a course of prosperity and ease has an unhappy tendency to make us cold and formal, especially in our secret devotions. But when troubles rouse the spirit, we are constrained to call upon the Lord in good earnest, for we feel a need of that help which none but God can supply.

Second. They tend to keep alive a conviction that all sublunary bliss is vain and unsatisfying, that here we have no abiding place of rest and therefore our thoughts should fly upward where true joys and permanent treasures are. The children of Israel would have laughed at Moses, or treated his invitation of going with him to the land of promise with coolness and, perhaps, contempt had they not been, at that time, sorely galled with the cruel yoke of uncommon oppression. Thus the Lord, by withering our gourds and breaking our cisterns, weakens our attachments to the present world and renders the thought of leaving it less painful and more welcome. This you seem sensible of when you say, two ties, etc. are broken. My paper reminds me of drawing to a conclusion, in which I have only to say sincerely that,

I am your real friend, D. Jarratt

3

SCRIPTURE

INTRODUCTION

Scripture has always been central to the Christian faith. The texts of this section examine both how and why evangelicals interacted with Scripture. Since they affirmed the divine nature and inspiration of the Bible, they believed that it contained God's dynamic and transformative word. Reading Scripture could make one wise, alert to sin, and offer the good news of salvation by Jesus Christ. People were warned not to neglect Scripture because of its ability to correct and comfort anyone in need. Due to this distinctiveness, Scripture was read, prayed, studied, and preached; it formed the basis for commentaries, created the themes and images for hymns and letters, and became a source of conversation among people from every walk of life because it contained guidance for Christian living. Evangelicals also demonstrated a broad spectrum for engaging Scripture. They recognized the role of the Holy Spirit in illuminating and instructing their interaction with these holy words. Similar to many Christians in the early and medieval church, they prized humility and cautioned that a corrupt mind would distort the interpretation of the Bible. They approached the Scripture in both a literal and a historical manner but realized, especially in reading Old Testament passages, the need for a spiritual or typological reading. Additionally, some authors in this section, always looking for the teaching or reinforcement of Jesus' life and ministry, encouraged the christological reading of Scripture. Other writers instructed people to read passages slowly, meditatively, dwelling over a few verses to soak up the maximum meaning. Engaging Scripture was often combined with other spiritual practices, especially prayer and fasting, to sensitize the readers to the presence of God in their daily lives. Each individual had a personal responsibility to come to know Jesus; thus all people were expected to search the Scriptures for the truth that would liberate them.

THE TEXTS

George Whitefield, "The Duty of Searching the Scriptures," John 5:39[1]

When the Sadducees came to our blessed Lord and put to him the question, whose wife a woman should be in the next life who had seven husbands in this, he told them they erred, not knowing the Scriptures. And if we would know whence all the errors that have overspread the Church of Christ first arose, we should find they in a great measure flowed from the same fountains, an ignorance of the word of God.

Our blessed Lord, though he was the eternal God, yet as man made it his constant rule and guide, and therefore, when he was asked by the lawyer which was the great commandment of the law, he referred him to his Bible for an answer: "What readest thou?" And thus, when led by the Spirit to be tempted by the devil, he repelled all his assaults, with "It is written." A sufficient confutation this of their opinion who say, "The Spirit only," and not "The Spirit by the Word is to be our rule of action." If so, our Savior, who had the Spirit without measure, needed not always have referred to the written word. But how few copy after the example of Christ! How many are there who do not regard the word of God at all, but throw the sacred oracles aside as an antiquated book, fit only for unlearned and illiterate people?

Such do greatly err, not knowing what the Scriptures are and for what they are designed. I shall, therefore, in the following discourse, first show that it is every one's duty to search them. And secondly, lay down some directions how to search them with advantage.

By the Scriptures I understand the Law and the Prophets and all those books which have in all ages been accounted canonical, and which make up that book commonly called the Bible. These are emphatically styled the Scriptures, and, in one place, the Scriptures of truth, as though no other books deserved the name of true writings or scriptures in comparison of them. They are not of any private interpretation, authority, or invention, but holy men of old wrote them, as they were moved by the Holy Ghost.

The foundation of God's revealing himself thus to humanity was our fall in Adam, and the necessity of our new birth in Christ Jesus. And if we search the Scriptures as we ought, we shall find the sum and substance, the alpha and omega, the beginning and end of them has no other tendency but to lead us to a knowledge of these two great truths. All the threats, promises, and precepts, all the exhortations and doctrines contained therein, all the rights and ceremonies and sacrifices appointed under the Jewish law; no, almost all the historical parts of Holy Scripture suppose our being fallen in Adam, and either point out to us a Mediator to come, or speak of him as already come in the flesh.

Had humanity continued in a state of innocence, he would not have needed an outward revelation, because the law of God was so deeply written in the tables of his heart. But having eaten of the forbidden fruit, he incurred the divine displeasure and lost the divine image and, therefore, without an outward revelation, could never tell how God would be reconciled unto him, or how he should be saved from the misery and darkness of his fallen nature.

That these truths are so, I need not refer you to any other book than that of your own hearts. For unless we are fallen creatures, whence come those abominable corruptions which daily arise in our hearts? We could not come thus corrupt out of the hands of our Maker, because he being goodness itself could make nothing but what is like himself: holy, just, and good. And that we want to be delivered from these disorders of our nature is evident, because we find an unwillingness within ourselves to own we are thus depraved and are always striving to appear to others of a quite different frame and temper of mind than what we are.

I appeal to the experience of the most learned disputer against divine revelation, whether he does not find in himself that he is naturally proud, angry, revengeful, and full of other tempers contrary to the purity, holiness and long suffering of God. And is not this a demonstrable proof that some way or other he is fallen from God?...Here then God by his word steps in, and opens to his view such a scene of divine love and infinite goodness in the Holy

Scriptures, that no one but of such corrupt and reprobate minds as our modern Deists would shut their eyes against it. For what does God in his written word do more or less, than show thee, O man, how thou art fallen into that blindness, darkness, and misery thou feelest and complainest of? And, at the same time, points out the way to what thou desirest, how thou mayest be redeemed out of it by believing in and copying after the Son of his love.

For as I told you before, so I tell you again, upon these two truths hangs all divine revelation. It being given us for no other end, but to show us our misery, and our happiness; our fall and recovery; or, in one word, after what manner we died in Adam, and how in Christ we may again be made alive.

Hence then arises the necessity of searching the Scriptures. For since they are nothing else but the grand character of our salvation, a revelation of a covenant made by God with humanity in Christ, a light to guide them into the way of peace, it follows that all are obliged to read and search them, because all are equally fallen from God, all equally stand in need of being informed what they must do to be restored to, and again united with him....

But this discourse is not designed so much for them that believe not, as for them who both know and believe that the Scriptures contain a revelation that came from God, and that it is their duty, as being chief parties concerned, not only to read but search them also. I pass on, therefore, as was proposed in the second place, to lay down some directions how to search them with advantage.

And first, have always in view the end for which the Scriptures were written to show us the way of salvation, but Jesus Christ. Search the Scriptures, says our blessed Lord, for they are they that testify of me. Look, therefore, always for Christ in the Scripture. For he is the treasure hid in the field, both of the Old and New Testaments. In the Old you'll find him hid under prophecies, types, sacrifices and shadows. In the New, manifested in the flesh to become a propitiation for our sins, as a priest, and as a prophet to reveal the whole will of his heavenly Father. Have Christ, and to become a principle then of new life to our souls, thus always in view when you are reading the word of God, and this, like the star in the east, will guide you to the Messiah, will serve as a key to everything that is obscure, and unlock to you the wisdom and riches of all the mysteries of the kingdom of God.

Secondly, search the Scriptures with a humble child-like disposition. For whosoever does not read them with this temper shall in no wise enter into the knowledge of the things contained therein. For God hides the sense of them from those that are wise and prudent in their own eyes, and reveals them only to babes in Christ, who think they know nothing yet as they ought to know who hunger and thirst after righteousness and humbly desire to be fed with the sincere milk of the word, that they may grow thereby.

Fancy yourselves, therefore, when you are searching the Scriptures, especially when you are reading the New Testament, to be with Mary, sitting at the feet of the Holy Jesus, and be as willing to learn what God shall teach you, as Samuel was, when he said, "Speak, Lord, for thy servant heareth."

And oh, that the unbelievers would pull down every high thought and imagination that exalts itself against the revealed will of God! Oh that they would, like new-born babes, desire to be fed with the pure milk of the word! Then we should have them no longer scoffing at divine revelation, nor would they read the Bible any more with the same intent (the Philistines brought out Sampson) to make sport at it, but they would see the divine image and superscription written upon every line of it. They would hear God speaking unto their souls by it, and, consequently, be built up in the knowledge and fear of him who is the author of it.

Thirdly, search the Scriptures with a sincere intention to put in practice what you read. For a desire to do the will of God is the only way to know it; if any one will do my will, says Jesus Christ, he shall know of my doctrine whether it be of God or whether I speak of myself. As he also speaks in another place to his disciples, to you who are willing to practice your duty, it is given to know the mysteries of the kingdom of God, but to those that are without, who only want to raise cavils against my doctrine, all these things are spoken in parables, that seeing they may see and not understand, and hearing they may hear and not perceive. For it is but just in God to send those strong delusions, that they may believe a lie, and to conceal the knowledge of himself from all such as do not seek him with a single intention.

Jesus Christ is the same now as formerly. To those who desire to know from his word who he is that they may believe on and live by and to him, he will reveal himself as clearly as he did to the woman of Samaria, when he said, "I that speak to thee am he," or as he did to the man that was born blind, whom the Jews had cast out for his name's sake, "He that talketh with thee is he." But to those who consult his word with a desire neither to know him or keep his commandments, but either merely for their entertainment or to scoff at the simplicity of the manner in which he is revealed, to those, I say, he never will reveal himself, though they should search the Scriptures to all eternity. As he never would tell those whether he was the Messiah or not who put that question to him either out of curiosity, or that they might have whereof to accuse him.

Fourthly, in order to search the Scriptures still more effectually, make an application of everything you read to your own hearts. For whatever was written in the book of God was written for our learning. And what Christ said unto those aforetime, we must look upon as spoken to us also. For since the Holy Scriptures are nothing but a revelation from God how fallen humanity is to be restored by Jesus Christ. All the precepts, threats, and promises belong to us and to our children, as well as to those to whom they were immediately made known.

Thus the Apostle, when he tells us that he lived by the faith of the Son of God, adds, who died and gave himself for me. For it is this application of Jesus Christ to our hearts that makes his redemption effectual to each of us. And it is this application of all the doctrinal and historical parts of Scripture, when we are reading them over, that must render them profitable to us, as they were designed for reproof, for correction, for instruction in righteousness, and make every child of God perfect, thoroughly furnished to every good work....

For this is the way God now reveals himself to people, not by making new revelations but by applying general things that are revealed already to every particular sincere reader's heart. And this, by the way, answers an objection made by those that say, "The Word of God is not a perfect rule of action, because it cannot direct us how to act or how to determine in particular cases, or what place to go to, when we are in doubt, and therefore the Spirit, and not the Word, is to be our rule of action." But this I deny and affirm on the contrary that God at all times, circumstances, and places, though never so minute, never so particular, will, if we diligently seek the assistance of his Holy Spirit, apply general things to our hearts, and thereby to use the words of the Holy Jesus, will lead us into all truth, and give us the particular assistance we want.

But this leads me to a fifth direction, how to search the Scriptures with profit, labor to attain that Spirit by which they were wrote. "For the natural man discerneth not the words of the Spirit of God, because they are spiritually discerned; the words that Christ hath spoken they are Spirit, and they are life," and can be no more understood as to the true hidden sense and meaning of them by the mere natural man, than a person who never had learnt a language can understand another speaking in it. The Scriptures therefore have not unfitly been compared by some to the cloud which went before the Israelites: they are dark and hard to be understood by the natural man, as the cloud appeared dark to the Egyptians, but they are light, they are life to Christians indeed, as that same cloud which seemed dark to Pharaoh and his house appeared bright and altogether glorious to the Israel of God....

How should it be otherwise, for God being a Spirit he cannot communicate himself any otherwise than in a spiritual manner to human hearts, and consequently if we are strangers to his Spirit, we must continue strangers to his word, because it is altogether like himself spiritual; labor, therefore, earnestly for to attain this blessed Spirit, for otherwise, your understandings will never be opened to understand the Scriptures aright, and because prayer is one of the most immediate means to get this Holy Spirit.

Sixthly, let me advise you before you read the Scripture to pray that Christ according to his promise would send his Spirit to guide you into all truth; intersperse short ejaculations while you are engaged in reading, pray over every word and verse if possible, and when you close up the Book most earnestly beseech God that the words which you then have read may be inwardly engrafted into your hearts, and bring forth in you the fruits of good living.

Do this and you will, with a holy violence, draw down God's Holy Spirit into your hearts, and you will experience his gracious influence and feel him enlightening, quickening, and inflaming your souls by the word of God; you will then not only read, but mark, learn, and inwardly digest what you read, and the word of God will be meat indeed, and drink indeed unto your souls; you then will be as Apollos was powerful in the Scriptures, be scribes ready instructed to the kingdom of God, and bring out of the good treasures of your hearts things both from the Old and New Testaments, to entertain all you converse with.

One direction more, which shall be the last. Seventhly, read the Scripture constantly, or to use our Savior's expression in the text, search the Scriptures, dig in them as for hid treasure, for here's a manifest allusion to those who dig in mines, and our Savior would thereby teach us that we must take as much pains in constantly reading his word, if we would grow thereby, as those who dig for gold and silver. The Scriptures contain the deep things of God, and therefore can never be sufficiently searched into by a careless, superficial, cursory way of reading them, but by an industrious, close, and humble application.

The Psalmist therefore makes it the property of a good person that he mediates on God's law day and night. And this book of the law, says God to Joshua, "shall not go out of thy mouth, but thou shalt meditate therein day and night, for then thou shalt make thy way prosperous, and then thou shalt have good success." Search, therefore, the Scriptures not only devoutly but daily, for in them are the words of eternal life; wait constantly at Wisdom's gate, and she will then, and not till then, display and lay open to you her heavenly treasures. You that are rich are without excuse if you do not and you that are poor ought to take heed that little time have. For by the Scriptures you are to be acquitted, and by the Scriptures you are to be condemned at the last day.

But, perhaps, you have no taste for this despised book; perhaps plays and romances, books of polite entertainment suit your taste better. But if this be your case, give me leave to tell you, your taste is vitiated, and unless corrected by the Spirit and word of God, you shall never enter into his heavenly kingdom, for unless you delight in God here, how will you be made meet to dwell with him hereafter? Is it a sin then you'll say to read useless impertinent books? I answer, yes. And that for the same reason as it is a sin to indulge useless conversation, because both immediately tend to grieve and quench that Spirit by which alone we can be sealed to the day of redemption; but you may reply, how shall we know this?...In short, you will then be guided by God's wisdom here, and conducted by the light of his divine word into glory hereafter.

Thomas Walsh, An Extract from His Diary[2]

Sunday, 22d [1757?]. All the day long my Lord was wonderfully present with me in every ordinance. Truly my soul longed vehemently to be, and live, like my Savior, the holy Jesus. This indeed is the thing I aim at and I believe, according to the sure word of promise, I shall attain. O, what depths and heights of holiness do I discern attainable in this world....

My soul was mightily encouraged, while I expounded John 14:21–23. Inward and constant liberty is what I want: to be always recollected, having my mind stayed upon God. I would live like an angel below. For some moments, indeed, I often love and rejoice in a wonderful manner, but, alas how soon it dies! I become comparatively cold, and can neither pray with freedom, nor rejoice with reverence.

Prayer and reading the Scriptures are my daily delight.

O Jesus, you holy lover of my soul, unite me more closely to your self. Be my glory, my joy. You are my all in all.

Still, nature, the devil, and grace are striving with me. Christ, however, has the upper hand; but I want him "to live and reign, the Lord of every motion of my soul."

I prayed with my kindred at taking my leave of them.* My brother and sister were ill, and my mother weeping after me. I found a great struggle and believe I should have stayed, but for those Scriptures: "He that loveth father or mother more than me is not worthy of me" (Matt 10:37) and, "Let the dead bury their dead; but go thou and preach the kingdom of God" (Luke 9:60). My heart felt pain and sorrow; but I took up my cross, and went immediately to Ballygarane (where were a colony of Germans), and preached that night. O, what is needful for a minister of Jesus! what faith, love, purity, divine light, life, and strength, to finish his course with joy!

---

*He was then going to England the third, and which was the last, time.

Meeting the penitents, I could hardly speak in the last prayer. I was so overpowered with the presence and majesty of God.

I arose early this morning, after watering my pillow with my tears more than ever I remember to have done before. Throughout the various exercises of the day, I had strong assurance that the Lord would eternally save me; especially as I sat at dinner, conversing with my brethren on the things of God.

Having this evening to myself without preaching (a rare thing with him), I shut myself up, and sought the Lord with prayers and tears. Show me, my Lord, your glory; or let me die that I may see you! If I cannot perfectly love you, and do your will upon earth, send for me, and take my soul to heaven. But, Lord God, have you not spoken by Moses, Deuteronomy 30:6; and by Ezekiel 36:23–32? If these are your words and promises, I pray and plead that they may be fulfilled in me, according to their utmost extent. O, come, and baptize me with fire!

At prayer with some friends, the Lord applied powerfully to my heart, "Go, and sin no more." Now the Lord has answered for himself. I believe it is his will that I should sin no more, and that I should have such a faith, as never to depart, from this moment, from Christ, in thought, word, or deed; that so, being inseparably one with him, I should walk in the Spirit, and sing and praise him evermore! Angels, praise my Savior!

Sunday, 1757. All the day I was happy in my Lord, rejoicing in confidence that he would save me eternally. I could pray, and love, and weep. It was a day of great blessing and of great trials. I came home through much snow and rain. But it was all sweet with Christ. I called on the strong for strength; and, after meditation, lay me down in peace.

Thursday. I employed all the day in reading the Hebrew and Greek Scriptures, save some time which I spent in endeavoring to convince a man (who contended much,) that there is salvation for a person, though he does not make use of the Church of England's liturgy. I had many comforts, with strong temptation.

With a heart full of matter, I preached on Ephesians 6:11. I could truly say that "the law of Thy mouth is dearer unto me than thousands of gold and silver."...

At dinner my soul was sweetly drawn out after God. I felt such an assurance of eternal salvation as I never had before, not with such a degree of clearness of evidence. I wept and prayed before the Lord that he would make me entirely pure in heart, and bless all his children. It was a happy day.

I felt great love to all humanity. My soul pleaded with God in their behalf. O Jesus, hasten your kingdom. Come, and put a period to sin and misery! O my God, suffer not a vain thought to live in me. I never can rest, till Jesus has poured his humble, pure, and happy mind into my soul. For some moments I did taste of the felicity of heaven; but, through pain and unbelief, it was of short continuance.

Friday. It being the public fast, I preached on Isaiah 58:3. It was a day of feasting to my soul. With great delight I rested in my God; and it seemed to me, that the people of God were not yet to suffer....

I seek perfection, and uninterrupted communion with the blessed God, Father, Son, and Holy Ghost. True, I am not worthy of the crumbs under your table; yet I look, through your rich grace, for all the precious and eternal blessings of the new covenant.

Sunday. This was a glorious day indeed. Great and marvelous were the blessings which God bestowed upon me. He blesses me in every duty, all is useful, all works together for my good. I go on my way singing the hundred and thirty-eighth Psalm: "They shall sing in the ways of the Lord; for great is the glory of the Lord."

Jesus was with me in all I did. He gave me light, love, help, joy, peace, and strength in all. In his Spirit I went to rest. Wherever I was, and in whatsoever I did, my soul delighted in God; never had I deeper or more sweet manifestations of his gracious presence. I could not but praise him, and thirst for more perfect union with him! Surely this is the foretaste of glory! O, if Christians did but rightly understand the nature, power, and extent of "the kingdom of God" in the soul, I am persuaded they would not rest satisfied with the bare pardon of sin, and some joy and peace, when they may have perfect and uninterrupted rest! If once sin be totally destroyed, and the spirit filled with the light and love of God, it is then neither hurt nor hindered by any person or thing; but steadily goes on its heavenly journey, uniting to Christ more and more daily. "It does not yet appear what we shall be," even in this world.

O Christ! What have you done for me? What shall I say of or unto you? This I say, that I love you! O, let it be with all my heart, and soul, and mind, and strength! At intercession, I felt such a degree of the presence of God as utterly amazed me. O glorious Lord, how shall I bless you?

My heart continually rested in God, and drank of the living waters; yes, my very body was supported by the joy where my soul was refreshed; so that after preaching three times to-day, beside visiting the sick and well, my strength was more than when I arose in the morning.

Friday. A day of fasting. (A frequent practice of his.) At prayer with brother M—n, my soul was greatly humbled before God. Entire resignation, without much joy, was the state of my heart this day....

Sunday, 13th. I conversed with one today who told me that for fourteen years last past she never found any unhappiness, but always rejoiced in the love of God. Before and after sacrament, I found such desire as almost made my heart break. My soul and flesh cried, mourned, and wept for the perfect love of God. There is a beauty and excellence in holiness which has quite won my heart.

I felt a deep necessity of constant and habitual preparation for death.

All day, both in reading, prayer, and conversation, I felt something of that promise, John 4:14. I look for religion to possess, and entirely to change, me. I see and feel that Christianity is something divine, living, generous, powerful, and internal. It is God dwelling in the soul of a person (2 Cor 6:16).

Friday, 18th. I prayed and read till twelve. My body began then to complain. It does not like fasting; but my soul did banquet on the rich delicacies of the love and promises of God. I am in the way to heaven; but I want a heavenly nature, heaven within me. My soul can be satisfied with nothing less than God. Jesus, my blessed Jesus, let me ever esteem your blood and righteousness above the whole world! Through you I come to God. By you I enter heaven; you are heaven.

From the labor of this day I was truly tired in body; but thankful and serene in spirit. I had no ravishing joy nor overflowing of love....

There is, there can be, no higher, no better, no sweeter divinity than this, "My Beloved is mine, and I am His!" O my soul, rest in this! Be satisfied and safe in the protecting, sanctifying, and reviving love of Immanuel, God with us.

The 33d chapter of Exodus came in my course of reading today. And, O, what pleading and communion between Moses and his God! Happy man! who conversed with the glorious Jehovah face to face.* And yet St. John seems to express something higher and sweeter than even this, 1st Epistle 1:3. For, certainly, eternal union with God and a fullness of his Spirit are more excellent than any external manifestation can be. This was one of my blessed days, wherein I had a foretaste of the powers and glory of the world to come.

I retired a few minutes after five, to wait for the coming of Jesus. My soul is all desire after Christ. I am resolved to love and serve him so as I have never yet done. Come, Holy Ghost, and kindle the fire within my breast.

From a quarter after four this morning till ten, I spent in prayer, and reading the Scriptures; and such humiliation of soul, such a sense of my vileness, I hardly ever felt. It was genuine, godly sorrow, indeed, with a clear sight of the odiousness of sin. I believe the first time I ever sinned was brought to my remembrance. My head was as waters, and my heart as wax before the fire. But all the time, I had a clear sense of the love of God, a witness that I was accepted in the Beloved; and all the day after, my soul delighted itself in the Lord.

Henry Venn, "Four Guidelines for Reading Scripture"[3]

Further, the infinite concern which we all have in the subject matter of holy writ most evidently obliges us to read and acquaint ourselves with it; for what the Scripture contains is, by the unanimous confession of all Christians, of everlasting moment. The articles of faith are proposed under the most awful sanctions to prove the necessity of receiving them; the precepts of life it prescribes are

---

*That is, with a degree of familiarity and access which was not allowed to any of the other patriarchs or prophets. For, strictly speaking, "no man hath seen God at any time."

essentially requisite to our safety; the promises to encourage our hope, to animate to increasing diligence; the threatnings [*sic*] to alarm us in a season of peculiar temptation, that we may stand in awe and sin not. He therefore who is able to read, and neglects to search the Scripture in order to know what is the will of God, openly professes his scorn of his Maker, and that he cares for nothing but the enjoyments of this perishing life.

The will of God therefore in this matter is so plainly revealed that none will avow or justify their neglect of reading the Scripture who have opportunity of doing it, except such as are base enough to doubt its heavenly origin. But then amongst those who read their Bible, allowances no doubt are to be made for different capacities, and different situations in life; for these things make a great difference with respect to the time which can be given up to so delightful an employment, and with respect to understanding God's word. But the principal thing which all sorts and conditions of persons are to regard is the avoiding formality in this duty; for most common it has been in all ages and ever alas will be for persons to read constantly the Scripture, yet in such a way as to be neither wiser nor better for it in any degree. To secure therefore to ourselves some spiritual advantage and real edification in this devotional duty of reading the Scripture, we should observe the following rules.

Whenever we open the sacred, the inestimable book of God, we should lift up our hearts to him to teach us the true meaning and sense of what we are going to read. This is necessary because the doctrines which are the very glory of Scripture offend our natural pride, and its precepts contradict our dearest lusts. To receive the one therefore with humility and thankfulness, and to submit to be governed by the other, requires assistance from heaven and a blessing from the Father and Fountain of lights. Accordingly in the Bible we are frequently taught that we cannot know the excellency of its doctrines, nor rely on them with such a persuasion as to honor God by hazarding every thing sooner than deny his truth, unless he opens our understandings; for no one, says St. Paul, can say that "Jesus Christ is Lord, but by the Holy Ghost." And when he speaks of those believers in Christ who knew the things which were freely given of God to them, he declares they received "the Spirit which is of God, that they might know them." So deeply sensible were the holy men of old, of their own natural incapacity of reaping any profitable knowledge from the Scripture without the teachings of God obtained by prayer, that with the Bible open before them they continually made request for illumination of their minds to understand it aright: "I am a stranger upon earth, O hide not thy commandments from me; I am thy servant, give me understanding that I may know thy statutes. Open thou mine eyes that I may behold wondrous things out of thy law." These blessed servants of God we must imitate, and depend on the Spirit for light and instruction when we read God's word; not indeed expecting a new light, as that signifies a new revelation either distinct from the Scripture rule, or supplemental to it; nor laying aside our reason and understanding, relying upon an immediate inspiration to interpret Scripture. Either of these things is weak enthusiasm. But with the greatest sobriety we may expect, and ought to pray for the Spirit's help to give us real advantage and improvement while we are reading the word of God, because the Spirit is promised to abide with the church for ever as a spirit of wisdom and revelation in the knowledge of the things of God, nor shall we ever know them so as to feel their power and authority on the heart, without internal revelation.

There is indeed a knowledge of divine truths, there is an assent to Scripture propositions attained without any influence of the Spirit, attained sometimes by persons of parts and application, though they may be very bad, in a degree of eminence above what even true Christians of lower capacities do in general attain. But then this knowledge is speculative, this assent is worthless, resting in the head, and never changing the heart. And so must all knowledge of divine things be, unless the influence of the Spirit of God gives them power to command and sway the soul; because whatever way we come to be certain of any thing contrary to the bent of our own wicked hearts, we need much more than the brightest possible external evidence of the truth of the thing, to make it efficacious to determine our will against its own strong and corrupt propensity....We turn aside from the known commandments of our God; we prefer the service of some vile lust to our bounden duty, while we allow the Scripture to be a divine revelation, and read it as such, till we read it with prayer, imploring the God whose word it is, to grant, by the illumination of his Spirit, that his word may be put into our mind, and exert a sovereign sway over it.

If there be any to whom this rule and advice is not grateful, they must be left to their own apprehensions. In the mean time this doctrine is of the utmost importance, for, once take away the influences of the Holy Spirit from the members of the church, and then the very gospel of Christ will be no more than a sublime speculation, as ineffectual to change the heart or reform the world as the pagan philosophy. The Holy Spirit, the Comforter, is the inestimable promise made to the church; if therefore we would read the Bible for our reproof, our correction, our instruction in righteousness, we must before, and as we read, pray to God for his influence and teaching.

A second rule no less worthy of our constant and careful observation is to read but a small portion at one time. It is common for those who have the character of being very devout to set themselves such a quantity, suppose two or three chapters, to read every day; a much larger portion this than they can sufficiently attend to, except it be in some of the historical parts of the Bible. Hence, though they converse much in this manner with the word of God, they remain as shamefully ignorant of its contents, at least as much unrenewed in their minds as those who never look into it.* We must by no means therefore content ourselves with having the words and expressions of God before our eyes, or in our mouths. On the contrary, we must pause and deliberate much on the things signified by the words; we must labor to fix the true import of the divine expressions deep in our minds; so that the very spirit of the Bible may be as it were, transcribed into them.

It is true in this method we shall read but a little, and our progress in going through all the principal parts of the sacred volume will be slow compared with those who can read many chapters in a day. But then the singular benefit of such a method will amply reward our pains and prove its preference; for while in much recollection and silent meditation we take God's word into our hands and place ourselves as it were before him for instruction, we shall find the meaning of it beautifully unfolding; and the knowledge of what we

---

*Venn cautions parents to set the proper example of reading Scripture to their children in family devotions to not create a "formal, lifeless reading of it."

gain in this manner will come with a transforming efficacy. It will also remain with us, and be our own for use and recollection at all times, while the comments and explanations of other men, and our own hasty readings, however they may seem to instruct us, are soon forgotten, because they have no root in us....

Nearly allied to this careful meditation on the word of God is another important rule which we must observe when we read any principal part of it; that is, to exact of ourselves correspondent affections, and if we do not experience them, to lament and bewail the poverty and misery of our condition. For instance, when the character of God is before us, when we are reading such passages as describe him infinite in power, glorious in holiness, continually adored by the host of heaven, yet more tender and affectionate than any father to the faithful in Christ Jesus, and interesting himself in all the most minute circumstances that can affect the welfare of those that love him—to read such descriptions of God will be to very little purpose, unless we pause and ask ourselves whether we in this manner really behold the glory of the Lord and the excellency of our God; whether we have such views of him who is thus represented, as to make him indeed our delight, as to satisfy us of his good and gracious intentions toward ourselves in particular, and lead us with comfort to rely on him for all we want. In like manner, when we read the Scripture representations of the glory, the offices, and the temper of the Redeemer, with the inestimable promises he makes to them who trust in his name, little will it profit us unless we also at the same time search and try our souls, whether these representations make us eager to embrace a Savior thus altogether lovely unfeignedly thankful to God for this unspeakable gift, and able without doubt or wavering to yield ourselves up to his service, and to trust him as the guardian of our eternal interests. Also when we meet with many Scripture assertions of the weakness, blindness, guilt, and depravity of fallen humanity, in vain shall we assent to them, because found in the book of God, if we do not trace each of these branches of natural corruption as they have discovered themselves in our behavior, and behold some remains of them still in ourselves. When the self-denying tempers of the faithful in Christ, their deliverance from the dominion of worldly hopes and fears, their unfeigned love to God and others, their real imitation of Jesus in the abhorrence of all evil, is the subject before us, in vain we read of these spiritual attainments unless we examine in what degree the infinitely desirable transformation has taken place in our own hearts.

Unless we thus read all Scripture with self-application, we shall do just enough to flatter and deceive ourselves that we are something, when we are nothing; enough to make us imagine we have a great regard to Scripture, when in fact it has no weight at all with us to form our judgment or determine us in the grand object of our pursuit. It is our duty therefore not only to read the word of God with frequency, but like people in earnest, who know every thing is to be determined by it; like people who know he only is blessed whom that word blesses, and he most assuredly cursed whom that word curses. It is our duty to labor and pray to have the lively signatures of Scripture impressed in all our sentiments, breathing in all our desires, living in all our conduct; so that all may see, and we ourselves most delightfully prove, that the word of the Lord is pure, converting our souls.

Lastly, we must read those portions of Scripture most frequently which relate to subjects of the greatest moment. For, as in the frame of our body God has ordained some parts absolutely necessary to its life, others to its comfort and ease, others again to its ornament, in the same manner is the Scripture composed. As our greatest regard therefore is to such parts of the body as are most vital, so our most frequent contemplation must dwell on those parts of Scripture which most nearly concern the glory of God, our own eternal salvation, and the good of others. The Scriptures therefore which delineate the perfections of God, his jealous regard for his own honor, the necessity of living in willing subjection to his authority, the certain insupportable miseries of the unconverted and the unbelieving, of the earthly and the sensual, call for our frequent perusal; for in such a world as this, and with hearts disposed as ours are, in vain we attempt to observe the commands of God, if we are not immovably persuaded of these truths, and constantly reminded of them. The Scriptures also, which describe the miseries of our fallen state, the evil bias that is upon our will, our utter impotence on this every account to recover ourselves, are in a very eminent degree deserving our frequent meditation. And of the same important nature are all those passages in holy writ which declare what the Savior is in his own personal excellency; what he has done and suffered on earth; what he is now doing in heaven for his church; which acquaint us with his gracious calls and his tender expostulations; which instruct us in the knowledge of our indispensable need of him in his offices of prophet, priest and king. No one can look into the Bible without perceiving with what peculiar emphasis these subjects are treated, how they project to our view, and are insisted upon and extoled as the glorious display of God's wisdom and love. A deep intimate acquaintance therefore with these things is a principal end for which Scripture was given, and therefore should be so in our perusing it. What is said also of the influences and operations of the Spirit must be closely attended to and frequently read by us, that we may know whether we are led by the Spirit, or walk according to the influence of our corrupt nature....

PRAYER:

...Finally, O God, as you have caused all Holy Scripture to be written for our reproof, for our correction, for our instruction in righteousness, teach us, we beseech you, the true meaning and interpretation thereof. Let us not go wrong out of the way of your commandments, by leaning to our own understanding, or by calling any man master. Give us to delight in reading your word and pondering it in our hearts. And as we read, may we drink deep into its spirit, be molded by it in all our sentiments, tempers and practice; that in the end we may enjoy that eternal life, which is revealed in your word, and promised to all them that obey it. Hear our prayers, and do abundantly for us above all we can ask or think, through Jesus Christ our Lord. Amen.

Phillis Wheatley, "On the Death of the Rev. Mr. George Whitefield, 1770"[4]

Hail, happy saint, on thine immortal throne,
Possessed of glory, life, and bliss unknown;
We hear no more the music of thy tongue,
Thy wonted auditories cease to throng.
Thy sermons in unequall'd accents flow'd,

And ev'ry bosom with devotion glow'd;
Thou didst in strains of eloquence refin'd
Inflame the heart, and captivate the mind.
Unhappy we the setting sun deplore,
So glorious once, but ah! It shines no more.

Behold the prophet in his tow'ring flight!
He leaves the earth for heav'n's unmeasur'd height,
And worlds unknown receive him from our sight.
There Whitefield wings with rapid course his way,
And sails to Zion through vast seas of day.
Thy pray'rs, great saint, and thine incessant cries
Have pierc'd the bosom of thy native skies.
Thou moon hast seen, and all the stars of light,
How he has wrestled with his God by night.
He pray'd that grace in ev'ry heart might dwell,
He long'd to see America excel;
He charg'd its youth that ev'ry grace divine
Should with full lustre in their conduct shine;
That Savior, which his soul did first receive,
The greatest gift that ev'n a God can give,
He freely offer'd to the num'rous throng,
That on his lips with list'ning pleasure hung.

"Take him, ye wretched, for your only good,
Take him ye starving sinners, for your food;
Ye thirsty, come to this life-giving stream,
Ye preachers, take him for your joyful theme;
Take him my dear Americans, he said,
Be your complaints on his kind bosom laid:
Take him, ye Africans, he longs for you,
Impartial Savior is his title due:
Wash'd in the fountain of redeeming blood,
You shall be sons, and kings, and priests to God."

Great Countess,* we Americans revere
Thy name, and mingle in thy grief sincere;

---

*The Countess of Huntingdon, to whom Mr. Whitefield was Chaplain.

New England deeply feels, the Orphans mourn,
Their more than father will no more return.

   But, though arrested by the hand of death,
Whitefield no more exerts his lab'ring breath,
Yet let us view him in th' eternal skies,
Let ev'ry heart to this bright vision rise;
While the tomb safe retains its sacred trust.
Till life divine re-animates his dust.

Augustus Toplady, "A Contemplation: Suggested by Revelation 7:9–17"[5]

Part 1.

   I saw, and lo! A countless throng,
Th'-elect of ev'ry nation, name, and tongue,
Assembled round the everlasting throne;
With robes of white endu'd
(The righteousness of God);
And each a palm sustain'd
In his victorious hand;
When thus the bright melodious choir begun:
"Salvation to thy name,
Eternal God, and co-eternal Lamb,
In pow'r, in glory, and in essence, One!"

   So sung the saints. Th' angelic train
Second the anthem with a loud Amen
(These in the outer circle stood,
The saints were nearest God);
And prostrate fall, with glory overpow'r'd,
And hide their faces with their wings,
And thus address the King of kings:
"All-hail, by thy triumphant church ador'd!
Blessing and thanks and honor too
Are thy supreme, thy everlasting due,
Our Tri-une Sov'reign, our propitious Lord!"

While I beheld th' amazing sight,
A seraph pointed to the saints in white,
And told me who they were, and whence they came:
"These are they, whose lot below
Was persecution, pain, and woe:
These are the chosen purchas'd flock,
Who ne'er their Lord forsook;
Through his imputed merit, free from blame;
Redeem'd from ev'ry sin;
And, as thou seest, whose garments were made clean,
Wash'd in the blood of yon exalted Lamb.

Sav'd by his righteousness alone,
Spotless they stand before the throne,
And in th' ethereal temple chant his praise:
Himself among them deigns to dwell,
And face to face his light reveal:
Hunger and thirst, as heretofore,
And pain, and heat, they know no more;
Nor need, as once, the sun's prolific rays.
Immanuel, here, his people feeds,
To streams of joy perennial leads,
And wipes, for ever wipes, the tears from ev'ry face."

Anne Steele, "The Excellency of the Holy Scriptures"[6]

1. Father of mercies, in thy word
    What endless glory shines?
Forever be thy name ador'd
    For these celestial lines.

3. Here, may the wretched sons of want
    Exhaustless riches find:
Riches, above what earth can grant,
    And lasting as the mind.

4. Here, the fair tree of knowledge grows,
    And yields a free repast;
Sublimer sweets than nature knows,
    Invite the longing taste.

9. Here, the Redeemer's welcome voice,
    Spreads heavenly peace around;
And life, and everlasting joys
    Attend the blissful sound.

11. O may these heavenly pages be
    My ever dear delight,
And still new beauties may I see,
    And still increasing light.

12. Divine instructor, gracious Lord,
    Be thou forever near,
Teach me to love thy sacred word,
    And view my Savior there.

Thomas Scott, "Notes for 2 Timothy 3:14–17 and Hebrews 4:12–13"[7]

Notes for 2 Timothy 3:14–17: The Apostle therefore called on Timothy vigilantly to maintain, and persevere in, the profession and preaching of that doctrine which he had learned, and assuredly believed, knowing that he had received it from the Lord through his ministry and remembering that it accorded to the Holy Scriptures or writings of the prophets with which he had from his childhood been acquainted. These, when properly understood, were sufficient to render him wise unto salvation, and to instruct him in all things pertaining to it, as they all spoke of the promised Messiah, and prepared the mind for receiving him in faith, and submitting to his authority. For all the writings of Moses and the prophets (as well as those parts of the New Testament, which were then extant), were given by inspiration of God, to instruct us in divine things and every part of them was not only perfect truth, but profitable, to teach them sound doctrine respecting God and themselves, the eternal state, the way of acceptance, and other interesting and difficult subjects; to reprove and convince them of their errors and sins, that they might learn their guilt and danger, and so value and embrace the remedy proposed; to correct and regulate their affections, dispositions and conduct; and to instruct them in every part of universal righteousness, with the obligations, motives and encouragements to it. Thus they were suited, and sufficient, not only to make the Christian wise unto salvation, and to direct his whole behavior; but to perfect "the man of God," the faithful minister of Christ; and fully to supply him with knowledge and wisdom, and whatever could tend to his fitness for every good work in his private conduct and his public services. Doubtless this is still most emphatically true of the Sacred Scriptures, now the canon of the New Testament also is completed.

Practical Observations:

In order to escape and oppose such seductions, let us study to become well acquainted with the doctrine and the example of the Apostle; let us copy his manner of life, his purpose, faith, long-suffering and patience; let us frequently reflect on his persecutions, supports, and deliverances. Let us count our cost, and know assuredly, that "if any man will live godly in Christ Jesus," he must suffer persecution, in one way or other, as far as providence will permit the enmity of human hearts to break forth against him. Let us then continue in the things which we have learned, and professed to believe, endeavoring to get further acquaintance with the Holy Scriptures, "which are able to make us wise unto salvation, by faith in Jesus Christ" who is the principal subject both of the Old and New Testaments; and let us learn to reverence the whole Bible, as every sentence in it was given by inspiration from God, and is profitable, to instruct, reprove, correct, and guide us in the way of peace and holiness. Nothing more can be wanting to render the Christian, or the minster, perfectly qualified for every service required of him, and thoroughly furnished unto every good work, than a complete, believing, experimental, and practical knowledge of the whole Scriptures, in their genuine meaning, and connection, and the proportion of one part to another. All religious error springs from ignorance, perversion, or misunderstanding of the Scriptures; from overlooking, objecting to, or explaining away some part of them; or from adding human notions, inventions, superstitions, or new revelations to them, as of equal, or superior authority. The way therefore to oppose error is by promoting the solid knowledge of the word of truth, especially by the faithful preaching of the gospel, and the greatest kindness we can do our children is to make them early acquainted with the Bible. Thus we shall do something that may tend to preserve religion in the world, when we are removed out of it, and to perpetuate a succession of those, who are established in the faith, wise unto salvation, and thoroughly furnished unto every good work.

Notes Hebrews 4:12–13: It has been greatly controverted whether the Holy Scriptures or the personal word of God be meant in these verses, but it appears to me that the Apostle meant the written word, and that he gradually passed from the word spoken to him who spoke it. The Hebrews need not be surprised to find such deep and interesting truths couched under the typical events of their history, or contained in other parts of their scriptures; for they were the word of God. This was no lifeless, feeble, or formal instruction, like the traditions, and glosses of their scribes; but it was a living, active, energetic word, suited to be the instrument of the Holy Spirit in quickening those that were dead in sin, and in awakening, convincing, and alarming the most careless, and stupid of humanity. It was even sharper than any two-edged sword which would cut each way, for it would pierce the heart and conscience, like the irresistible lightning, forcing convictions and alarms upon the most haughty, and obstinate; showing people their past and present sins in all their odiousness, and ill desert; detecting the unsuspected pride, enmity, rebellion, ingratitude, and other evils of the heart; distinguishing people's characters with the clearest evidence; and exposing the base motives of their most specious actions. Thus, by exhibiting the glory of the divine perfections, human relations, and obligations to the great Creator; the spirituality, extent, excellency and sanction of the law; the evil and desert of sin; and the depravity of the human heart, etc., in a variety of ways, and a multiplicity of experiments, it forces conviction of guilt and danger upon the sinner, and compels him, as it were, to condemn himself, and seek deliverance, nor can any kind of delusion, or hypocritical profession stand before its penetrating energy, when experimentally and fully preached, and applied to human hearts, according to their various characters. It is, as it were, a sword, which can pierce so deep, and cut so keenly, as to divide between soul and spirit (1 Thess 5:23) and to penetrate the joints and marrow, which no other sword can reach; being in plain language a discerner of a person's most secret thoughts and intentions, so that it often shows them their most hidden purposes, and makes them afraid of being openly named and exposed, as if the preacher knew their hearts far better than they did themselves, and had a register before him even of those sins which they had forgotten. (Note: Jer 23:29; 1 Cor 14:24–25.) For in fact the Lord himself is the Speaker, when his own word is properly declared and applied; he discerns, and by his words detects the thoughts and intentions of the heart; nor is there any creature, who is not wholly manifest in every respect in his sight; before whom all things are naked, as stripped of all disguise, and open, being fully understood by Him with whom we have to do, as with our Lawgiver and Judge, and to whom we must at length render an account of all our conduct, and of all our secret thoughts and intents. The expressions "naked and open" are supposed to refer to the sacrifices, which were slayed, and opened; and then the whole of the intestines, that were before concealed, were exposed to the exact inspection of the priest.

Practical Observations:

While we find, by experience, that the word of God is quick and powerful, and sharper than any two-edged sword to penetrate the heart and conscience, let us remember that the Lord himself is the Discerner of the thoughts and intents of the heart before whom all creatures are manifest, and all things are naked and open. With him we have to do and to him we are accountable; and if, under faithful preaching, we find our hearts condemn us, we are sure that God is greater than our hearts and knows all things. Instead therefore of quarrelling with the heart-searching ministry, and choosing such lifeless feeble instructions, as are more like the shaking reed than a two-edged sword, let us lay open our inmost souls to the piercing strokes of the distinguishing word of God, that we may learn our need of that great High Priest, even the Son of God, who now pleads for us before his Father's throne in heaven.

Samuel Hopkins, "Concerning Divine Revelation"[8]

...Promises to those who believe and obey the truth, and threatenings to the disobedient and impenitent, run through all those writings; and the best and strongest conceivable motives are set before people, to deter them from sin, and excite them to fear and obey God.

Here two things may be observed:

1. What is revealed in the Scriptures concerning the perfections and works of God, his laws as the rule of duty, the nature and evil tendency of sin, and the description given of true virtue and religion, and their happy tendency and end, appears so reasonable and evident to every attentive person when revealed, that this, with the other evidences that have been mentioned, is sufficient to convince the reason and judgment of every one that this is a revelation from God, though their hearts be ever so corrupt and vicious, and has generally proved sufficient, unless where peculiar prejudices by education or otherwise have taken place.

2. The honest, virtuous mind only, which does discern and relish the beauty and excellence of truth and virtue, will see and feel the full force of this argument for the divinity of the Holy Scriptures. Such have true discerning to see the wonderful, excellent, glorious things revealed in the Holy Scriptures, which in themselves carry a most satisfying and infallible evidence of their truth and divinity. They see the divine stamp which this system of truth carries on it, and believe and are sure that this is the true God, and that here is eternal life. They therefore no longer need any other evidence but this which they find in the contents of the Holy Scriptures; in this they rest satisfied, and are assured that the writings contained in the Bible are the word of God.

Thus the Holy Scriptures are attended with the highest possible evidence that they came from God; they carry that external and internal evidence of their divinity to the reason and conscience of humanity which is sufficient to convince them, however corrupt their hearts may be; but the highest internal evidence is fully discerned only by the humble, honest mind, which is disposed to relish, love, and receive the truth. To such the true light shines from the Holy Scriptures with irresistible evidence, and their hearts are established in the truth. They believe from evidence they have within themselves, from what they see and find in the Bible. And as all might have this evidence and certainty that the contents of the Bible are from God, did they not exercise and indulge those unreasonable lusts which blind their eyes to the beauty and excellence of divine truth; unbelief is in every instance and degree of it wholly inexcusable and very criminal.

Having considered the abundant evidence there is that the writings contained in the Bible are given by divine inspiration, the following observations may be made concerning this sacred book.

1. This is a complete, unerring, and perfect rule of faith and practice, and the only rule. This being understood and believed, is sufficient to make us wise unto salvation; and we have no warrant to believe any religious truth, unless it be revealed or can be supported by the Holy Scriptures; and this is the only rule of our duty. We may be certain, if God has given us a revelation, it is in all respects complete, and in the best manner suited to answer the end: and must be the only standard of truth and duty.

2. Whatever may be justly and clearly inferred as a certain consequence from what is expressly revealed in the Scriptures must be considered as contained in divine revelation, as really as that which is expressed. For instance, if from any two or more truths, expressly revealed, another certainty follows, that other truth, by the supposition, is really contained in those expressly revealed, and, therefore, is in fact revealed or made known in the revelation of them.

3. The Holy Scriptures are not to be understood without a constant, laborious attention to them, and a careful

examination and search of them, in order to know the mind and will of God therein revealed. This is no evidence that the Scriptures are not plain and easy to be understood, as plain and intelligible as in the nature of things they can be, and adapted, in the best manner, to give instruction in those things about which they treat. For they cannot be instructed by the best possible means of instruction who will not attend and take pains. They only who "incline their ear unto wisdom, and apply their heart to understanding; who cry after knowledge, and lift up their voice for understanding; who seek her as silver, and search for her as for hid treasures," will understand the sacred writings.

4. The Holy Scriptures were never designed to be understood, especially in those things that are most important and excellent, by persons of corrupt minds whose hearts have no relish for these things, but do wholly oppose and hate them, and are determined in a course of disobedience to them. It is impossible, indeed, that such should understand the sublime holy truths that relate to the infinitely holy God, his holy law, gospel and kingdom. Therefore their not being understood by such is no argument that they are not sufficiently plain. It is no evidence that the sun does not shine clear and bright, because they who have no eyes, or if they have, refuse to open them, do not see the light, and discern the objects it plainly discovers. It is abundantly declared in Scripture that wicked evil humanity will not understand the things there revealed. "The wicked know not, neither will they understand: they walk on in darkness" (Ps 28:5). "Evil men understand not judgment" (Prov 18:5). "The natural man (that is, the man of a corrupt, carnal mind) receives not the things of the Spirit of God; for they are foolish unto him: neither can he know them, because they are spiritually discerned" (1 Cor 2:14)....Therefore, if the Scriptures be dark and unintelligible to any, especially in the most important matters there revealed, it is not owing to any defect or

darkness in them; but the fault is wholly in the persons themselves, and they are altogether inexcusable and criminal in not seeing what is revealed with sufficient clearness.

5. It can therefore be easily accounted for that these sacred writings should be so little understood by multitudes, and so greatly misunderstood by many; and that there should be so many different and opposite opinions respecting the doctrines and duties inculcated in the Bible among those who enjoy this revelation and profess to make it their rule. This is not the least evidence of any defect in the Scriptures, or that they are not sufficiently plain, and in the best manner suited to give instruction; but is wholly owing to the criminal blindness, corrupt propensities and unreasonable prejudices of persons who do not attend to the Bible with an honest heart. It is impossible that a revelation should be given that cannot be misunderstood and perverted to the worst purposes, and to support the greatest errors and delusions, by the prejudices, wicked blindness, and perverse inclinations of artful men. Nothing has taken place, with respect to this, but what might justly be expected, if persons are naturally as depraved and rebellious as the Scriptures represent them to be; and is perfectly consistent with the perfection of divine revelation....

6. The chief and greatest end of divine revelation is not yet answered. The Bible has been greatly neglected and abused, and not understood, and perverted to evil purposes by most of those who have enjoyed it. This light has hitherto shined, in a great measure, in vain, in the criminal darkness of this world, which has not comprehended, but abused and rejected it. And those few who have in some measure understood and received and practiced the truth have done it in a very imperfect degree, and the Bible has not been yet fully understood by any. But this same revelation informs us that it shall not always be so; but the time is coming, and is now just

at hand, when God will destroy the face of the covering cast over all people, and the veil that is spread over all nations, by causing the gospel to be preached to them all, and giving them a heart to discern and understand the truth....In that time the Bible shall be understood, and all the institutions and ordinances of the gospel shall have their proper, greatest and most happy effect, in the illumination and salvation of multitudes. All that precedes this time is but preparatory in order to introduce this day of salvation, in the reign of Christ on earth. The word of God shall then have free course, and be glorified, as it never was before, and shall fully answer the end for which it was given.

REFLECTIONS

1. What gratitude do we owe to God for giving such a complete revelation to us, every way suited to give instruction in every necessary and most important truth, and without which mankind must have remained in the grossest darkness! What gratitude do we owe to God, who has distinguished us from so great a part of humanity, in giving us to enjoy this inestimable privilege, while they are left to grope in the dark!

   The enemies of divine revelation have made this an objection against it, and said, if it were from God it would have been given equally to all people, and not confined to so small a part as this revelation has been....Among other things which might be and have been said in answer to this objection, it may be sufficient only to observe the following.

   1. God was under no obligation to enter on those designs of good and salvation, and do those things in favor of all people which are now made known; and therefore, could not be obliged to make this revelation. And if he is obliged to none, he may for good reasons, known to him, though we should not see them, order things so that but few shall enjoy it, as a

distinguishing sovereign favor, while others are left in that state of darkness in which all might have justly been left.

2. It is wholly owing to the fault of people that this revelation has been so long, and still is confined to such narrow bounds, and is known to so small a part of humanity. The most essential things in this revelation were made known to the first parents of all people. Had they been faithful, and all their posterity wise, and disposed to make a good improvement of the light, it would have continued, and increased, and every one of them would have enjoyed it. And after this light was abused and rejected, and almost wholly put out by human wickedness before the flood, it was again restored to the new world in the family of Noah; and was soon corrupted and extinguished by people, when they multiplied into nations, because they loved darkness, and hated this light. And when this revelation was renewed and enlarged, committed to writing and completed, had mankind been as desirous of knowing the truth, and as inquisitive after it as they ought to have been; and had they who enjoyed it been as ready and as much engaged to understand and practice it, and spread and communicate it to others, as was most reasonable and their duty, all nations would have enjoyed it fully soon after it was published. It is not therefore owing to divine revelation that it is so confined, and not universal, but the fault is wholly human. It is to be wholly ascribed to God's merciful, irresistible interposition and care, that it has not been wholly lost and destroyed by people, long before this time. Therefore the Scriptures being preserved as they have been, and handed down to this day, and put into our hands by God's merciful, wise, sovereign interposition, and direction, is both an argument that they are from God, and of our great obligations to gratitude to him for this unspeakable distinguishing favor.

3. It may be observed, that they who do not enjoy this revelation do not live up to the light they have, but misimprove and abuse it, and therefore have no reason to complain, that they have not greater light and advantages, but are most righteously given up to their chosen blindness and darkness. There cannot be a person that lives, or ever has lived in the heathen world, produced, who has fully improved, and lived up to the light he has had, or might have had, were it not his own fault. Divine revelation warrants this assertion: "The invisible things of God, from the creation of the world, are clearly seen, being understood by the things that are made, even his eternal power and divinity; so that they are without excuse; because that when they knew God, they glorified him not as God, neither were thankful, but became vain in their imaginations, and their foolish heart was darkened." Oh! let us not be unthankful, who enjoy so much greater light, which will render our ingratitude proportionably more criminal, and dreadful in its consequences. This leads to another reflection.

2. How very criminal, and wretched, are they who neglect or abuse this inestimable privilege of a revelation from God! Many not only disregard it in practice, but reject and despise it, and speak evil of it. How much will the Deists, who have been, and now are in the Christian world, have to answer for! What they call foolishness is the wisdom of God, and the wisdom of which they boast is the height of folly and madness. Would to God there were none who abused and despised the Holy Scriptures, but professed Deists! Multitudes, who profess to believe the Bible is a revelation from heaven, hold this truth in unrighteousness. They pay no proper regard to it, and constantly abuse it innumerable ways; and all the advantages they have by it, and concerns with it, will only serve to render their damnation greater, and unspeakably more dreadful. How much

lower will they sink in eternal misery, who by their folly and impenitence, perish from the countries enjoying divine revelation, than they who perish from heathen lands! This truth, though so obvious, solemn, and awakening, is too little thought of by those who enjoy, and yet disregard and abuse, the Holy Scriptures.

3. What obligations are we under to attend to this revelation, and make the best improvement of it? Surely we ought to study it with great diligence and care, and meditate therein day and night, looking to God, the Father of lights, with sincerity, earnestness, and constancy, that he would prevent our misunderstanding and perverting it, and direct and lead us to discern all the truths he has revealed, and give us a heart to conform to them in practice. We ought to pay a conscientious and sacred regard to all the directions and commands in the Bible, to turn our feet unto these testimonies, and to improve the words of God, as to make it a constant light to our feet, and lamp to our path. Blessed are they who thus watch daily at wisdom's gates, and wait at the posts of her doors; for they shall be wise unto salvation, obtain favor of the Lord, and find eternal life.

Thomas Adam, "The Scriptures"[9]

I dreamed I saw Christ curing a distempered person. I immediately applied to him for my own healing. He asked in what respect. I answered, I want spiritual healing and forgiveness of sins. He seemed to doubt whether I truly desired it. I fell upon my knees and besought him earnestly, on which he said, with a gracious look, "Thy sins are forgiven thee; go, and sin no more." I was transported at the words, and wept tears of joy in great abundance. My reflections on waking was that I had as full assurance from the word of God of the remission of sins, and as plain a command to sin no more, as if it was spoken to me by a voice from heaven, or Christ himself in person: "If they hear not Moses and the Prophets, neither will they be persuaded though one rose from the dead."

St. Augustine, in his *Confessions* (book 12, cap. 26) delivers himself to this purpose: "If I had been enjoined by God to write the book of Genesis, I should have chosen to have composed it in such a manner, for depth and eloquence, that they who did not understand creation, should nevertheless not be able to reject it for being above their capacity; and that whatever different truths any man, or number of men, might discover, or have discovered to them, should be contained in the conciseness of the text." This shows a vast reach of thought in St. Augustine, and opens to us an amazing extent of truth in Scripture, and seems to have been his real opinion of the book of Genesis.

The Scripture is light and truth from God; a clue put into my hands by him to guide me through the mazes of darkness and error; the instrument he works with in the destruction of sin and purification of my nature; and if I do but receive it as such, I am sure he will bless it to me in such ways as he knows to be best for me. My only prayer to the Father of mercies and God of all consolation is that he would give me a full conviction and certain apprehension of my faith and sincerity in the use of it; and all the rest, the measure of illumination, sensible comforts, and worldly accommodations I leave cheerfully to him.

Some people lie at catch with Scripture for examples or expressions to countenance their corruption. The design of the Christian religion is to change human views, lives, and tempers. But how? By the superior excellence of its precepts? By the weight of its exhortations, or the promise of its rewards? No, but by convincing people of their wretched guilt, blindness, and impotence; by inculcating the necessity of remission, supernatural light and assistance, and actually promising and conveying these blessings. And if it does not prove its divinity by its efficacy, let it be condemned as an imposture. This was one of its most operative convincing proofs at the beginning, and certainly is its greatest abiding proof.

The Scripture sends me to my heart; and my heart, well-known and considered, sends me back again to the Scripture, with great advantage for the understanding of it. It may be a dangerous snare to me, and I may go mourning all my life long, if I expect any thing from God that he has never promised. Eve was sadly mistaken in Cain, when she said she had gotten the man Jehovah, (the promised seed) and had got no better than a murderer. Perhaps this is a common mistake, and men think they have Christ, when they have nothing in them but the spirit of Cain.

If we had a voice from heaven, it would reveal no new Scripture to us, it would send us to the law and the testimony; why then should we not adhere to the word, and make a diligent use of it without? We should, if we believed it. The religion of most people is fixed from nature, that is, worldly ease and convenience, before they come to the reading of the Scripture. The consequence is plain. In all points where it exceeds their standard, it will be pared away. With what a mixture of fear, reverence, and holy joy should we open the Bible! The book of truth and happiness! God's heart opened to humanity! And yet the whole and every part of it secreted from him, and hid under an impenetrable veil till he opens his heart to God.

Before the coming of Christ, the law and the gospel were in one, but the latter so hid under the former that it was matter of some difficulty to discern it. After his coming, the gospel part of the law was taken out of it, and separated from it, and by being placed apart, in a conspicuous point of view, reflected back its own luster upon the law, discovered plainly that it was in it, and gave it a strength and vigor which it never had before.

The wisdom of this world is foolishness with God; consequently the wisdom of God is foolishness with people. The consequence of both is plain; all who adhere to divine wisdom and illumination must necessarily be fools in the eye of the world. The Scripture is unto us what the star was to the wise men; but if we spend all our time in gazing upon it, observing its motions, and admiring its splendor, without being led to Christ by it, the use of it will be lost to us. Perhaps it may be a good rule in the reading of Scripture not to run from one passage to another, or suppose it a duty to read a certain portion of it every day, but to dwell upon particular passages, till they have, in some measure, done their office.

Every one should apply Scripture to himself, as if it was written for him only. Scripture reading is a feast indeed, when we find in ourselves a disposition to receive it in truth and simplicity. "Son of man, can these dry bones live? Lord God, thou knowest." Show me a thought so interesting, so profound, so impressive, and so well expressed in a pagan author. Poison secretly conveyed into an antidote must be fatal, because no farther cure will be looked for. How many themselves poison their great antidote the Bible!

Look full at Scripture, especially the Beatitudes; do not be afraid of it, it is a sovereign cure for a sick soul; but then it must not be adulterated, as it is, with the spurious mixtures of human reason. We go to commentators for the most part, because we are afraid to take Christ and his apostles upon their own word. If we had a simple faith, we should seldom want others to explain their meaning. It is an awful, dreadful thing to come full into the light of Scripture, and be upon a foot of sincerity with God.

Our spiritual progress is greatly hindered by running from one thing to another. When any thought, discovery, or passage of Scripture makes a strong impression, and, as it were, seizes upon the mind, consider it as of God, and give it time and opportunity to work its effect, by excluding every thing else for a season. It would be of infinite use to keep an exact history of such inward workings; their rise, continuance, declension, and revival; and the communication and comparison of many such histories would not only afford matter of curious knowledge, great improvement, and mutual comfort, but, perhaps, be one of the strongest evidences of Christ's mission and the truth of Scripture.

The Scriptures are so darkened with expositions, and buried under such a heap of rubbish, that it is a kind of labor even for the Spirit of God to remove it. The minds of the poor, not being sophisticated by the false glosses which obscure the plain sense of Scripture, are in a much better condition for understanding it than the learned. It is no objection to the truth of Scripture that so many different sects find their own opinions in it; for, first, if they were all agreed in their sense of it, and submission to it, the testimony it brings against the blindness and corruption of mankind would be weakened. Secondly, it is no disparagement to a looking glass that all see something in it that is pleasing to themselves; the glass is true, the eye is partial.

It is said of Socrates that when he believed he was divinely admonished to do anything, it was impossible to make him take a contrary resolution. How does his example shame those who pretend to receive and believe the Scripture as a divine direction, and yet for the most part trample it under their feet? It is the great design of the Scripture to teach the best to despair of being self-saved; the worst not to despair of being saved by Christ, and to offer to all the help they want. The Scripture was written to be transcribed into the heart, and it has its effect when the heart is in such full consent and agreement therewith, that the Scripture might have been copied from it....

The design of revelation is to inform people that they are in a state of ruin, and under the divine displeasure by reason of sin, and to propose the means of their recovery to the favor of God and the hope of eternal life, by faith in a Redeemer, and submission to his teaching and authority. Setting aside St. Paul, I should think Mr. Law right in his notion of regeneration; but when I look into the Scripture I am sure he is wrong.

Many assent to the truth of Scripture, and make use of it to paint their faces, but will not suffer it to get within them, nor come too near the heart. How can I be discontented or low-spirited, want employment or enjoyment, when I have the Scripture to go to? I have the writings of a most invaluable estate in my hands, made over to me as my own property; and whenever I open the New Testament, and think of the unsearchable riches of Christ, therein conveyed to every believer, I may look down with contempt on all earthly possessions, and deserve to forfeit my interest in the gospel treasure if I do not.

There is but one kind of happiness in nature for intelligent creatures, namely that by which God is happy. God is happy in his own will; therefore intelligent creatures can only be happy by their knowledge of, and conformity to, that will. The question, where is this knowledge to be had is easily answered; and the necessity of a revelation for this purpose, together with the helps it offers for bringing mankind to that conformity, appear at once.

John Newton, Letters to the Rev. Mr. B——, October 1778[10]

My dear friend, October 1778.

Your letters are always welcome, the last doubly so for being unexpected. If you never heard before of a line of yours being useful, I will tell you for once that I get some pleasure and instruction whenever you write to me. And I see not but your call to letter writing is as clear as mine, as least when you are able to put pen to paper.

I must say something to your queries about 2 Samuel 14. I do not approve of the scholastic distinctions about inspiration, which seem to have a tendency to explain away the authority and certainty of one half of the Bible at least. Though the penmen of Scripture were ever so well informed of some facts, they would, as you observe, need express, full, and infallible inspiration to teach them which the Lord would have selected and recorded for the use of the church, amongst many others, which to themselves might appear equally important.

However, with respect to historical passages, I dare not pronounce positively that any of them are, even in the literal sense, unworthy of the wisdom of the Holy Ghost and the dignity of inspiration. Some, yes many of them, have often appeared trivial to me; but I check the thought, and charge it to my own ignorance and temerity. It must have some importance, because I read it in God's book. On the other hand, though I will not deny that they may all have a spiritual and mystical sense (for I am no more qualified to judge of the deep things of the Spirit, than to tell you what is passing this morning at the bottom of the sea); yet if, with my present modicum of light, I should undertake to expound many passages in a mystical sense, I fear such a judge as you would think my interpretations fanciful, and not well supported. I suppose I should have thought the Bible complete, though it had not informed me of the death of Rebekah's nurse or where she was buried. But some tell me that Deborah is the law, and that by the oak I am to understand the cross of Christ, and I remember to have heard of a preacher who discovered a type of Christ crucified in Absalom hanging by the hair on another oak. I am quite a mole when compared with these eagle-eyed divines, and must often content myself with plodding upon the lower ground of accommodation and allusion, except when the New Testament writers assure me what the mind of the Holy Ghost was. I can find the gospel with more confidence in the history of Sarah and Hagar than in that of Leah and Rachel; though without Paul's help I should have considered them both as family squabbles, recorded chiefly to illustrate the general truth that vanity and vexation of spirit are incident to the best men in the most favored situations. And I think there is no part of Old Testament history from which I could not (the Lord helping me) draw observations that might be suitable to the pulpit, and profitable to his people, so I might perhaps from Livy or Tacitus. But then with the Bible in my hands I go upon sure grounds: I am certain of the facts I speak from, that they really did happen. I may likewise depend upon the springs and motives of actions, and not amuse myself and my hearers with speeches which were never spoken, and motives which were never thought of, till the historian rummaged his pericranium for something to embellish his work. I doubt not but were you to consider Joab's courtly conduct only in a literal sense, how it tallied with David's desire, and how gravely and graciously he granted himself a favor, while he professed to oblige Joab; I say, in this view you would be able to illustrate many important scriptural doctrines, and to show that the passage is important to those who are engaged in the studying the anatomy of the human heart.

Andrew Fuller, "A Solemn Vow, or Renewal of Covenant with God," January 10, 1780[11]

O my God! (let not the Lord be angry with his servant, for thus speaking!) I have, thou knowest, heretofore sought thy truth. I have earnestly entreated thee, that thou wouldest lead me into it, that I might be rooted, established, and built up in it, as it is in Jesus. I have seen the truth of that saying, "It is a good thing to have the heart established with grace"; and now, I would this day, solemnly renew my prayer to thee, and also enter afresh into covenant with thee.

O Lord God! I find myself in a world where thousands profess thy name: some are preaching, some writing, some talking about religion. All profess to be searching after truth, to have Christ and the inspired writers on their side. I am afraid, lest I should be turned aside from the simplicity of the gospel. I feel my understanding full of darkness, my reason exceedingly imperfect, my will ready to start aside, and my passions strangely volatile. O illumine my understanding; teach my reason, reason; my will, rectitude; and let every faculty of which I am possessed, be kept within the bounds of thy service!

O let not the sleight of the wicked, who lie in wait to deceive, nor even the pious character of good men and women (who yet may be under great mistakes), draw me aside. Nor do thou suffer my own fancy to misguide me. Lord, thou hast given me a determination to take up no principle at secondhand, but to search for every thing at the pure fountain of thy word. Yet, Lord, I am afraid, seeing that I am as liable to err as others, lest I should be led aside from truth, by mine own imagination. Hast thou not promised, "The meek wilt thou guide in judgement, and the meek wilt thou teach thy way?" Lord, thou knowest that, at this time, my heart is not haughty, nor are mine eyes lofty. O guide me by thy counsel, and afterward receive me to glory!

One thing, in particular, I would pray for: namely, that I may not only be kept from erroneous principles, but may so love the truth as never to keep it back. O Lord, never let me, under the specious pretense of preaching holiness, neglect to promulge [i.e., promulgate] the truths of thy word; for this day I see, and have all along found that holy practice has a necessary dependence on sacred principle. O Lord, if thou wilt open mine eyes to behold the wonders of thy word, and give me to feel their transforming tendency, then shall the Lord be my God; then let my tongue cleave to the roof of my mouth, if I shun to declare, to the best of my knowledge, the whole counsel of God!

4

SPIRITUAL PRACTICES

INTRODUCTION

Early evangelicals inherited the Puritan threefold classification of spiritual practices or duties, as they normally referred to them. These three classes were the following: (1) the closet or secret and personal prayer practiced by a single individual, (2) private prayer done within a more intimate social structure, such as a family or religious society, and (3) public, which was the broadest gathering for cultivation of one's faith with others, particularly in worship. Spiritual practices were highly prized because they had the potential to bring the individuals or groups of people into God's presence. Proper motivation and focus was critical. Because ministers and friends alike understood that spiritual practices were about God and not about the individual, the person would seek to come with the best posture of his or her heart. Many ministers served as spiritual directors to their church members and other curious individuals who sought counsel through letters or personal sessions. Common wisdom recognized that it was not possible to create a standard rule that would guide everyone. Rather, flexibility and experimentation was encouraged, with the reminder to consult one's own temperament. These texts reveal many spiritual practices that are commonly used today, such as reading and praying Scripture, prayer and fasting, keeping a journal, meditation on creation, spiritual friendship, family worship, self-examination, spiritual direction, retreats, public worship, celebrating the sacraments, and listening to sermons. But they also include practices that have been lost—for example, public days for prayer and fasting around national or state emergencies; but perhaps even more, the preparation displayed in the Scottish communion weekends seems missing today. Significantly, a number of the authors speak personally of their pattern of withdrawal and return.

This demonstrates Jesus' earlier balance of contemplation and loving adoration of God that then returns to serve as an active representative of Christ in a broken and needy world.

THE TEXTS

John Cennick, "Before Meat" and "After Meat"[1]

Be present at our Table, Lord;
Be here, and ev'ry where ador'd;
Thy creatures bless, and grant that we
May feast in paradise with Thee.

We bless thee, Lord, for this our food;
But more for Jesus' flesh and blood;
The manna to our spirits giv'n,
The living bread sent down from heav'n;
Praise shall our grateful lips employ,
While life and plenty we enjoy;
'Till worthy, we adore thy name,
While banqueting with Christ, the Lamb.

Anne Dutton, Excerpt from
Thoughts on the Lord's Supper[2]

To approach his presence in this ordinance, with a particular view to Christ as our great Redeemer. We are called to the immediate exercise of faith on [*sic*] Christ, as spiritually present in his own appointment, to sit with the King at his table, and to draw near obediently, reverently, and joyfully, with a view to him, a look of faith cast upon him as our great Redeemer. Let us consider, when called to partake of the Lord's Supper, that we are going to court into the awful presence of the King of Glory, who in condescending grace to his favorites is pleased to appear in his palace royal, the church below, and invites us, as his Beloved, to feast with him on the royal banquet which infinite love has prepared. By which he admits us into the nearest approach to his glorious self that we can make in an ordinance way on the earth, on this side the presence of his glory in heaven. And putting on by faith our royal apparel, the wedding garment, Redeemer's righteousness, let us approach our Royal Bridegroom, to feast with him and upon him as our great Redeemer. And as such, cast our wondering eyes upon the infinite greatness of his person, as "Emanuel, God with us!" And the infinite greatness of his love, that "he who being in the form of God, thought it no robbery to be equal with God," should yet for us vile worms humble his great and glorious self to become a man, our kinsman, that he might become a fit Redeemer! And in our believing on Christ as such, we ought to view him in his work of redemption, both by price and power, as the former is complete and the latter shall be; and particularly we should reflect upon what we are redeemed from, and upon what we are redeemed to; or, upon those depths of misery in a state of alienation from God, whence redeeming love took us, and upon those heights of glory in the enjoyment of God, unto which thereby we are and shall be raised. Again, in our right partaking of the Lord's Supper, we are to do this in remembrance of our dear Redeemer in his death and sufferings for us, which he holds forth in this ordinance. We are called to view our great Redeemer by faith, in the greatness of his redeeming love, in that, having assumed our nature, taken upon him, who was the Lord of all, the form of a servant, he humbled himself therein for us and became obedient unto death, even the death of the cross! He fulfilled the law's command and endured its penalty, obeyed and died in our room; to redeem us from under the law's servitude as a covenant of works, and from its curse as a broken law, to make us righteous before God, to reconcile us to him; and to bring us to the enjoyment of him, both in grace and glory, through time and to eternity. We are called in this ordinance to look upon our Redeemer's sufferings for us, even from his birth to his death, which in a lively manner are represented therein, while he condescends to our senses, that he may assist our faith, and gives us the signs, the bread and wine, to be received by our bodies, that our souls may feast upon his body and blood, the things signified thereby. And when we see the broken bread with our eyes, we are to look upon Christ therein by faith, as the bread of life, provided and broken for us. The bread represents the person of our Redeemer; the blessing of the bread, the setting of him apart for the work of redemption; and the breaking of the bread, the breaking of his body. The wine holds forth our Redeemer's blood, and the pouring of it out, his pouring out his soul unto death for us. And both the bread and wine show the whole of his sufferings for our sins, under the law and justice of God, to prepare him to be our food, his body broken and his blood shed, to be our meat and drink unto life eternal. And the giving of the bread and wine hold forth the giving of our crucified Lord, our great Redeemer, for us and to us. And thus while our natural eyes behold the signs, we should look with the eye of faith unto the things thereby signified. While we hear the voice of Christ in this ordinance, in the giving of the bread, saying, "Take, eat; this is my body, which is given and broken for you"; when we stretch out our hands to receive the broken bread, we should at the same moment stretch out the hand of faith, to receive our crucified Lord as given and broken for us. When we eat the broken bread in this ordinance, we should, at the same instant, feed upon Christ crucified as given to death for our eternal life. And so, when we hear our Lord's voice at the giving of the wine, "Drink ye all of it; for this cup is the New Testament in my blood, which is shed for you, for the remission of sins," at the same time that we take the cup with our hands and drink of it with the mouth of our bodies, our souls therein and thereby should receive and drink our Savior's blood by faith. We should stretch out the hand of faith and receive the blood of Christ, given to us by infinite love, and open the mouth of faith, to drink it, that we may live forever. And oh what a large, what a soul-reviving draught, does our Redeemer give, and should our faith receive, while we hear him say of the wine at his blessed Supper, "Drink ye all of it; for this cup is the New Testament in my blood!" We should, at the same instant that we drink the wine, receive the blood of Jesus and, in and with it, all the grace of the New Covenant, of the New Testament, all the promises of grace, and all the grace of the promises, the grace of life; of pardon, of justification, of adoption, of sanctification, of consolation, and of glorification; of all good things, for our souls and bodies, both here, and hereafter. Yes, "the God of all grace," given us in Christ as the God of our life, as our present and eternal all. And see the whole of our vast inheritance, confirmed forever to us in the Lamb's blood....

Let us, attracted, allured, enkindled by the power of infinite love, cast our little drop into love's vast ocean, our little shining spark into love's vehement flame, into love's adorable brightness! While the Lord our Redeemer in love unknown gives himself to us in this ordinance, let us, in all the love we are capable of, give up ourselves to him to be entirely and forever his! Let us mourn that we can love him no more. That the Lord, our Lover, will call our kindness. Let us confess before him and bewail all our sins whereby we have pierced him....Thus, after the exercise of every grace, we should labor, while partaking of the Lord's Supper, to honor and delight the Lord our lover. And while the King of Glory sits at his table and honors us with the presence of his grace, our spikenard, through his influence, does and will cast forth its smell.

I should, under this head of the right partaking of the Lord's Supper, just give a hint as to the time of it. And it seems as if the primitive churches used to observe this ordinance every Lord's Day....It plainly appears to be the mind of Christ that his churches should frequently observe his solemn supper, to show his death thereby, till he come, or until his second coming at the end of the world. And as a crucified Jesus, the sacrificed Lamb, the Passover Lamb is there set forth as a continual feast to satisfy and solace the saints, it shows that this ordinance should be observed often. I humbly think, once a month at least, on the Lord's Day, and in the decline of the day, to answer the name and nature of a supper. And as this solemn appointment is a church ordinance, to be administered in church assembly, I likewise think that it ought not to be administered in private houses to sick persons near the time of their death. For as such persons are very unfit at that time rightly to partake of this ordinance, so there is no warrant from the word of God to administer the same to them, not one single text that hints any such thing. This is all besides and without the rule of leaders, and not of God.

I might also add that the Lord 's Supper, if rightly partook of, must be received in both kinds, in both the elements of bread and wine, as appears by our Lord's giving both the bread and wine to his disciples and commanding them to "do this in remembrance of" Him....I humbly think that as the bread and wine are to be considered in their nature and essence as such, before they are broken and poured out; so the person of Christ, God-Man, is to be considered in both parts of his human nature, in his soul and body, as in union to his divine nature, with respect to the active obedience of his life, to the mandatory part of the law, or in his fulfilling the law's command for us, to make us righteous before God. And as both the bread and wine are given to us, broken and poured out, so a whole Christ, in the whole of his obedience, active and passive, in the obedience of his life to the law's command, to make us righteous, and in his obedience unto death, by which he endured the law's penalty and satisfied for our sins is, in and under the broken bread and poured out wine, given to and ought to be together with both, received by us. And, what God hath joined together, let no one put asunder....

And while our glorious Bridegroom says, "I come quickly," let us his longing bride reply, "Amen, Even so come Lord Jesus!" Now we go in and out, to and from the house of God, his church militant, to get a glimpse of our Beloved in this special ordinance....Now the dear saints, to celebrate the Lord's Supper in the church militant, meet in diverse assemblies; but at the marriage supper of the Lamb, in the church triumphant, all the saints shall meet as the happy participants in one general assembly....Now, at the Lord's Supper we sometimes feel a sad contraction of all our graces. But at the marriage supper of the Lamb, our hearts shall be joyfully enlarged and all our graces made perfect in glory. And now, if at times while we sit with our Lord, the King at his table, our hearts are not contracted but our graces upon the flow, yet how are we straightened while in this mortal state, and pained, that we can neither see, nor love, enjoy, nor praise the Lord our Redeemer as we would! But at the Lamb's marriage feast, we shall be immortalized; mortality shall be swallowed up of life....O how sweetly do these words sound: the marriage supper of the Lamb! Then, believers, you will behold the Lamb of God as you never saw him before. You will feast upon the sacrificed Lamb as you never did before. No more darkness, no more distance shall then attend you. The Lamb's face you shall see, the Lamb's presence, his glorious presence you shall be in. No more doubts of your relation to the Lamb then, nor want of the enjoyment of relation love. No, no, the Lamb will bring you as his bride into the bride chamber, and set you as married to the Lord, to feast with him at his marriage supper; and then he will open all his heart and tell you such stories of his and of his Father's love as you never before heard, the one half, the thousandth part of which had not been told you....Love then will have its full vent on both sides: the Bridegroom of the church will then love the church freely, ineffably, infinitely and eternally, her Sun shall no more withdraw its shine; and the church, the Lamb's bride, shall love the Lamb, perfectly and forever. And oh what mutual joys, what raptures of delight, in and with each other, will be between them; while wondering angels assist the joy, and join the praise, unto endless ages!

Philip Doddridge, Chap. 19, "Directions for Daily Walking with God"[3]

Some more particular directions for maintaining continual communion with God, or being in his fear all the day long.

I would hope that upon serious consideration, self-examination, and prayer, the reader may by this time be come to a resolution to attend the table of the Lord and to seal his vow there....I say (and desire it may be observed) that I wish my reader may act on these directions so far as they may properly suit his capacities and circumstances in life; for I would be far from laying down the following particulars as universal rules for all, or for any one person in the world at all times. Let them be practiced by those that are able, and when they have leisure. And when you cannot reach them all, come as near the most important of them as you conveniently can....

1. Since you desire my thoughts in writing, and at large, on the subject of our late conversation, "By what particular methods in our daily conduct, a life of devotion and usefulness may be most happily maintained, and secured?" I set myself with cheerfulness to recollect and digest the hints which I then gave you, hoping it may be of some service to you in your most important interests, and may also fix on my own mind a deeper sense of my obligations, to govern my own life by the rules I offer to others....

2. The directions you will expect from me on this occasion naturally divide themselves into three heads: how we are to regard God in the beginning, the progress, and the close of the day. I will open my heart freely to you with regard to each, and leave you to judge how far these hints may suit your circumstances....

3. In the beginning of the day it should certainly be our care to lift up our hearts to God as soon as we wake, and while we are rising; and then to set ourselves seriously and immediately to the secret devotions of the morning.

4. For the first of these, it seems exceedingly natural. There are so many things that may suggest a great variety of pious reflections and ejaculations which are so obvious that one would think a serious mind could hardly miss them. The ease and cheerfulness of our mind at our first awakening; the refreshment we find from sleep; the security we have enjoyed in that defenseless state; the provision of warm and decent apparel;...Any of these particulars, and many more which I do not mention, may furnish us with matter of pleasing reflection and cheerful praise, while we are rising....

5. For the exercise of secret devotion in a morning, which I hope will generally be our first work, I cannot prescribe an exact method to another. You must, my dear friend, consult your own taste in some measure....Were I to propose a particular model for those who have half or three quarters of an hour at command (which with prudent conduct I suppose most may have), it should be this.

6. To begin the stated devotions of the day with a solemn act of praise offered to God on our knees, and generally with a low yet distinct voice; acknowledging the mercies we had been reflecting on while rising; never forgetting to mention Christ as the great foundation of all our enjoyments and our hopes, or to return thanks for the influences of the blessed Spirit which have led our hearts to God, or are then engaging us to seek him....This address of praise may properly be concluded with an express renewal of our covenant with God, declaring our continued repeated resolution of being devoted to him and particularly of living to his glory the ensuing day.

7. It may be proper, after this, to take a prospect of the day before us, so far as we can probably foresee in the general, where and how it may be spent; and seriously to reflect, "How shall I employ myself for God this Day? What Business is to be done, and in what Order?"...

8. After this review, it will be proper to offer up a short prayer, begging that God would quicken us to each of these foreseen duties; that he would fortify us against each of these apprehended dangers; that he would grant us success in such or such a business undertaken

for his glory; and also, that he would help us to discover and improve unforeseen opportunities, to resist unexpected temptations, and to bear patiently, and religiously, any afflictions which may surprise us in the day on which we are entering.

9. I would advise you after this to read some portion of Scripture; not a great deal, nor the whole Bible in its course, but some select lessons out of its most useful parts, perhaps ten or twelve verses, not troubling yourself much about the exact connection or other critical niceties which may occur (though at other times I would recommend them to your enquiry, as you have ability and opportunity), but considering them merely in a devotional and a practical view....

10. It might be proper to close these devotions with a psalm or hymn. And I rejoice with you that through the pious care of Dr. Watts and some other sacred poets we are provided with so rich a variety for the assistance of the closet and family on these occasions, as well as for the service of the sanctuary.

11. The most material directions which have occurred to me relating to the progress of the day are these: that we be serious in the devotions of the day; that we be diligent in the business of it, that is, in the prosecution of our worldly callings; that we be temperate and prudent in the recreations of it; that we carefully remark the providences of the day; that we cautiously guard against the temptations of it; that we keep up a lively and humble dependence upon the divine influence, suitable to every emergency of it; that we govern our thoughts well in the solitude of the day, and our discourses well in the conversations of it....

12. For seriousness in devotion, whether public or domestic, let us take a few moments before we enter upon such solemnities to pause and reflect on the perfections of the God we are addressing to, on the importance of the business we are coming about, on the pleasure and advantage of a regular and devout attendance, and on the guilt and folly of an hypocritical formality. When engaged, let us maintain a strict watchfulness over our own spirits and check the first wanderings of thought....

13. As for the hours of worldly business; whether it be, as with you, that of the hands, or whether it be the labor of a learned life not immediately relating to religious matters, let us set to the

prosecution of it with a sense of God's authority, and with a regard to his glory....

14. For seasons of diversion let us take care that our recreations be well chosen; that they be pursued with a good intention, to fit us for a renewed application to the labors of life; and thus, that they be only used in subordination to the honor of God, the great end of all our actions. Let us take heed that our hearts be not estranged from God by them; and that they do not take up too much of our time....

15. For the observation of providences it will be useful to regard the divine interposition in our comforts and in our afflictions. In our comforts, whether more common or extraordinary...these should be regarded as providential favors, and due acknowledgments should be made to God on these accounts, as we pass through such agreeable scenes. On the other hand, providence is to be regarded in every disappointment, in every loss, in every pain, in every instance of unkindness from those who have professed friendship....It is a reflection which we should particularly make with relation to those little cross accidents (as we are ready to call them) and those infirmities and follies in the temper and conduct of our intimate friends which may else be ready to discompose us....

16. For watchfulness against temptation it is necessary, when changing our place or our employment, to reflect, "What snares attend me here?" And as this should be our habitual care, so we should especially guard against those snares which in the morning we foresaw....

17. As for dependence on divine grace and influence, it must be universal and, since we always need it, we must never forget that necessity. A moment spent in humble fervent breathings after the communications of the divine assistance may do more good than many minutes spent in mere reasoning....Let us therefore always call upon God and say, for instance, when we are going to pray, "Lord, fix my attention! Awaken my holy affections, and pour out upon me, the Spirit of grace and of supplication (Zech 12:10)!"...When addressing ourselves to any worldly business, "Lord, prosper thou the work of mine hands upon me (Ps 90:17), and give thy blessing to my honest endeavors!" When going to any kind of recreation, "Lord, bless my refreshments! Let me not forget thee in them, but still keep thy glory in view!"...

18. For the government of our thoughts in solitude let us accustom ourselves, on all occasions, to exercise a due command over our thoughts. Let us take care of those entanglements of passion, and those attachments to any present interest and view, which would deprive us of our power over them. Let us set before us some profitable...verse of Scripture, which we had met with in the morning, and to treasure it up in our mind, resolving to think of that at any time when we are at a loss for matter of pious reflection, in any intervals of leisure for entering upon it....

19. Lastly, for the government of our discourse in company, we should take great care that nothing may escape us which can expose us or our Christian profession to censure and reproach....And in pauses of discourse, it may not be improper to lift up an holy ejaculation to God, that his grace may assist us and our friends in our endeavors to do good to each other, that all we say and do may be worthy the character of reasonable creatures and of Christians.

20. The directions for a religious closing of this day, which I shall here mention, are only two. Let us see to it that the secret duties of the evening be well performed; and let us lie down on our beds in a pious frame.

21. For our secret devotion in the evening, I would propose a method something different from that in the morning....I should, sir, advise to read a portion of Scripture in the first place, with suitable reflections, and prayer, as above. Then to read a hymn, or psalm. After this to enter on self-examination, to be followed by a longer prayer, than that which followed reading, to be formed on this review of the day....

22. Before I quit this head, I must take the liberty to remind you that self-examination is so important a duty that it will be worth our while to spend a few words upon it....I offer you therefore the following queries, which I hope you will, with such alterations as you may judge requisite, keep near you for daily use. "Did I wake as with God this morning, and rise with a grateful sense of his goodness? How were the secret devotions of the morning performed? Did I offer my solemn praises, and renew the dedication of myself to God, with becoming attention and suitable affections? Did I lay my scheme for the business of the day wisely and well? How did I read the Scripture, and any other devotional or practical piece which I

might afterward conveniently review? Did it do my heart good, or was it a mere amusement? How have the other stated devotions of the day been attended, whether in the family or in public? Have I pursued the common business of this day with diligence and spirituality, doing every thing in season, and with all convenient dispatch, and as unto the Lord (Col 3:23)? What time have I lost this day, in the morning, or the forenoon, in the afternoon, or the evening?" (for these divisions will assist your recollection). "And what has occasioned the loss of it? With what temper, and under what regulations, have the recreations of this day been pursued? Have I seen the hand of God in my mercies, health, cheerfulness, food, clothing, books, preservation in journeys, success of business, conversation and kindness of friends, etc.? Have I seen it in afflictions, and particularly in little things which had a tendency to vex and disquiet me? And with regard to this interposition, have I received my comforts thankfully and my afflictions submissively? How have I guarded against the temptations of the day, particularly against this or that temptation which I foresaw in the morning? Have I maintained an humble dependence on divine influences? Have I lived by faith in the Son of God (Gal 2:20) and regarded Christ this day as my Teacher and Governor, my Atonement and Intercessor, my Example and Guardian, my Strength and Forerunner? Have I been looking forward to death and eternity this day, and considered myself as a probationer for heaven, and through grace an expectant of it? Have I governed my thoughts well, especially in such or such an interval of solitude? How was my subject of thought this day chosen, and how was it regarded?…With what attention and improvement have I read the Scripture this evening? How was self-examination performed the last night, and how have I profited this day by any remarks I then made on former negligence and mistakes? With what temper did I then lie down and compose myself to sleep?"

23. You will easily see, sir, that these questions are so adjusted as to be an abridgment of the most material advices I have given in this letter; and I believe I need not, to a person of your understanding, say any thing as to the usefulness of such enquiries....

24. The sentiments with which we should lie down and compose ourselves to sleep. Now here it is obviously suitable to think of the divine goodness in adding another day and the mercies of it to

the former days and mercies of our life;…thus may our sleeping, as well as our waking hours, be in some sense devoted to God.…

25. I am persuaded, the most important of them have, in one form or another, been long regarded by you and made governing maxims of your life. I shall greatly rejoice if the review of these, and the examination and trial of the rest, may be a means of leading you into more intimate communion with God and so of rendering your life more pleasant and useful, and your eternity, whenever that is to commence, more glorious.…

Jonathan Edwards, "Personal Narrative"[4]

The first that I remember that ever I found anything of that sort of inward, sweet delight in God and divine things that I have lived much in since, was on reading those words, 1 Timothy 1:17: "Now unto the King eternal, immortal, invisible, the only wise God, be honor and glory for ever and ever, Amen." As I read the words, there came into my soul, and was, as it were, diffused through it, a sense of the glory of the divine being, a new sense, quite different from anything I ever experienced before. Never any words of Scripture seemed to me as these words did. I thought with myself, how excellent a being that was; and how happy I should be if I might enjoy that God, and be wrapt up to God in heaven, and be as it were swallowed up in him. I kept saying and, as it were, singing over these words of Scripture to myself, and went to prayer, to pray to God that I might enjoy him, and prayed in a manner quite different from what I used to do; with a new sort of affection. But it never came into my thought that there was anything spiritual, or of a saving nature in this.

From about that time, I began to have a new kind of apprehensions and ideas of Christ, and the work of redemption, and the glorious way of salvation by him. I had an inward, sweet sense of these things that at times came into my heart, and my soul was led away in pleasant views and contemplations of them. And my mind was greatly engaged to spend my time in reading and meditating on Christ, and the beauty and excellency of his person, and the lovely way of salvation by free grace in him. I found no books so delightful to me as those that treated of these subjects. Those words Canticles 2:1 used to be abundantly with me: "I am the Rose of Sharon, the Lily of the Valley." The words seemed to me sweetly to represent the loveliness and beauty of Jesus Christ. And the whole Book of Canticles used to be pleasant to me, and I used to be much in reading it, about that time. And found, from time to time, an inward sweetness that used, as it were, to carry me away in my contemplations in what I know not how to express otherwise than by a calm, sweet abstraction of soul from all the concerns of this world, and a kind of vision, or fixed ideas and imaginations, of being alone in the mountains, or some solitary wilderness, far from all people, sweetly conversing with Christ, and wrapt and swallowed up in God. The sense I had of divine things would often, of a sudden as it were, kindle up a sweet burning in my heart, an ardor of my soul that I know not how to express.

Not long after I first began to experience these things, I gave an account to my father of some things that had passed in my mind. I was pretty much affected by the discourse we had together. And when the discourse was ended, I walked abroad alone, in a solitary place in my father's pasture, for contemplation. And as I was walking there and looked up on the sky and clouds, there came into my mind a sweet sense of the glorious majesty and grace of God that I know not how to express. I seemed to see them both in a sweet conjunction, majesty and meekness joined together; it was a sweet and gentle and holy majesty, and also a majestic meekness, an awful sweetness, a high and great and holy gentleness.

After this my sense of divine things gradually increased and became more and more lively and had more of that inward sweetness. The appearance of everything was altered; there seemed to be, as it were, a calm, sweet cast, or appearance of divine glory, in almost everything. God's excellency, his wisdom, his purity and love, seemed to appear in everything: in the sun, moon, and stars; in the clouds and blue sky; in the grass, flowers, trees; in the water, and all nature, which used greatly to fix my mind. I often used to sit and view the moon for a long time, and so in the day time spent much time in viewing the clouds and sky, to behold the sweet glory of God in these things, in the meantime singing forth with a low voice my contemplations of the Creator and Redeemer. And scarce anything, among all the works of nature, was so sweet to me as thunder and lightning. Formerly, nothing had been so terrible to me. I used to be a person uncommonly terrified with thunder and it used to strike me with terror when I saw a thunderstorm rising. But now, on the contrary, it rejoiced me. I felt God at the first appearance of a thunderstorm and used to take the opportunity at such times to fix myself to view the clouds, and see the lightning play, and hear the majestic and awful voice of God's thunder, which often times was exceeding entertaining, leading me to sweet contemplations of my great and glorious God. And while I viewed, used to spend my time, as it always seemed natural to me, to sing or chant forth my meditations; to speak my thought in soliloquies, and speak with a singing voice.

I felt then a great satisfaction as to my good estate. But that did not content me. I had vehement longings of soul after God and Christ and after more holiness, wherewith my heart seemed to be full and ready to break, which often brought to my mind the words of the Psalmist, Psalm 119:28: "My soul breaketh for the longing it hath." I often felt a mourning and lamenting in my heart that I had not turned to God sooner, that I might have had more time to grow in grace. My mind was greatly fixed on divine things; I was almost perpetually in the contemplation of them. Spent most of my time in thinking of divine things, year after year. And used to spend abundance of my time in walking alone in the woods and solitary places for meditation, soliloquy and prayer, and converse with God. And it was always my manner, at such times, to sing forth my contemplations. And was almost constantly in ejaculatory prayer, wherever I was. Prayer seemed to be natural to me, as the breath by which the inward burnings of my heart had vent.

The delights which I now felt in things of religion were of an exceeding different kind from those aforementioned that I had when I was a boy. They were totally of another kind and what I then had no more notion or idea of than one born blind has of pleasant and beautiful colors. They were of a more inward, pure, soul-animating and refreshing nature. Those former delights never reached the heart and did not arise from any sight of the divine excellency of the things of God, or any taste of the soul satisfying, and life-giving good, there is in them.

My sense of divine things seemed gradually to increase until I went to preach at New York, which was about a year and a half after they began. While I was there, I felt them very sensibly, in a much higher degree than I had done before. My longings after God and holiness were much increased. Pure and humble, holy and heavenly Christianity appeared exceeding amiable to me. I felt in me a burning desire to be in everything a complete Christian, and conformed to the blessed image of Christ, and that I might live in all things according to the pure, sweet and blessed rules of the Gospel. I had an eager thirsting after progress in these things....

The heaven I desired was a heaven of holiness; to be with God, and to spend my eternity in divine love and holy communion with Christ. My mind was very much taken up with contemplations on heaven and the enjoyments of those there, and living there in perfect holiness, humility and love. And it used at that time to appear a great part of the happiness of heaven that there the saints could express their love to Christ. It appeared to me a great clog and hindrance and burden to me that what I felt within I could not express to God and give vent to as I desired. The inward ardor of my soul seemed to be hindered and pent up, and could not freely flame out as it would. I used often to think how in heaven this sweet principle should freely and fully vent and express itself. Heaven appeared to me exceeding delightful as a world of love. It appeared to me that all happiness consisted in living in pure, humble, heavenly, divine love....

Holiness, as I then wrote down some of my contemplations on it, appeared to me to be of a sweet, pleasant, charming, serene, calm nature. It seemed to me it brought an inexpressible purity, brightness, peacefulness and ravishment to the soul and that it made the soul like a field or garden of God, with all manner of pleasant flowers; that is, all pleasant, delightful and undisturbed, enjoying a sweet calm and the gently vivifying beams of the sun. The soul of a true Christian, as I then wrote my meditations, appeared like such a little white flower as we see in the spring of the year, low and humble on the ground, opening its bosom to receive the pleasant beams of the sun's glory; rejoicing as it were, in a calm rapture; diffusing around a sweet fragrancy; standing peacefully and lovingly in the midst of other flowers round about it; all in like manner opening their bosoms, to drink in the light of the sun....

On January 12, 1723, I made a solemn dedication of myself to God and wrote it down, giving up myself and all that I had to God; to be for the future in no respect my own; to act as one that had no right to himself, in any respect. And solemnly vowed to take God for my whole portion and felicity, looking on nothing else as any part of my happiness, nor acting as if it were, and his law for the constant rule of my obedience, engaging to fight with all my might, against the world, the flesh and the devil, to the end of my life. But have reason to be infinitely humbled, when I consider how much I have failed of answering my obligation.

I had then abundance of sweet religious conversation in the family where I lived, with Mr. John Smith and his pious mother. My heart was knit in affection to those in whom were appearances of true piety; and I could bear the thoughts of no other companions but such as were holy and the disciples of the blessed Jesus.

I had great longings for the advancement of Christ's kingdom in the world. My secret prayer used to be in great part taken up in praying for it. If I heard the least hint of anything that happened in any part of the world that appeared to me, in some respect or other, to have a favorable aspect on the interest of Christ's kingdom, my soul eagerly catched at it, and it would much animate and refresh me. I used to be earnest to read public news letters, mainly for that end, to see if I could not find some news favorable to the interest of religion in the world.

I very frequently used to retire into a solitary place on the banks of Hudson's River, at some distance from the city, for contemplation on divine things and secret converse with God, and had many sweet hours there. Sometimes Mr. Smith and I walked there together to converse of the things of God, and our conversation used much to turn on the advancement of Christ's kingdom in the world and the glorious things that God would accomplish for his church in the latter days.

I had then, and at other times, the greatest delight in the Holy Scriptures of any book whatsoever. Oftentimes in reading it, every word seemed to touch my heart. I felt a harmony between something in my heart and those sweet and powerful words. I seemed often to see so much light exhibited by every sentence, and such a refreshing ravishing food communicated, that I could not get along in reading. Used often times to dwell long on one sentence, to see the wonders contained in it; and yet almost every sentence seemed to be full of wonders....

In September 1725 was taken ill at New Haven; and endeavoring to go home to Windsor, was so ill at the North Village that I could go no further, where I lay sick for about a quarter of a year. And in this sickness, God was pleased to visit me again with the sweet influences of his Spirit. My mind was greatly engaged there on divine, pleasant contemplations and longings of soul....

It has often appeared sweet to me to be united to Christ, to have him for my head and to be a member of his body, and also to have Christ for my teacher and prophet. I very often think with sweetness and longing and panting of soul of being a little child, taking hold of Christ, to be led by him through the wilderness of this world. That text, Matthew 18 at the beginning, has often been sweet to me: "Except ye be converted, and become as little children, etc."...

Sometimes only mentioning a single word causes my heart to burn within me, or only seeing the name of Christ or the name of some attribute of God. And God has appeared glorious to me on account of the Trinity. It has made me have exalting thoughts of God, that he subsists in three persons: Father, Son, and Holy Ghost.

The sweetest joys and delights I have experienced have not been those that have arisen from a hope of my own good estate, but in a direct view of the glorious things of the gospel. When I enjoy this sweetness, it seems to carry me above the thoughts of my own safe estate. It seems at such times a loss that I cannot bear, to take off my eye from the glorious, pleasant object I behold without me, to turn my eye in upon myself and my own good estate....

I have sometimes had a sense of the excellent fullness of Christ and his meekness and suitableness as a Savior, whereby he has appeared to me, far above all, the chief of ten thousands. And his blood and atonement has appeared sweet, and his righteousness sweet, which is always accompanied with an ardency of spirit, and inward struggling and breathing and groaning, that cannot be uttered, to be emptied of myself and swallowed up in Christ.

Once, as I rid [sic] out into the woods for my health, Anno 1737, and having lit from my horse in a retired place, as my manner commonly has been, to walk for divine contemplation and prayer, I had a view that for me was extraordinary of the glory of the Son of God as Mediator between God and man; and his wonderful, great, full, pure and sweet grace and love, and meek and gentle condescension. This grace, that appeared to me so calm and sweet, appeared great above the heavens. The person of Christ appeared ineffably excellent, with an excellency great enough to swallow up all thought and conception. Which continued, as near as I can judge, about an hour; which kept me, the bigger part of the time, in a flood of tears, and weeping aloud. I felt withal an ardency of soul to be what I know not otherwise how to express than to be emptied and annihilated, to lie in the dust, and to be full of Christ alone; to love him with a holy and pure love; to trust in him; to live upon him; to serve and follow him, and to be totally wrapt up in the fullness of Christ; and to be perfectly sanctified and made pure, with a divine and heavenly purity. I have several other times had views very much of the same nature, and that have had the same effects.

I have many times had a sense of the glory of the third Person in the Trinity in his office of Sanctifier, in his holy operations communicating divine light and life to the soul. God in the communications of his Holy Spirit has appeared as an infinite fountain of divine glory and sweetness, being full and sufficient to fill and satisfy the soul, pouring forth itself in sweet communications like the sun in its glory, sweetly and pleasantly diffusing light and life....

I have greatly longed of late for a broken heart and to lie low before God. And when I ask for humility of God, I can't bear the thoughts of being no more humble than other Christians. It seems to me that though their degrees of humility may be suitable for them, yet it would be a vile self-exaltation in me not to be the lowest in humility of all people. Others speak of their longing to be humbled to the dust. Though that may be a proper expression for them, I always think for myself that I ought to be humbled down below hell. It is an expression that it has long been natural for me to use in prayer to God. I ought to lie infinitely low before God....

Though it seems to me that in some respects I was a far better Christian for two or three years after my first conversion than I am now and lived in a more constant delight and pleasure, yet of late years I have had a more full and constant sense of the absolute sovereignty of God and a delight in that sovereignty, and have had more of a sense of the glory of Christ as a Mediator, as revealed in the gospel.

Joseph Hart, "Buried in Baptism"[5]

Buried in baptism with our Lord,
We rise with him, to life restor'd:
Not the base life in Adam lost,
But richer far; for more it cost.

Water can cleanse the flesh, we own;
But Christ well knows, and Christ alone,
How dear to him our cleansing stood,
Baptiz'd with fire, and bath'd in blood.

His was a baptism deep indeed,
O'er feet and body, hands and head.
He in his body purg'd our sin;
A little water makes us clean.

Not but we taste his bitter cup;
But only he could drink it up.
To burn for us was his desire:
And he baptizes us with fire.

This fire will not consume, but melt.
How soft, compar'd with that he felt!
Thus cleans'd from filth, and purg'd from dross,
Baptized Christian, bear the cross.

Isaac Backus, Excerpt from
Family Prayer Not to Be Neglected[6]

To the reader (February 6, 1766),

New England has formerly been a place famous for religion in general and for family worship in particular; but of late the neglect of this, as well as of other religious duties, has evidently been growing upon us, which has caused much grief to pious souls; yet I have not heard that any discourse has been published upon this subject here these many years and as there have lately been numbers

172

remarkably awakened in some parts of the land that were trained up in the neglect of family prayer, who are still at a loss about the Scripture authority for the daily practice thereof. Therefore the following considerations, by the advice of friends, are humbly offered to the public....

Other hindrances I shall have occasion to speak of in my addresses to several sorts of persons, to which I now proceed. And,

To heads of families who neglect the daily practice of family worship.

Dear sirs, will you permit an unworthy instrument to ask you a few serious questions about this matter? As,

1. Is this neglect because you see no warrant for this duty? If so, pray then review the case again, and in the fear of God search his word, and consider well if there is not as plain evidence for it, both by precept and example, as there is for almost any point of Christian practice. And consider also if it is not our reasonable service that we should seek the Lord, and that daily, since it is "in him we live, move, and have our being" (Acts 27:28); yes, and whether such as neglect it don't act more absurdly than irrational animals; for we are told that the "young lions roar after their prey and seek their meat from God: and that, He giveth to the beast his food, and the young ravens that cry" (Pss 104:21; 147:9). Or,

2. Is your neglect owing to a want of a disposition to such exercises? Surely the thought of that might well alarm your soul; "for the wrath of God is revealed from heaven against all ungodliness, and unrighteousness of men, who hold the truth in unrighteousness." It is a great truth that God is a spirit and is to be worshiped spiritually; yet this truth is held in unrighteousness, while it is held as an excuse from our daily acknowledgements of his favors; "for (says the Apostle) the invisible things of him from the creation of the world, are clearly seen, being understood by the things that are made, even his eternal power, and God-head; so that they are without excuse, because that when they knew

God, they glorified him not as God, neither were thankful" (Rom 1:18, 20–21). And the following part of the chapter shows that for this cause they were given up to the most amazing blindness and awful abominations that mortals ever knew. Or,

3. Do you allege the ill behavior of any that practice family prayer as an excuse for your neglect, as I have known some to do? I think you will be ashamed, in open daily light, to stand in this one minute. Who ever acted more abominably about prayer than the Pharisees? Yet how far was that from hindering the abundant practice of it by Christ and his followers?

4. Is this neglect caused by things being out of order in your family? O then rest not without having those disorders rectified, for a family that will not admit of the worship of God in it must be a dreadful place, and one may justly say of it, as Jacob did of Simeon and Levi, O my soul, come not thou into their secret; unto such a family, mine honor be not thou united. Joshua's resolution with regard to himself and family deserves our warmest regard: "As for me and my house we will serve the Lord" (Josh 24:15)....

5. Do any excuse themselves because of the smallness of their gifts? I would only ask such, whether that prevented them from coming in their childhood to their earthly parents for what they wanted? If not, then why should it hinder us from coming to him who knows what we have need of before we ask him (Matt 6:8)?

Before I take my leave of you who profess religion, and yet neglect the daily practice of social worship, I would earnestly desire you to view the inconsistency that there is between your profession and practice. It is generally allowed that a leading point in the profession of Christianity is the ordinance of baptism, notwithstanding one's different judgments about the time and manner of administering of it....Baptism is a "putting on Christ" and contains an engagement to "walk in newness of life" (Rom 6:4). But if we think that one act, without living such a life, will answer, we shall find ourselves greatly mistaken. No doubt but you will find that many outward difficulties and inward struggles will rise against prayer as well as other duties; but if you will neglect them because of that, I leave you to answer it to him who has said, "Whosoever doth not bear his cross, and come after me, cannot be my disciple" (Luke 14:27).

I would say a few words to them that practice family worship and my address to you shall be by way of advice and exhortation. And,

1. Rest not in the mere external performances of this duty. James tells us that while many receive not because they ask not, others ask and receive not, because they ask amiss, that they may consume it upon their lusts; and he says, "God resisteth the proud, but giveth grace unto the humble." And among other things which he advances on this subject he brings in the example of Elijah, who, though a man of like passions with us, yet he prayed earnestly and he repeatedly obtained his request. He prayed earnestly, or as it is in the margin, he prayed in his prayer (Jas 4:2–3, 6; 5:17–18). So, my friends, if we pray in our prayers, we shall find it not to be in vain.

2. Take good heed to your walk. Obedient children will come to their parents, not only for food but for instruction about what they should do, and will be as much concerned to obey their commands as to obtain their help. So says our Apostle, "As obedient children, not fashioning yourselves according to the former lusts in your ignorance: but as he which hath called you is holy, so be ye holy, in all manner of conversation" (1 Pet 1:14–15)....

3. Content not yourself with family prayer alone. We are to pray always with all prayer, and watch thereunto with all perseverance. Therefore,

4. Beware of turning back from these ways; for if any person draw back, Christ's soul will have no pleasure in him; which is set in a very striking light in the 81st Psalm, where God reminds his people of the wonders

which he had done for them and says, "Thou calledst in trouble, and I delivered thee. Hear, O my people, and I will testify unto thee: There shall no strange god be in thee; I am the Lord thy God: open thy mouth wide and I will fill it." As if he had said, "Thou hast found me to be a God hearing prayer, and I am ever the same: therefore regard no others, but open thy mouth wide, enlarge thy desires to me as much as thou wilt, and I will fill them." But instead of continuing their regard to him, he goes on to say, "My people would not hearken to my voice: and Israel would none of me; so I gave them up unto their own heart's lusts; and they walked in their own counsels" (vv. 7, 12). O tremendous case! to be given up to one's heart's lusts is one of the greatest judgments on this side of hell. What need have we then to cry daily, "Lead us not into temptation, but deliver us from evil!"

My address shall be to young persons. And what I have at present to say to such is, learn the importance of setting out as well as traveling through the world with God....Take heed, dear youth! You are called upon from two very different quarters: Satan promises you the kingdoms and glories of this world, if you will take his ways of deceit, vanity, and iniquity; and on the other hand, here are these calls from heaven to choose the way of truth and holiness, and the promise thereupon of all blessings, both in this life and that which is to come; and which will you believe? Which will you regard?

John Witherspoon, "Fast Day Sermon on Psalm 76:10," Preached at Princeton, on the 17th of May, 1776[7]

In the first place, I would take the opportunity on this occasion and from this subject to press every hearer to a sincere concern for his own soul's salvation. There are times when the mind may be expected to be more awake to divine truth, and the conscience more open to the arrows of conviction, than at others. A season of public judgment is of this kind, as appears from what has been already said. That curiosity and attention at least are raised in some degree is plain from the unusual throng of this assembly. Can you have a clearer view of the sinfulness of your nature, than when the rod of the oppressor is lifted up, and when you see men putting on the habit of the warrior and collecting on every hand the weapons of hostility and instruments of death? I do not blame your ardor in preparing for the resolute defense of your temporal rights. But consider, I beseech you, the truly infinite importance of the salvation of your souls. Is it of much moment whether you and your children shall be rich or poor, at liberty or in bonds? Is it of much moment whether this beautiful country shall increase in fruitfulness from year to year, being cultivated by active industry and possessed by independent freemen, or the scanty produce of the neglected fields shall be eaten up by hungry publicans while the timid owner trembles at the tax gatherers approach? And is it of less moment, my brethren, whether you shall be the heirs of glory or the heirs of hell? Is your state on earth for a few fleeting years of so much moment? And is it of less moment what shall be your state through endless ages? Have you assembled together willingly to hear what shall be said on public affairs and to join in imploring the blessing of God on the councils and arms of the united colonies, and can you be unconcerned what shall become of you for ever, when all the monuments of human greatness shall be laid in ashes, for "the earth itself and all the works that are therein shall be burnt up"?

Wherefore my beloved hearers, as the ministry of reconciliation is committed to me, I beseech you in the most earnest manner to attend to the things that belong to your peace before they are hid from your eyes. How soon and in what manner a seal shall be set upon the character and state of every person here present it is impossible to know, for he who only can know does not think proper to reveal it. But you may rest assured that there is no time more suitable, and there is none so safe as that which is present, since it is wholly uncertain whether any other shall be yours. Those who shall first fall in battle have not many more warnings to receive. There are some few daring and hardened sinners who despise eternity itself and set their maker at defiance, but the far greater number, by staving off their convictions to a more convenient season, have been taken unprepared and thus eternally lost. I would therefore earnestly press the Apostle's exhortation: "Now is the day of salvation" (2 Cor 6:1–2).

Suffer me to beseech you, or rather to give you warning not to rest satisfied with a form of godliness, denying the power thereof. There can be no true religion till there be a discovery of your lost state by nature and practice, and an unfeigned acceptance of Christ Jesus as he is offered in the gospel. Unhappy they who either despise his mercy or are ashamed of his cross! Believe it, "there is no salvation in any other. There is no other name under heaven given amongst men by which we must be saved." Unless you are united to him by a lively faith, not the resentment of a haughty monarch but the sword of divine justice hangs over you, and the fullness of divine vengeance shall speedily overtake you....The fear of others may make you hide your profanity; prudence and experience may make you abhor intemperance and riot; as you advance in life, one vice may supplant another and hold its place; but nothing less than the sovereign grace of God can produce a saving change of heart and temper, or fit you for his immediate presence.

From what has been said upon this subject, you may see what ground there is to give praise to God for his favors already bestowed on us, respecting the public cause. It would be a criminal inattention not to observe the singular interposition of providence hitherto in behalf of the American colonies. It is, however, impossible for me in a single discourse, as well as improper at this time, to go through every step of our past transactions....

While we give praise to God, the supreme disposer of all events, for his interposition in our behalf, let us guard against the dangerous error of trusting in or boasting of an "arm of flesh." I could earnestly wish that while our arms are crowned with success, we might content ourselves with a modest ascription of it to the power of the highest. It has given me great uneasiness to read some ostentatious, vaunting expressions in our newspapers, though happily I think much restrained of late. Let us not return to them once again. If I am not mistaken, not only the Holy Scripture in general, and the truths of the glorious gospel in particular, but the whole course of providence seems intended to abase the pride of people, and lay the vainglorious in the dust....

From what has been said you may learn what encouragement you have to put your trust in God and hope for his assistance in the present important conflict. He is the Lord of hosts, great in might and strong in battle. Whoever has his countenance and approbation shall have the best at last. I do not mean to speak prophetically, but agreeably to the analogy of faith and the principles of God's moral government. Some have observed that true religion, and in her train dominion, riches, literature, and arts, have taken their course in a slow and gradual manner from east to west since the earth was settled after the flood, and from thence forbode the future glory of America. I leave this as a matter rather of conjecture than certainty, but observe that if your cause is just, if your principles are pure, and if your conduct is prudent, you need not fear the multitude of opposing hosts.

If your cause is just you may look with confidence to the Lord and entreat him to plead it as his own. You are all my witnesses that this is the first time of my introducing any political subject into the pulpit. At this season, however, it is not only lawful but necessary, and I willingly embrace the opportunity of declaring my opinion without any hesitation, that the cause in which America is now in arms is the cause of justice, of liberty, and of human nature. So far as we have hitherto proceeded, I am satisfied that the confederacy of the colonies has not been the effect of pride, resentment, or sedition, but of a deep and general conviction that our civil and religious liberties, and consequently in a great measure the temporal and eternal happiness of us and our posterity, depended on the issue....

You shall not, my brethren, hear from me in the pulpit what you have never heard from me in conversation, I mean railing at the king personally, or even his ministers and the Parliament and people of Britain, as so many barbarous savages. Many of their actions have probably been worse than their intentions. That they should desire unlimited dominion if they can obtain or preserve it is neither new nor wonderful. I do not refuse submission to their unjust claims because they are corrupt or profligate, although probably many of them are so, but because they are human and therefore liable to all the selfish bias inseparable from human nature. I call this claim unjust of making laws to bind us in all cases whatsoever, because they are separated from us, independent of us, and have an interest in opposing us. Would any person who could prevent it give up his estate, person, and family to the disposal of his neighbor, although he had liberty to choose the wisest and the best master? Surely not. This is the true and proper hinge of the controversy between Great Britain and America. It is however to be added that such is their distance from us that a wise and prudent administration of our affairs is as impossible as the claim of authority is unjust. Such is and must be their ignorance of the state of things here, so much time must elapse before an error can be seen and remedied, and so much injustice and partiality must be expected from the arts and misrepresentation of interested persons, that for these colonies to depend wholly upon the legislature of Great Britain would be like many other oppressive connections, injury to the master, and ruin to the slave.

Phillis Wheatley, "To the Rev. Dr. Thomas Amory on Reading His Sermons on Daily Devotion, in Which That Duty Is Recommended and Assisted"[8]

To cultivate in ev'ry noble mind
Habitual grace, and sentiments refin'd.
Thus while you strive to mend the human heart,
Thus while the heav'nly precepts you impart.
O may each bosom catch the sacred fire,
And youthful minds to virtue's throne aspire!

When God's eternal ways you set in sight,
And virtue shines in all her native light,
In vain would vice her works in night conceal,
For wisdom's eye pervades the sable veil.

Artists may paint the sun's effulgent rays,
But Amory's pen the brighter God displays:
While his great works in Amory's pages shine,
And while he proves his essence all divine.
The atheist sure no more can boast aloud
Of chance, or nature, and exclude the God;
As if the clay without the potter's aid
Should rise in various forms, and shapes self-made,

Or worlds above with orb o'er orb profound
Self-mov'd could run the everlasting round.
It cannot be—unerring wisdom guides
With eye propitious, and o'er all presides.

    Still prosper, Amory! Still may'st thou receive
The warmest blessings which a muse can give,
And when this transitory state is o'er,
When kingdoms fall, and fleeting fame's no more,
May Amory triumph in immortal same,
A nobler title, and superior name!

William McCulloch, "An Account of the Second Sacrament at Cambuslang: In a Letter from Mr. McCulloch to a Brother"[9]

Reverend and dear brother,

You know that we had the sacrament of the Lord's Supper dispensed here on the eleventh of July last. It was such a sweet and agreeable time to many that a motion was made by Mr. Webster and immediately seconded by Mr. Whitefield that we should have another such occasion again in this place very soon. The motion was very agreeable to me, but I thought it needful to deliberate before coming to a resolution. The thing proposed was indeed extraordinary, but so had the work in this place been for several months past. Care was therefore taken to acquaint the several meetings for prayer with the motion who relished it well and prayed for direction to these concerned to determine in this matter. The session met next Lord's day, and taking into consideration the divine command to celebrate this ordinance often, joined with the extraordinary work that had been here for some time past; and understanding that many who had met with much benefit to their souls at the last solemnity had expressed their earnest desires of seeing another in this place shortly; and hearing that there were many who intended to have joined at the last occasion but were kept back through inward discouragements or outward obstructions, and were wishing soon to see another opportunity of that kind here to which they might have access, it was therefore resolved (God willing) that the sacrament of the Lord's Supper should be again dispensed in this parish on the third Sabbath of August then next to come, being the fifteenth day of that month....

The design of these meetings, and the business which they were accordingly employed in (besides singing of psalms and blessing the name of God together), was to ask mercy of the God of heaven to ourselves to pray for the Seceders* and others who unhappily oppose this work of God here and in some other parts where it takes place, that God would forgive their guilt in this matter, open their eyes, remove their prejudices, and convince them that it is indeed his work, and give them repentance to the acknowledgment of this truth that the Lord would continue and increase the blessed work of conviction and conversion here, and in other places where it is begun, in a remarkable measure, and extend it to all the corner of the land, and that he would eminently countenance the dispensing of the sacrament of the holy supper a second time in this place, and thereby to make the glory of this latter solemnity to exceed that of the former. Much of the Lord's gracious presence was enjoyed at these meetings for prayer, returns of mercy were vouchsafed in part, and are still further expected and hoped for.

This second sacrament occasion did indeed much excel the former, not only in the number of ministers, people and communicants, but, which is the main thing, in a much greater measure of the power and special presence of God, in the observation and sensible experience of multitudes that were attending.

The ministers that assisted at this solemnity were Mr. Whitefield....All of them appeared to be very much assisted in

---

*Scottish Presbyterians led by Ralph and Ebenezer Erskine who opposed the Cambuslang Revival, thinking it was the work of the "evil one."

their work. Four of them preached on the fast day, four on Saturday; on Sabbath I cannot well tell how many, and five on Monday, on which last day it was computed that above twenty-four ministers and preachers were present. Old Mr. Bonner, though so frail that he took three days to ride eighteen miles from Torphichen to Cambuslang, yet his heart was so set upon coming here that he could by no means stay away, and when he was helped up to the tent, preached three times with great life and returned with much satisfaction and joy. Mr. Whitefield's sermons on Saturday, Sabbath and Monday were attended with much power, particularly on Sabbath night about ten, and that on Monday, several crying out, and a very great but decent weeping and mourning was observable through the auditory. On Sabbath evening while he was serving some tables he appeared to be so filled with the love of God as to be in a kind of ecstasy or transport, and communicated with much of that blessed frame. Time would fail me to speak of the evidences of the power of God coming along with the rest of the assistants, and I am in part prevented by what is noticed by Mr. Robe in his *Narrative*.

The number of people that were there on Saturday and Monday was very considerable. But the number present at the three tents on the Lord's day was so great that, so far as I can hear, none ever saw the like since the Revolution in Scotland, or even anywhere else, at any sacrament occasion; some have called them fifty thousand, some forty thousand; the lowest estimate I hear of, with which Mr. Whitefield agrees, who has been much used to great multitudes, and forming a judgment of their number, makes them to have been upward of thirty thousand.

The number of communicants appears to have been about three thousand. The tables were double, and the double table was reckoned to contain one hundred and fourteen, or one hundred and sixteen, or one hundred and twenty communicants. The number of tables I reckoned had been but twenty-four, but I have been since informed that a man who sat near the tables and kept a pen in his hand, and carefully marked each service with his pen, assured that there were twenty-five double tables or services, the last table wanting only five or six persons to fill it up. And this account seems indeed the most probable, as agreeing nearly with the number of tokens distributed, which was about three thousand. And some worthy of credit, and that had proper opportunities to know, gave it as their opinion that there was such a blessed frame fell upon the people that if there had been access to get tokens, there would have been a thousand more communicants than what were.

This vast concourse of people, you may easily imagine, came not only from the city of Glasgow and other places nearby, but from many places at a considerable distance.…There was a great deal of outward decency and regularity observable about the tables. Public worship began on the Lord's day just at half past eight in the morning. My action sermon, I think, was reasonably short; the third or fourth table was a serving at twelve o'clock and the last table was a serving about sunset; when that was done, the work was closed with a few words of exhortation, prayer and praise, the presenter having so much daylight as to let him see to read four lines of a psalm.…

But what was most remarkable was the spiritual glory of this solemnity, I mean the gracious and sensible presence of God. Not a few were awakened to a sense of sin and their lost and perishing condition without a Savior. Others had their bands loosed, and were brought into the marvelous liberty of the sons of God. Many of God's dear children have declared that it was a happy time to their souls, wherein they were abundantly satisfied with the goodness of God in his ordinances and filled with all joy and peace in believing. I have seen a letter from Edinburgh, the writer of which says, "That having talked with many Christians in that city, who had been here at this sacrament, they all owned, that God had dealt bountifully with their souls at this occasion." Some that attended here declared that they would not for a world have been absent from this solemnity. Others cried, "Now let thy

184

servants depart in peace, from this place, since our eyes have seen thy salvation here." Others wishing, if it were the will of God, to die where they were attending God in his ordinances, without ever returning again to the world or their friends that they might be with Christ in heaven, as that which is incomparably best of all.

I thought it my duty to offer these few hints concerning this solemnity, and to record the memory of God's great goodness to many souls at that occasion. And now, I suppose you will by this time find yourself disposed to sing the ninety-eighth Psalm at the beginning, or the close of the seventy-second Psalm, or some other psalm of praise. May our exalted Redeemer still go on from conquering to conquer, until the whole earth be filled with his glory. Amen, so let it be. In him, I am, yours, William McCulloch.

Francis Asbury, ["On Spiritual Practices"][10]

Tuesday 14 [July 1772]. Went to the Jerseys and preached at friend T.'s to near 100 people, though in the time of harvest; and while preaching from these words, "Ye were sometimes darkness, but now are ye light in the Lord," many felt the power of truth, when the darkness and its properties were explained. After describing true religion to about 100 souls, at J.C.'s, I went on Wednesday to Greenwich and felt much shut up while preaching to about the same number, on "Fear not, little flock," etc. I then proceeded to Gloucester, which is one of the dullest places I have seen in this country. The same night went to Haddonfield, and the next day preached at J.T.'s to a few attentive hearers who seemed somewhat affected by the truths of God, especially one S.K., who was greatly concerned on account of his past life, as he had been much devoted to company and liquor. I felt afraid that his concern would not be permanent. However, he accompanied me to the ferry....

Wednesday, July 22. In meeting the small society of about 19 persons, I gave them tickets and found it a comfortable time. They are a serious people, and there is some prospect of much good being done in this place. After preaching on Tuesday morning over the ferry, and in the evening at Trenton, I took leave of them on Wednesday morning and set off for Philadelphia. Left Philadelphia on the Lord's day evening after preaching on these words, "If I come again, I will not spare"; and on Monday met with brother B. Went thence to New Mills, where I preached on Tuesday night and Wednesday morning, and found the people there very affectionate; then returned to Burlington and found many friends from Philadelphia....

August 4. My soul felt life, and power, and renewed courage. Discovering the unfaithfulness of some who first spoil a person and then condemn him, I intend to keep such at a proper distance. In the love feast this evening, I found that the living could not bear the dead....

Thursday 7. Preached in York from Philippians 1:24–25: "To abide in the flesh is more needful for you. And having this confidence, I know that I shall abide and continue with you all, for your furtherance and joy of faith." Found liberty in my mind while addressing the people, and am determined, in the strength of the Lord, to aim at promoting his glory and to seek nothing but him.

Friday 8. After preaching in the morning, I found the Lord near and had great peace at intercession. It pleases me much to see the people diligent in attending the word and find myself favored with liberty and the power of God in my labors among them; and humbly hope that God will make known his power among this people, and drive Satan from them, and that we shall yet see good days in this place.

Saturday 9. I found a degree of life in my soul; and on the Lord's day had power, and light, and life, and love, in speaking on those words, "Ye were sometimes darkness, but now are ye light in the Lord: walk as children of light." The congregations are steady, and we look for the power of God both in our own souls and among the people. O, my God, make bare your arm! After preaching in the evening of the Lord's day, with some opening of heart and to a full house, I met the society and then set out on Monday morning for New Rochelle, and preached the same night at friend D.'s ....

Tuesday 12. My soul does not forget God; but my desire is still toward him and the remembrance of his name. On Wednesday I found my mind somewhat engaged, but on Thursday had some fears of coming short of eternal life. A cloud rested on my mind which was occasioned by talking and jesting. I also feel at times tempted to impatience and pride of heart, but the Lord graciously blest me with life and power in preaching at night, and I afterward found my mind fixed on God and an earnest longing to be always holy in heart and life....Preached also this evening with some satisfaction, but found broken classes and a disordered society, so that my heart was sunk within me; but it is still my desire to commit myself to God.

Lord's Day 17. Preached in the morning, and then went to preach at New Town, about 12 miles distant, in the evening. Friend S. was in company with me, and we were obliged to lodge at a tavern, but we were more serious than usual, and spent our time in useful conversation....In this journey I have found my soul comfortable and alive to God, a sacred nearness to God, and power to withstand temptations, though in the afternoon of the next day I had cause to blame myself for trifling conversation at noon.

Monday 18. This has been a day of distress to my soul. I was opposed for meeting the society, because one or two classes met at that time, which seemed to me a very weak objection, as those classes might meet at another time.

August 21. Preached this morning with great life in my soul, and felt a strong desire to be devoted to God and more and more engaged to promote his glory both in heart and life. O that my soul could be more intimately and sweetly united to the Lord! In the evening I preached with power; but have found my soul troubled within me on account of a party spirit which seems to prevail too much in this place. But they must answer for their own conduct. My business is, through the grace of God, to go straight forward, acting with honesty, prudence, and caution, and then leave the event to him.

Lord's Day, August 24. Preached morning and evening and had peace in my own soul. In the evening I met the society and read Mr. Wesley's letter....

Lord's Day 28 [July 1776]. My soul is kept in the love of God but longs for an increase of the divine gift. The workers of iniquity are not so bold as they were; some of them have had convictions but lost them. Others seem stiffly to oppose the influences of divine grace. Mr. H., who is commonly called the high priest on account of his height, preached today, and I stood clerk for him; but he seemed much dashed, and it was with difficulty he proceeded in his discourse, which was very dry. While I was preaching my heart was drawn out in compassion to the people, and as the word was pointedly applied to their consciences, I believe some good was done. So much public speaking is almost more than my frame can at present bear, but the Spirit within me constrains me. I feel indeed the want of retirement in this place, yet I make a substitute of family exercises and find communion with God. My soul has lately been much drawn out toward God in reading the life of Mr. Brainard, and longs to be like him and every other faithful follower of Jesus Christ.

Monday 29. My present mode of conduct is as follows: to read about a hundred pages a day; usually to pray in public five times a day; to preach in the open air every other day; and to lecture in prayer meeting every evening. And if it were in my power, I would do a thousand times as much for such a gracious and blessed Master. But in the midst of all my little employments I feel myself as nothing, and Christ to me is all in all.

Tuesday 30. My spirit was grieved to see so little of the fear of God and such a contempt of sacred things as appeared in many of the people in this place. An enmity against God and his ways reigns in the hearts of all the unawakened, from the highest to the lowest...

Wednesday 31. Spent some time in the woods alone with God, and found it a peculiar time of love and joy. O delightful employment! All my soul was centered in God! The next day I unexpectedly met with brother W. and, while preaching at 3 o'clock to an increased company, the word produced great seriousness and attention. And we had a happy, powerful meeting in the evening at Mr. G.'s....

Friday August 2. My soul was in a serious, solemn frame, but earnestly desired to be more universally devoted to God....I am afraid my friends begin to grow somewhat languid in their spirits. How watchful, devout, and heavenly should we be, to keep up the power of inward religion in the midst of such a company of sinners of diverse principles and manners! For my own part, I have had cause to lament the want of more watchfulness. Lord, help us to be faithful in all things, to all persons, and in all places!...

Monday 5. Having withdrawn to the woods for the purpose of self-examination, and pouring out my heart in prayer to God, I found myself much melted. Glory to God, for a comfortable sense of the divine favor! But alas! How serious, how solemn should I be when so many immortal souls on every side are posting down to everlasting fire!...

John Fletcher, Letter to Miss Hatton, on Recollection, March 5, 1764[11]

Miss Hatton, Madeley, March 5th, 1764.

You see, madam, not to have a clear idea of the happiness of the love of Jesus, or, at least, of your privilege of loving him again. Your dullness in private prayer arises from the want of familiar friendship with Jesus. To obviate it, go to your closet, as if you were going to meet the dearest friend you ever had; cast yourself immediately at his feet, bemoan your coldness before him, extol his love to you, and let your heart break with a desire to love him, till it actually melts with his love. Be you, if not the importunate widow, at least the importunate virgin, and get your Lord to avenge you of your adversary—I mean your cold heart. You ask me some directions to get a mortified spirit, in order to get it, get recollection.

Recollection is a dwelling within ourselves, a being abstracted from the creature and turned toward God. Recollection is both outward and inward. Outward recollection consists in silence from all idle and superfluous words, and in solitude or a wise disentanglement from the world, keeping to our own business, observing and following the order of God for ourselves and shutting the ear against all curious and unprofitable matters. Inward recollection consists in shutting the door of the sense in a deep attention to the presence of God, and in a continual care of entertaining holy thoughts for fear of spiritual idleness.

Through the power of the Spirit, let this recollection be steady even in the midst of hurrying business; let it be calm and peaceable and let it be lasting. "Watch and pray, lest you enter into temptation." To maintain this recollection, beware of engaging too deeply, and beyond what is necessary, in outward things; beware of suffering your affections to be entangled by worldly desire, your imagination to amuse itself with unprofitable objects, and indulging yourself in the commission of what are called small faults.

For want of continuing in a recollected frame all the day, our times of prayer are frequently dry and useless, imagination prevails, and the heart wanders; whereas we pass easily from recollection to delightful prayer. Without this spirit there can be no useful self-denial, nor can we know ourselves; but where it dwells, it makes the soul all eye, all ear, traces and discovers sin, repels its first assaults, or crushes it in its earliest risings.

In recollection let your mind act according to the drawings of grace, and it will probably lead you either to contemplate Jesus as crucified and interceding for you, etc., or to watch your senses and suppress your passions, to keep before God in respectful silence of heart, and to watch and follow the motions of grace and feed on the promises.

But take care here to be more taken up with the thoughts of God than of yourself, and consider how hardly recollection is sometimes obtained, and how easily it is lost. Use no forced labor to raise a particular frame, nor tire, fret, and grow impatient, if you have no comfort; but meekly acquiesce and confess yourself unworthy of it; lie prostrate in humble submission before God, and patiently wait for the smiles of Jesus.

May the following motives stir you up to the pursuit of recollection: (1) We must forsake all and die to all first by recollection. (2) Without it God's voice cannot be heard in the soul. (3) It is the altar on which we must offer up our Isaacs. (4) It is instrumentally a ladder (if I may be allowed the expression) to ascend into God. (5) By it the soul gets to its center, out of which it cannot rest. (6) A person's soul is the temple of God, a recollection of the holy of holies. (7) As the wicked by recollection find hell in their hearts, so faithful souls find heaven. (8) Without recollection all means of grace are useless, or make but a light and transitory impression.

If we would be recollected, we must expect to suffer. Sometimes God does not speak immediately to the heart; we must then continue to listen with a more humble silence. Sometimes assaults of the heart or of the tempter may follow, together with weariness and desire to turn the mind to something else; here we must be patient; by patience unwearied we inherit the promises....

As dissipation always meets its punishment, so recollection never fails of its reward. After patient waiting comes communion with God and the sweet sense of his peace and love. Recollection is a castle, an inviolable fortress against the world and the devil; it renders all times and places alike, and is the habitation where Christ and his bride dwell.

I give you these hints not to set Christ aside, but that you may, according to the light and power given to you, takes these stones and place them upon the chief corner stone, and cement them with the blood of Jesus, until the superstructure in some measure answers to the excellence of the foundation. I beg an interest in your prayers for myself and those committed to my charge, and am, with sincerity, madam, your servant for Christ's sake, J. F.

John Fletcher, "The Test of a New Creature, or Heads of Examination for Adult Christians"[12]

Examine yourselves, whether ye be in the faith. (2 Cor 13:5)

...Heads of Examination:

1. Do I feel any pride, or am I a partaker of the meek and lowly mind that was in Jesus? Am I dead to all desire of praise? If any despise me, do I like them the worse for it? Or if they love and approve me, do I love them more on that account? Am I willing to be accounted useless and of no consequence, glad to be made of no reputation?

Do humiliations give me real pleasure, and is it the language of my heart?...

2. Does God bear witness in my heart that it is purified that, in all things, I please him?

3. Is the life I live by the faith of the Son of God, so that Christ dwells in me? Is Christ the life of all my affections and designs, as my soul is the life of my body? Is my eye single, and my soul full of light,...all eye within and without...always watchful?

4. Have I always the presence of God? Does no cloud come between God and the eye of my faith? Can I rejoice evermore, pray without ceasing, and in every thing give thanks?

5. Am I saved from the fear of people? Do I speak plainly to all, neither fearing their frowns nor seeking their favors? Have I no shame of religion, and am I always ready to confess Christ, to suffer with his people, and to die for his sake?

6. Do I deny myself at all times and take up my cross as the Spirit of God leads me? Do I embrace the cross of every sort, being willing to give up my ease and convenience to oblige others, or do I expect them to conform to my hours, ways, and customs? Does the cross sit light upon me, and am I willing to suffer all the will of God? Can I trample on pleasure and pain?...

7. Are my bodily senses, and outward things, all sanctified to me? Do I not seek my own things, to please myself? Do I seek grace more for God than myself, preferring the glory of God to all in earth or heaven, the giver to the gift?

8. Am I poor in spirit? Do I take pleasure in infirmities, necessities, distresses, reproaches, so that out of weakness, want, and danger I may cast myself on the Lord? Have I no false shame in approaching God? Do I seek to be saved, as a poor sinner, by grace alone?

9. Do I not lean to my own understanding? Am I ready to give up the point, when contradicted, unless conscience forbid, and am I easy to be persuaded? Do I

esteem every one better than myself? Am I as willing to be a cypher as to be useful, and does my zeal burn bright, notwithstanding this willingness to be nothing?

10. Have I no false wisdom, goodness, strength, as if the grace I feel were my own? Do I never take that glory to myself which belongs to Christ? Do I feel my want of Christ as much as ever, to be my all; and do I draw near to God, as poor and needy, only presenting before him his well beloved Son?…Do I find joy in being thus nothing, empty, undeserving, giving all the glory to Christ: or do I wish that grace made me something, instead of God all?

11. Have I meekness? Does it bear rule over all my tempers, affections, and desires so that my hopes, fears, joy, zeal, love, and hatred, are duly balanced? Do I feel no disturbance from others, and do I desire to give none? If any offend me, do I still love them and make it an occasion to pray for them? If condemned by the world, do I entreat;….if condemned by the godly, am I one in whose mouth there is no reproof, replying only as conscience and not as impatient nature dictates? If in the wrong, do I confess it? If in the right, do I submit (being content) to do well, and suffer for it?…

12. Do I possess resignation, am I content with whatever is or may be, seeing that God, the author of all events, does, and will do, all for my good? Do I desire nothing but God, willing to part with all, if the Lord manifest his will for my so doing? Do I know how to abound and yet not gratify unnecessary wants, but being content with things needful, do I faithfully and freely dispose of all the rest for the help of others? Do I know how to suffer need, is my confidence in God unshaken, while I feel the distress of poverty and have the prospect of future want?…

13. Am I just, doing in all things as I would others should do unto me? Do I render due homage to those above me, not presuming on their lenity and condescension? As a superior, do I exercise no undue authority, taking

no advantage of the timidity, respect, or necessity of any person? Do I consider the great obligation superiority lays me under, of being lowly and kind and of setting a good example?

14. Am I temperate, using the world and not abusing it? Do I receive outward things in the order of God, making earth a seal to heaven? Is the satisfaction I take in the creation consistent with my being dead to all below, and a means of leading me more to God? Is the turn of my mind and temper in due subjection, not leading me to any extreme, either of too much silence, or of too much talkativeness, of reserve or freedom?

15. Am I courteous, not severe; suiting myself to all with sweetness; striving to give no one pain, but to gain and win all for their good?

16. Am I vigilant, redeeming time, taking every opportunity of doing good, or do I spare myself, being careless about the souls and bodies to which I might do good? Can I do no more than I do? Do I perform the most servile offices, such as require labor and humiliation, with cheerfulness? Is my conversation always seasoned with salt, at every time administering some kind of favor to those I am with?

17. Do I love God with all my heart? Do I constantly present myself, my time, substance, talents, and all that I have, a living sacrifice? Is every thought brought into subjection to Christ? Do I like, or dislike, only such things as are pleasing, or displeasing, to God?

18. Do I love God with all my strength, and are my spiritual faculties always vigorous? Do I give way to no sinful languor? Am I always on my watch? Do not business, worldly care, and conversation damp my fervor and zeal for God?

19. Do I love my neighbor as myself...every person for Christ's sake, and honor all people as the image of God? Do I think no evil, listen to no groundless surmises, nor judge from appearances? Can I bridle my tongue, never speaking of the fault of another, but with a view to do

good, and when I am obliged to do it, have I the testimony that I sin not? Have I that love which hopes, believes, and endures all things?

20. Do I bear the infirmities of age or sickness without seeking to repair the decays of nature by strong liquors, or do I make Christ my sole support, casting the burden of a feeble body into the arms of his mercy? Many consider that perfect love which castes out fear as instantaneous, all grace is so; but what is given in a moment is enlarged and established by diligence and fidelity. That which is instantaneous in its descent is perfective in its increase. This is certain...too much grace cannot be desired or looked for, and to believe and obey with all the power we have is the high way to receive all we have not. There is a day of Pentecost for believers, a time when the Holy Ghost descends abundantly. Happy they who receive most of this perfect love and of that establishing grace which may preserve them from such falls and decays as they were before liable to.

Jesus, Lord of all, grant your purest gifts to every waiting disciple. Enlighten us with the knowledge of your will, and show us the mark of the prize of our high calling. Let us die to all you are not; and seek you with our whole heart, till we enjoy the fullness of the purchased possession. Amen!

5

LOVE FOR GOD

INTRODUCTION

Early evangelicals had a deep desire for communion with the triune God. This was possible because they had first experienced God's love in union with Christ, which they frequently referred to as spiritual marriage. Many of the following texts embody the varieties of vivid imagery of spiritual intimacy used in the Song of Songs. This bridal language was popular both in the early Western Catholic tradition and among the Puritans and Pietists of the seventeenth century. Since believers in Jesus Christ had already experienced God's presence, their desires for a deeper delight and enjoyment of God were awakened. This created a yearning for heaven, not as a means of escaping the challenges of earth but rather as a fulfillment for their longings to know God more fully. Drawing from Scripture, evangelicals realized both the importance of a proper motivation for seeking God and the barriers and obstacles that they would face along their earthly pilgrimage. These early evangelicals valued the beauty, mystery, and ineffable nature of God. In responding to this awareness, they fully appreciated the proper posture of surrender to God, expressed through obedience, regular self-examination and scrutiny of their soul, desire to grow in holiness, praise and glorifying worship, and grateful gazing on God in contemplation. But they were not naïve; they recognized the reality of residual sin following conversion and spiritual conflict that arose from persistent temptations of the world, the flesh, and the devil. Periods of spiritual dryness were not uncommon, and friends were honest in confessing their struggles or offering words of encouragement to one another.

THE TEXTS

Anne Dutton, Letter 33 to Mr. W——t[1]

My dear brother in Christ,

Where are you? Have you left your first love? Have you
forgotten your Maker, your husband, and gone after other
lovers? The love of Christ to you is still the same. O return
unto the Lord, you backsliding child; for he will heal your
backsliding, and will love you freely. He will not cause his
anger to fall upon you; for he is merciful: Yea, I am married
unto you, saith the Lord. Have you loved strangers, and said,
after them will I go? Your dear Lord Jesus rests in his love to
you; his heart is at rest in you, as his, and his Father's choice.
He will never seek another object of his love, instead of you;
no, not for all your unkindness to him, nor cast you off, for all
that you have done. For thus the Lord the God of Israel saith:
He hateth putting away. He had betrothed you unto himself
forever, in judgment. He well knew what he did, when he took
you to be his; he knew you would deal very treacherously, and
yet he resolved to be gracious, to set his heart upon you, and
to love you to the end....And you shall know the Lord. You
shall enjoy Jehovah-Jesus, as your own God, in the nearest
relation, unto full consolation, both in this world, and in that
which is to come.

And is not Christ enough, my brother, to satisfy your soul?
Is not he the sum of your desires, and the all of your delights?
Can you want any joy that is not to be found in Christ? Is not
he your exceeding joy? Is not Christ better to you than ten
sons? Than all the creatures! What, love a creature, more than
the Creator? Choose satisfaction from a drop of pleasure,
rather than from the ocean of delights? From a drop of
sweetness, full of bitter mixture, rather than from those pure,

unmixed ineffable sweets, which are as a bottomless, boundless, endless sea, in the Lord your Maker, your Husband? Yes, what [sic] choose a creature, a drop of being, that can have no pleasure in it, unless the Creator, the Lord your Husband puts it there for you, rather than himself, the fountain of being, the infinite ocean of all delights? O never let this be said of you, a soul that is espoused unto the altogether lovely Jesus! Unto him who is all desires! Unto him who is the joy and wonder of saints and angels, throughout all times and to all eternity? Yes, unto him who from everlasting to everlasting is the Father's delight! If there is enough in Christ to fill the heart of God with infinite and endless joy, is there not much more than enough in him to fill your heart? To fill every corner of your soul brimful, running over full, of new joys, unto new praises, through time and to eternity? Say then, my dear brother, return unto thy rest, O my soul, for the Lord hath dealt bountifully with thee!

And delighting in the Lord as your portion, choose no creature but what he gives you. If he gives you comfort in any creature; see that you love it in and for himself alone. And if he denies you of any creature comfort you desire; say, "Father, thy will be done. Thou art the all of my bliss; and if I mayn't taste of Thee in that stream, I'll drink at the fountainhead, and delight myself in Thee, where pleasures are pure, full, and forever new." And believe it, my brother, the Lord does that which is best for you, whether you can at present see how it is best for you, or not. Whatever the Lord denies us of is done in infinite wisdom and love. He well knows that that creature or thing he denies, or at that time in which he is not pleased to give it, would not be for our good, but our hurt. Let us then say in faith and love, choose our inheritance for us. That the peace of God which passeth all understanding may keep your heart and mind thro' Christ Jesus is the earnest desire of, yours in the Lord.

George Whitefield, "Christ the Believer's Husband," Isaiah 54:5, "For thy Maker is thy Husband"[2]

Although believers by nature are far from God, and children of wrath, even as others, yet it is amazing to think how nigh they are brought to him again by the blood of Jesus Christ. Eye has not seen, or ear heard, neither has it entered into the heart of any person living fully to conceive, the nearness and dearness of that relation, in which they stand to their common head. He is not ashamed to call them brethren. Behold, says the blessed Jesus in the days of his flesh, my mother and my brethren. And again after his resurrection, Go tell my brethren. No, sometimes he is pleased to term believers his friends. Henceforth I call you no longer servants, but friends. Our friend Lazarus is asleep. And what is a friend? Why, "there is a friend that is nearer than a brother," even, as near as one's own soul, and your friend, says God in the Book of Deuteronomy, which is as your own soul. Kind and endearing appellations these, that undoubtedly speak a very near and ineffably intimate union between the Lord Jesus and the true living members of his mystical body! But, I think, the words of our text point out to us a relation which not only comprehends but, in respect to nearness and dearness, exceeds all other relations whatsoever. I mean that of a husband. For thy Maker is thy Husband. The Lord of Hosts is his name, and thy Redeemer the Holy One of Israel, the God of the whole earth shall he be called....

But, before I proceed to this, it may not be improper to observe that if any of you, amongst whom I am now preaching the kingdom of God, are enemies to inward religion, and explode the doctrine of inward feelings as enthusiasm, cant and nonsense, I shall not be surprised if your hearts rise against me while I am preaching, for I am about to discourse on true vital and internal piety, and an inspired Apostle has told us that the natural man discerneth not the things of the Spirit, because they are spiritually discerned. But, however, be noble as the Bereans were; search the Scriptures as they did; lay aside prejudice; hear like Nathaniel, with a true Israelitish ear; be willing to do the will of God; and then you shall, according to the promise of our dearest Lord, know of the doctrine, whether it be of God, or whether I speak of myself.

I would further observe, that if any here expect fine preaching from me this day, they will in all probability go away disappointed. For I came not here to shoot over peoples' heads, but, if the Lord shall be pleased to bless me, to reach their hearts. Accordingly, I shall endeavor to clothe my ideas in such plain language, that the meanest Negro or servant, if God is pleased to give a hearing ear, may understand me; for I am certain, if the poor and unlearned can comprehend, the learned and rich must....

Now that we may discourse more pertinently and intelligibly upon this point, it may not be amiss, under this head, to consider what is necessary to be done before a marriage between two parties amongst ourselves can be said to be valid in the sight of God and men and women. And that will lead us in a familiar way to show what must be done, or what must pass between us and Jesus Christ, before we can say our Maker is our Husband.

And first, in all lawful marriages, it is absolutely necessary that the parties to be joined together in that holy and honorable estate are actually and legally freed from all preengagements whatsoever. A woman is bound to her husband, saith the Apostle, so long as her husband liveth. The same law holds good in respect to the man. And so likewise, if either party be betrothed and promised, though not actually married to another, the marriage is not lawful till that preengagement and promise be fairly and mutually dissolved. Now, it is just thus between us and the Lord Jesus. For we are all by nature born under, and wedded to the law, as a covenant of works. Hence it is that we are so fond of, and artfully go about, in order to establish a righteousness of our own. It is as natural for us to do this as it is to breathe.

Our first parents, Adam and Eve, even after the covenant of grace was revealed to them in that promise [that] the seed of the woman shall bruise the serpent's head, reached out their hands, and would again have taken hold of the tree of life, which they had now forfeited, had not God drove them out of paradise, and compelled them, as it were, to be saved by grace. And thus all their descendants naturally run to the tree of life, and want to be saved, partly at least, if not wholly, by their works. And even gracious souls, who are inwardly renewed, so far as the old man abides in them, find a strong propensity this way. Hence it is that natural men and women are generally so fond of Arminian principles. Do and live, is the native language of a proud, self-righteous heart. But before we can say our Maker is our Husband, we must be divorced from our old husband the law; i.e., we must renounce our own righteousness, our own doings and performances, in point of dependence, either in whole or part, as dung and dross, for the excellency of the knowledge of Christ Jesus our Lord. For thus speaks the Apostle Paul to the Romans (Rom 7:4): "Ye also are become dead to the law (i.e., as a covenant of works) by the body of Christ, that ye should be married to another, even to him, who is raised from the dead." As he also speaks in another place, "I have espoused you, as a chaste virgin to Jesus Christ." This was the Apostle's own case. While he depended on his being a Hebrew of the Hebrews, and thought himself secure because, as to the outward observation of the law, he was blameless, he was an entire stranger to the divine life; but when he began to experience the power of Jesus Christ's resurrection, we find him, in his Epistle to the Philippians, absolutely renouncing all his external privileges and all pharisaical righteousness; yes, he says, doubtless, and I count all things but loss, nay but dung, that I may win Christ, and be found in him, not having mine own righteousness, which is of the law, but that which is through the faith of Jesus Christ, the righteousness which is of God by faith. And thus it must be with us, before we can say our Maker is our Husband. Though we may not be wrought upon in that extraordinary way in which the Apostle was, yet we must be dead to the law, we must be espoused as chaste virgins to Jesus Christ, and count all external privileges, and our most splendid performances (as was before observed) only as dung and dross, for the excellency of the knowledge of Jesus Christ our Lord.

But further, before a marriage among us can stand good in law, both parties must not only be freed from all preengagements, but there must be a mutual consent on both sides. We are not used to marry people against their wills. This is what the Jews called betrothing, or espousing, a thing previous to the solemnity of marriage. Thus we find [that] the Virgin Mary is said to be espoused to Joseph before they actually came together (Matt 1:18). And thus it is among us. Both parties are previously agreed, and as it were espoused to each other, before we publish what we call the banns of marriage concerning them. And so it will be in the spiritual marriage between

Jesus Christ and our souls. Before we are actually married or united to him by faith—or, to keep to the terms of the text, before we assuredly can say that our Maker is our Husband—we must be made willing people in the day of God's power, we must be sweetly and effectually persuaded by the Holy Spirit of God, that the glorious Emanuel is willing to accept of us just as we are, and also that we are willing to accept of him upon his own terms, yes, upon any terms. And when once it comes to this, the spiritual marriage goes on apace, and there is but one thing lacking to make it complete. And what is that? An actual union.

This is absolutely necessary in every lawful marriage among people. There must be a joining of hands before witnesses, before they can be deemed lawfully joined together. Some indeed of corrupt minds are apt to look upon this as a needless ceremony, and think it sufficient to be married, as they term it, in the sight of God. But when people get such divinity, I know not. I am positive not from the Bible; for we there read that even at the first marriage in paradise, there was something of outward solemnity, God himself (if I may so speak) being there the priest. For we are told (Gen 2:22) that, after God had made the woman, he brought her unto the man. And indeed, to lay aside all manner of outward ceremony in marriage would be to turn the world into a den of brute beasts. Men would then take, or forsake, as many wives as they pleased, and we should soon sink into as bad and brutal state as those nations are now in among whom such practices are allowed of, and who are utterly destitute of the knowledge of our Lord and Savior Jesus Christ. Whoever has experienced the power of his resurrection, I am persuaded will never plead for such a licentious practice. For the terms made use of in Scripture to represent the mystical union between Christ and his Church, such as our being joined to the Lord and married to Jesus Christ, are all metaphorical expressions, taken from some analogous practices amongst men and women. And as persons when married, though before twain, are now one flesh, so those that are joined to the Lord, and can truly say our Maker is our Husband, in the Apostle's language, are one Spirit.

This was typified in the original marriage of our first parents. When God brought Eve to Adam, he received her with joy at his hands, and said, this is bone of my bone, and flesh of my flesh. They had there primarily but one name. For thus speaks the sacred historian in Genesis 5:1–2. In the day that God created man, he blessed them, and called their name *Adam*. And why? Because they were one flesh, and were to have but one heart. The self-same terms are made use of in Scripture to express the believer's union with Jesus Christ. We are called *Christians*, after Christ's name, because made partakers of Christ's nature. Out of his fullness, believers receive grace for grace. And therefore, the marriage state, especially by the Apostle Paul, is frequently made use of to figure out to us the real, vital union between Jesus Christ and regenerate souls. This is termed by the Apostle a great mystery (Eph 5:32). But great as it is, we must all experience it before we can say assuredly that our Maker is our Husband. For what says our Lord in that prayer he put up to his Father before his bitter passion? "Father, I will that those whom thou hast given me, shall be where I am, that they may be one with thee; even as thou, O Father, and I are one, I in them, and they in me, that we all may be made perfect in One." Oh infinite condescension! Oh ineffable union! Hence it is that believers are said to be members of his body, of his flesh, and of his bones. Hence it is that the Apostle, speaking of himself, says, I live, yet not I, but Christ liveth in me. What an expression is that? How much does it comprehend? And that we might not think this was something peculiar to himself, he puts this close question to the Corinthians: "Know ye not, that Christ is in you, unless you be reprobates?" Agreeable to what he says in his Epistle to the Colossians, "Christ in you, the hope of glory." And hence it is that our church, in the communion office, directs the minister to acquaint all those that receive the sacrament worthily that they are one with Christ, and Christ with them; that they dwell in Christ, and Christ in them. Words that deserve to be written in letters of gold, and which evidently show what our reformers believed all persons must experience, before they could truly and assuredly say that their Maker is their Husband.

From what then has been delivered, may not the poorest and most illiterate person here present easily know whether or not he is really married to Jesus Christ? Some indeed, I am afraid, are so presumptuous as to affirm, at least to insinuate, that there is no such thing as knowing, or being fully assured, while here below, whether we are in Christ or not. Or at least, if there be such a thing, it is very rare, and only the privilege of the primitive believers. Part of this is true, and part of this absolutely false. That this glorious privilege of a full assurance is very rare is too, too true. And so it is equally too true that real Christians, comparatively speaking, are very rare also. But that there is no such thing, or that this was only the privilege of the first followers of our blessed Lord, is directly opposite to the word of God. "We know," says St. John, speaking of believers in general, "that we are his, by the Spirit which he hath given us"; and, "he that believeth hath the witness in himself"; "because you are sons," saith St. Paul, "God hath sent forth his Spirit into your hearts, even the Spirit of adoption, whereby we cry, Abba Father." Not that I dare affirm that there is no real Christian, but what has this full assurance of faith, and clearly knows that his Maker is his Husband. In speaking thus, I should undoubtedly condemn some of the generation of God's dear children who, through the prevalence of unbelief, indwelling sin, spiritual sloth, or it may be, for want of being informed of the privileges of believers, may walk in darkness and see no light. Therefore, though I dare not affirm that a full assurance of faith is absolutely necessary for the very being, yet I dare assert that it is absolutely necessary for the well-being of a Christian. And for my own part, I cannot conceive how any persons that pretend to Christianity can rest satisfied or contented without it. This is indeed stopping short, on this side of Jordan, with a witness. And gives others too much reason to suspect that such persons, however high their profession may be, have, as yet, no true saving grace at all. Those whose hearts are set on this world's goods, or, to use our Lord's language, the children of this world, act not so....To affirm, therefore, that there is no such thing as knowing that our Maker is our Husband, or that it is a privilege peculiar only to the first Christians, to speak in the mildest terms is both irrational and unscriptural. Not that all who can say their Maker is their Husband, can give the same clear and distinct account of the time, manner, and means of their being spiritually united and married by faith, to the blessed bridegroom of the church.

Some there may be now, as well as formerly, sanctified from the womb. And others in their infancy and nonage as it were silently converted. Such perhaps may say, with a little Scotch maiden now with God, when I asked her whether Jesus Christ had taken away her old heart and given her a new one? Sir, it may be, said she, I cannot directly tell you the time and place, but this I know, it is done. And indeed it is not so very material, though no doubt it is very satisfactory, if we cannot relate all the minute and particular circumstances that attended our conversion, if so be we are truly converted now, and can say the work is done, and that Our Maker is our Husband. And I question whether there is one single adult believer, now on earth, who lived, before conversion, either in a course of secret or open sin, but can, in a good degree, give an account of the beginning and progress of the work of grace in his heart. What do you think? Need I tell any married persons in this congregation that they must go to the university and learn the languages before they can tell whether they are married or not? Or, if their marriage was to be doubted, could they not, think you, bring their certificates, to certify the time and place of their marriage, and the minister that joined them together in that holy state? And if you are adult, and are indeed married to Jesus Christ, though you may be unlearned, and what the world terms illiterate persons, cannot you tell me the rise and progress, and consummation of the spiritual marriage between Jesus Christ and your souls? Know you not the time when you were first under the drawings of the Father, and Jesus began to woo you for himself? Tell me, O man, tell me, O woman, know you not the time, or at least, know you not that there was a time when the blessed Spirit of God stripped you of the fig leaves of your own righteousness, hunted you out of the trees of the garden of your performances, forced you from the embraces of your old husband the law, and made you to abhor your own righteousness as so many filthy rags? Can you not remember when, after a long struggle with unbelief, Jesus appeared to you as altogether lovely, one mighty and willing to save? And can you not reflect upon a season when your own stubborn heart was made to bend, and you were made willing to embrace him, as freely offered to you in the everlasting gospel? And can you not, with pleasure unspeakable, reflect on some happy period, some certain point of time, in which a sacred something (perhaps you could not then well tell what) did captivate, and fill your heart, so that you could say, in a rapture of holy surprise, and ecstasy of divine love, My Lord and my God; my Beloved is mine, and I am his; I know that my Redeemer liveth; or, to keep to the words of our text, my Maker is my Husband. Surely, amidst this great and solemn assembly, there are many that can answer these questions in the affirmative. For these are transactions not easily to be forgotten; and the day of our espousals is, generally, a very remarkable day, a day to be had in everlasting remembrance.

And can any of you indeed, upon good grounds say that your Maker is your Husband? May I not then (as it is customary to wish persons joy who are just entered into the marriage state) congratulate you upon your happy change, and wish you joy with all my heart? Sure am I that there was joy in heaven on the day of your espousals. And why should not the blessed news occasion joy on earth? May I not address you in the language of our Lord to the women that came to visit his sepulcher, All hail! for ye are highly favored. Blessed are ye among men, blessed are ye among women! All generations shall call you blessed. What? Is your Maker your Husband? The Holy One of Israel your Redeemer? Sing, O heavens, and rejoice, O earth! What an amazing stoop is this! What a new thing has God created on the earth! Do not your hearts, O believers, burn within you when meditating on this unspeakable condescension of the high and lofty One that inhabits eternity? While you are musing, does not the sacred fire of divine love kindle in your souls? And, out of the abundance of your hearts, do you not often speak with your tongues, and call upon all that is within you, to laud and magnify your Redeemer's holy Name? Is not that God-exalting, self-abasing expression frequently in your mouths: Why me, Lord, why me? And are you not often constrained to break out into that devout exclamation of Solomon, when the glory of the Lord filled the temple, and will God indeed dwell with man? Ungrateful, rebellious, ill, and hell-deserving person! Oh, my brethren, my heart is enlarged towards you! Tears, while I am speaking, are ready to gush out. But they are tears of love and joy. How shall I give it vent? How shall I set forth your happiness, O believer, you bride of God! And is your Maker thy Husband? Is his name the Lord of Hosts? Whom then should you fear?...

When you meditate on these things, are you not frequently ready to cry out, what shall we render unto the Lord for all these mercies, which of his free unmerited grace he hath been pleased to bestow upon us? For, though you are dead to the law, as a covenant of works, yet you are alive to the law as a rule of life, and are in, or under the law (for either expression seems to denote the same thing) to your glorious Husband, Jesus Christ.

Joseph Bellamy, "What Is implied in Love to God"[3]

...2. Another thing implied in love to God is esteem. Esteem, strictly speaking, is that high and exalted thought of and value for anything which arises from a sight and sense of its own intrinsic worth, excellency and beauty. So a sense of the infinite dignity, greatness, glory, excellency and beauty of the most high God begets in us high and exalted thoughts of him, and makes us admire, wonder and adore. Hence, the heavenly hosts fall down before the throne, and under a sense of his effable glory, continually cry, Holy, holy, holy Lord God Almighty, the whole earth is full of thy glory. And saints here below, while they behold as in a glass the glory of the Lord, are ravished; they esteem, they admire, they wonder and adore; and under some feebler sense of the ineffable glory of the divine nature, they begin to feel as they do in heaven, and to speak their language, and say, "Who is a God like unto thee! Thy Name alone is excellent, and thy glory is exalted above the heavens." This high esteem of God disposes and inclines the heart to acquiesce, yes, to exult, in all the high prerogatives God assumes to himself.

God, from a consciousness of his own infinite excellency, his entire right to and absolute authority over all things, is disposed to take state to himself, and honor and majesty, the kingdom, the power and the glory; and he sets up himself as the most high God, supreme Lord and sovereign governor of the whole world, and bids all worlds adore him, and be in the most perfect subjection to him, and that with all their hearts; and esteems the wretch, who does not account this his highest happiness, worthy of eternal damnation. God thinks it infinitely becomes him to set up himself for a God, and to command all the world to adore him, upon pain of eternal damnation. He thinks himself fit to govern the world, and that the throne is his proper place, and that all love, honor and obedience are his due. "I am the Lord, (says he,) and besides me there is no God. I am the Lord, that is my Name, and my glory will I not give to another. And thus and thus shall ye do, for I am the Lord. And cursed be every one that continues not in all things written in the book of the law to do them." Now it would be infinitely wicked for the highest angel in heaven to assume any of this honor to himself, but it infinitely becomes the most high God thus to do. And when we see his infinite dignity, greatness, glory and excellency, and begin rightly to esteem him, then his conduct in all this will begin to appear infinitely right and fit, and so infinitely beautiful and ravishing, and worthy to be rejoiced and exulted in. "The Lord reigneth, let the earth rejoyce: Let the multitude of the isles be glad thereof" (Ps 97:1).

And a sight and sense of the supreme, infinite glory and excellency of the divine nature will not only make us glad that he is God and king and governor, but also exceeding glad that we live under his government, and are to be his subjects and servants, and to be at his disposal. It will show us the grounds and reasons of his law, how infinitely right and fit it is that we should love him with all our hearts and obey him in everything. How infinitely unfit and wrong the least sin is and how just the threatened punishment. And at the same time it will help us to see that all the nations of the earth are as a drop of the bucket, or small dust of the balance, before him, and that we ourselves are nothing and less than nothing in his sight. So that a right sight and sense of the supreme, infinite glory of God will make us esteem him, so as to be glad that he is on the throne, and we at his footstool; that he is King, and we his subjects; that he rules and reigns, and that we are absolutely in subjection, and absolutely at his disposal. In a word, we shall be glad to see him take all that honor to himself which he does, and shall be heartily reconciled to his government, and cordially willing to take our own proper places; and hereby a foundation will begin to be laid in our hearts for all things to come to rights....This is implied in a genuine love to God, not only the reason of the thing and the plain tenor of Scripture manifest, but it is even self-evident; for if we do not so esteem God as to be thus glad to have him take his place and we ours, it argues secret dislike, and proves that there is secret rebellion in our hearts. Thus therefore must we esteem the glorious God, or be reputed rebels in his sight.

3. Another thing implied in love to God may be called benevolence. When we are acquainted with any person, and he appears very excellent in our eyes, and we highly esteem him, it is natural now

208

heartily to wish him well; we are concerned for his interest, we are glad to see it go well with him, and sorry to see it go ill with him; and ready at all times cheerfully to do what we can to promote his welfare. Thus Jonathan felt towards David. And thus love to God will make us feel towards him, his honor and interest in the world. When God is seen in his infinite dignity, greatness, glory and excellency, as the most high God, supreme Lord, and sovereign Governor of the whole world; and a sense of his infinite worthiness is hereby raised in our hearts; this enkindles a holy benevolence, the native language whereof is, Let God be glorified, and "Be thou exalted, O God, above the heavens; let thy glory be above all the earth" (Ps 57:5, 11).

This holy disposition sometimes expresses itself in earnest longings that God would glorify himself, and honor his great Name, and bring all the world into an entire subjection to him. And hence this is the native language of true love: "Our Father which art in heaven, hallowed be thy Name, thy kingdom come, thy will be done, on earth as it is in heaven" (Matt 6:9–10). And hence, when God is about to bring to pass great and glorious things to the honor of his great name, it causes great joy and rejoicing. "Let the heavens rejoice, and let the earth be glad; let the sea roar, and the fullness thereof, let the field be joyful, and all that is therein. Then shall the trees of the wood rejoyce, before the Lord; for he cometh, for he cometh to judge the earth, he shall judge the world with righteousness, and the people with his truth" (Ps 96:11–13)....

Again, this divine benevolence or wishing that God may be glorified sometimes expresses itself in earnest longings that all worlds might join together to bless and praise the Name of the Lord. And it appears infinitely fit and right, and so infinitely beautiful and ravishing, that the whole intelligent creation should forever join in the most solemn adoration. Yes, and that sun, moon, stars; earth, air, sea; birds, beasts, fishes; mountains and hills; and all things should in their way display the divine perfections, and praise the Name of the Lord, because his Name alone is excellent and his glory is exalted above the heavens. And hence the pious Psalmist so often breathes this divine language: "Bless the Lord, ye his angels, that excel in strength, that do his commandments; hearkening unto the voice of his word. Bless ye the Lord, all ye his hosts, ye ministers of his that do his pleasure. Bless the Lord all his works, in all places of his dominion; bless the Lord, O my soul" (Ps 103:20–22). "Praise ye the Lord. Praise ye the Lord from the heavens; praise him in the heights. Praise him, all ye his angels; praise him, all his hosts. Praise him, sun and moon, &c. Let them praise the Name of the Lord; for his Name alone is excellent, &c." (Ps 148:1, 13). See also Psalms 95; 96; 97; 98.

Lastly, from this divine benevolence arises a free and genuine disposition to dedicate, consecrate, devote and give up our selves entirely to the Lord forever; to walk in all his ways, and keep all his commands, seeking his glory. For if we desire that God may be glorified, we shall naturally be disposed to seek his glory. A sight and sense of the infinite dignity, greatness, glory and excellency of God, the great Creator, Preserver and Governor of the world, who has an entire right unto, and an absolute authority over all things, makes it appear infinitely fit that all things should be for him, and him alone; and that we should be entirely for him, and wholly devoted to him; and that it is infinitely wrong to live to ourselves, and make our own interest our last end. The same views which make the godly earnestly long to have God glorify himself, and to have all the world join to give him glory, thoroughly engage them for their parts to live to God. After David had called upon all others to bless the Lord, he concludes with, Bless the Lord, O my soul. And this is the language of heaven: "Thou art worthy, O Lord, to receive glory, and honor, and power; for thou hast created all things, and for thy pleasure they are, and were created" (Rev 4:11). And it was their maxim in the apostles' days, whether they eat [sic] or drank, or whatever they did, all must be done to the glory of God (1 Cor 10:31). And it was their way, not to live to themselves, but to the Lord (2 Cor 5:15). Yea, whether they lived, to live to the Lord; or whether they died, to die to the Lord (Rom 14:7–8). This was what they commended (Phil 2:20–21). And this was what they enjoined, as that in which the very spirit of true religion consisted (Eph 6:5–7; 1 Cor 6:20; Rom 12:1; 7:4).

All rational creatures, acting as such, are always influenced by motives in their whole conduct. Those things are always the most powerful motives which appear to us most worthy of our choice. The principal motive to an action is always the ultimate end of the action. Hence, if God, his honor and interest, appear to us as the supreme good, and most worthy of our choice; then God, his honor and interest, will be the principal motive and ultimate end of all we do. If we love God supremely, we shall live to him ultimately. If we love him with all our hearts, we shall serve him with all our souls. Just as on the other hand, if we love our selves above all, then self-love will absolutely govern us in all things. If self-interest be the principal motive, then self-interest will be the last end, in our whole conduct. Thus then we see that if God be highest in esteem, then God's interest will be the principal motive and the last end of the whole conduct of rational creatures. And if self be highest in esteem, then self-interest will be the principal motive and last end. And hence we may observe that where self-interest governs men and women, they are considered in Scripture as serving themselves (Hos 10:1; Zech 7:5–6). And where God's interest governs, they are considered as serving the Lord (2 Cor 5:15; Gal 1:10; Eph 6:5–7; compared with Titus 2:9–10). To love God so as to serve him is what the law requires; to love self so as to serve self is rebellion against the majesty of heaven. And the same infinite obligations which we are under to love God above our selves, even the same infinite obligations are we under to live to God ultimately, and not to our selves. And therefore it is as great a sin to live to our selves ultimately, as it is to love our selves supremely.

4. And lastly. Delight in God is also implied in love to him. By delight we commonly mean that pleasure, sweetness and satisfaction which we take in anything that is very dear to us. When a person appears very excellent to us, and we esteem him, and wish him all good, we also at the same time feel a delight in him, and a sweetness in his company and conversation. We long to see him when absent; we rejoice in his presence; the enjoyment of him tends to make us happy. So when a holy soul beholds God in the infinite moral excellency and beauty of his nature, and loves him supremely, and is devoted to him entirely, now also he delights in him superlatively. His delight and complacency is as great as his esteem, and arises from a sense of the same moral excellency and beauty. From this delight in God arise longings after further acquaintance with him, and greater nearness to him....Finally, from this delight in God arises a holy disposition to renounce all other things, and live wholly upon him, and take up everlasting content in him, and in him alone.

"Whom have I in heaven but thee? And there is none upon earth I desire besides thee. My flesh and my heart faileth, but God is the strength of my heart and my portion for ever" (Ps 73:25–26). The vain person takes content in vain company; the worldly person takes content in riches; the ambitious person in honor and applause; the philosopher in philosophical speculations; the legal hypocrite in his round of duties; the evangelical hypocrite in his experiences, his discoveries, his joys, his raptures, and confident expectation of heaven; but the true lover of God takes his content in God himself (see Ps 4:6–7). And thus we see what is implied in love to God.

Jonathan Edwards, "A True Christian's Life, A Journey towards Heaven," September 1733[4]

> And confessed that they were strangers and pilgrims on the earth. For they that say such things, declare plainly that they seek a country. (Heb 11:13–14)

The Apostle is here setting forth the excellencies of the grace of faith by the glorious effects and happy issue of it in the saints of the Old Testament. He had spoken in the proceeding part of the chapter particularly of Abel, Enoch, Noah, Abraham and Sarah, Isaac and Jacob. Having enumerated those instances, he takes notice that "these all died in faith, not having received the promises, but having seen them afar off, and were persuaded of them and embraced them, and confessed that they were strangers," etc.

In these words the Apostle seems to have a more particular respect to Abraham and Sarah, and their kindred that came with them from Haran, and from Ur of the Chaldees, by the 15th verse, where the Apostle says, "And truly if they had been mindful of that country from whence they came out, they might have had opportunity to have returned." It was they that upon God's call left their own country.

Two things may be observed in the text.

1. What these saints confessed of themselves, namely "that they were strangers and pilgrims on the earth." Thus we have a particular account concerning

Abraham: "I am a stranger and a sojourner with you" (Gen 23:4). And it seems to have been the general sense of the patriarchs, by what Jacob says to Pharaoh. "And Jacob said to Pharaoh, the days of the years of my pilgrimage are an hundred and thirty years. Few and evil have the days of the years of my life been, and have not attained to the days of the years of the life of my fathers in the days of their pilgrimage" (Gen 47:9). "I am a stranger and a sojourner with thee, as all my fathers were" (Ps 39:12).

2. The inference that the Apostle draws from hence, namely that they sought another country as their home. "For they that say such things declare plainly that they seek a country." In confessing that they were strangers, they plainly declared that this is not their country, that this is not the country where they are at home. And in confessing themselves to be pilgrims, they declared plainly that this is not their settled abode, but that they have respect to some other country, that they seek and are traveling to as their home.

Doctrine: This life ought so to be spent by us as to be only a journey towards heaven.

Here I would observe,

1. That we ought not to rest in the world and its enjoyments, but should desire heaven.

This our hearts should be chiefly upon and engaged about. We should "seek first the kingdom of God" (Matt 6:33). He that is on a journey seeks the place that he is journeying to. We ought above all things to desire a heavenly happiness: to go to heaven and there be with God, and dwell with Jesus Christ. If we are surrounded with many outward enjoyments, and things that are very comfortable to us. If we are settled in families, and have those good friends and relations that are very desirable. If we have companions whose society is delightful to us. If we have children that are pleasant and hopeful, and in whom we see many promising qualifications. If we live by good neighbors; have much of the respect of others; have a good name; are generally beloved where we are known. And have comfortable and pleasant accommodations. Yet we ought not to take our rest in these things. We should not be willing to have these things for our portion, but should seek a higher happiness in another world. We should not merely seek something else in addition to these things, but should be so far from resting in them that we should choose and desire to leave these things for heaven, to go to God and Christ there. We should not be willing to live here always, if we could, in the same strength and vigor of body and mind as when in youth, or in the midst of our days, and always enjoy the same pleasure, and dear friends, and other earthly comforts. We should choose and desire to leave them all in God's due time, that we might go to heaven, and there have the enjoyment of God. We ought to possess them, enjoy and make use of them, with no other view or aim but readily to quit them, whenever we are called to it, and to change them for heaven. And when we are called away from them, we should go cheerfully and willingly.

He that is going a journey is not wont to rest in what he meets with that is comfortable and pleasing on the road. If he passes along through pleasant places, flowery meadows or shady groves; he don't [sic] take up his content in these things. He is content only to take a transient view of these pleasant objects as he goes along. He is not enticed by these fine appearances to put an end to his journey, and leave off the thought of proceeding. No, but his journey's end is in his mind; that is the great thing that he aims at. So if he meets with comfortable and pleasant accommodations on the road, at an inn, yet he doesn't rest there; he entertains no thoughts of settling there. He considers that these things are not his own, and that he is but a stranger; that, that is not allotted for his home....

So should we thus desire heaven so much more than the comforts and enjoyments of this life that we should long to change these things for heaven. We should wait with earnest desire for the time when we shall arrive to our journey's end. The Apostle mentions it as an encouraging, comfortable consideration to Christians, when they draw nigh their happiness. "Now is our salvation nearer than when we believed."...We ought to look upon these things as only lent to us for a little while, to serve a present turn; but we should set our hearts on heaven as our inheritance forever.

2. We ought to seek heaven, by traveling in the way that leads thither.

The way that leads to heaven is a way of holiness. We should choose and desire to travel thither in this way and in no other. We should part with all those sins, those carnal appetites that are as weights, that will tend to hinder us in our traveling toward heaven. "Let us lay aside every weight, and the sin which doth so easily beset us, and let us run with patience the race set before us" (Heb 12:1). However pleasant any practice or the gratification of any appetite may be, we must lay it aside, cast it away, if it be any hindrance, and stumbling block in the way to heaven.

We should travel on in a way of obedience to all God's commands, even the difficult as well as the easy commands. We should travel on in a way of self-denial, denying all our sinful inclinations and interests. The way to heaven is ascending; we must be content to travel uphill, though it be hard and tiresome, though it be contrary to the natural tendency and bias of our flesh that tends downward to the earth. We should follow Christ in the path that he has gone. The way that he traveled in was the right way to heaven. We should take up our cross and follow him. We should travel along in the same way of meekness and lowliness of heart, in the same way of obedience and charity, and diligence to do good, and patience under afflictions. The way to heaven is a heavenly life; we must be traveling toward heaven in a way of imitation of those that are in heaven: in imitation of the saints and angels there, in their holy employments, in their way of spending their time in loving, adoring, serving, and praising God and the Lamb. This is the path that we ought to prefer before all others if we could have any other that we might choose. If we could go to heaven in a way of carnal living, in the way of the enjoyment and gratification of our lusts, we should rather prefer a way of holiness and conformity to the spiritual self-denying rules of the gospel.

3. We should travel on in this way in a laborious manner.

The going of long journeys is attended with toil and fatigue, especially if the journey be through a wilderness. Persons in such a case expect no other than to suffer hardships and weariness, in traveling over mountains and through bad places. So we should travel in this way of holiness, in a laborious manner, improving our time and strength, to surmount the difficulties and obstacles that are in the way. The land that we have to travel through is a wilderness; there are many mountains, rocks, and rough places that we must go over in the way; and there is a necessity that we should lay out our strength.

4. Our whole lives ought to be spent in traveling this road.

1. We ought to begin early. This should be the first concern and business that persons engage in when they come to be capable of acting in the world in doing any business. When they first set out in the world, they should set out on this journey. And,

2. We ought to travel on in this way with assiduity. It ought to be the work of every day, to travel on toward heaven. We should often be thinking of our journey's end, and not only thinking of it, but it should be our daily work to travel on in the way that leads to it. As he that is on a journey is often think-

ing of the place that he is going to, and 'tis his care and business every day to get along, to improve his time, to get toward his journey's end....Thus should heaven be continually in our thought; and the immediate entrance or passage to it, namely death, should be present with us. And it should be a thing that we familiarize to ourselves, and so it should be our work every day to be preparing for death and traveling heavenward.

3. We ought to persevere in this way as long as we live; we should hold out in it to the end. "Let us run with patience the race that is set before us" (Heb 12:1). Though the road be difficult, and it be a toilsome thing to travel it, we must hold out with patience, and be content to endure the hardships of it. If the journey be long, yet we must not stop short; we should not give out in discouragement, but hold on 'till we are arrived to the place we seek. We ought not to be discouraged with the length and difficulties of the way, as the children of Israel were, and be for turning back again. All our thought and design should be to get along. We should be engaged and resolved to press forward 'till we arrive.

5. We ought to be continually growing in holiness and in that respect coming nearer and nearer to heaven.

He that is traveling towards a place comes nearer and nearer to it continually. So we should be endeavoring to come nearer to heaven, in being more heavenly, becoming more and more like the inhabitants of heaven, and more and more as we shall be when we have arrived there, if ever that be. We should endeavor continually to be more and more as we hope to be in heaven, in respect of holiness and conformity to God. And with respect to light and knowledge, we should labor to be growing continually in the knowledge of God and Christ, and clear views of the glory of God, the beauty of Christ, and the excellency of divine things, as we come nearer and nearer to the beatific vision.

We should labor to be continually growing in divine love, that this may be an increasing flame in our hearts, 'till our hearts ascend wholly in this flame. We should be growing in obedience and a heavenly conversation that we may do the will of God on earth as the angels do in heaven. We ought to be continually growing in comfort and spiritual joy, in sensible communion with God and Jesus Christ. Our path should be as "the shining light, that shines more and more to the perfect day" (Prov 4:18)....We ought to be hungering and thirsting after righteousness after an increase in righteousness. "As newborn babes desire the sincere milk of the word, that ye may grow thereby" (1 Pet 2:2). And we should make the perfection of heaven our mark....

6. All other concerns of life ought to be entirely subordinate to this.

As when a person is on a journey, all the steps that he takes are in order to further him in his journey, and subordinated to that aim of getting to his journey's end. And if he carries money or provision with him 'tis to supply him in his journey. So we ought wholly to subordinate all our other business, and all our temporal enjoyments to this affair of traveling to heaven. Journeying toward heaven ought to be our only work and business, so that all that we have and do should be in order to that. When we have worldly enjoyments, we should be ready to part with them, whenever they are in the way of our going toward heaven. We should sell all this world for heaven. When once anything we have becomes a clog and hindrance to us, in the way heavenward, we should quit it immediately. When we use our worldly enjoyments and possessions, it should be with such a view and in such a manner as to further us in our way heavenward. Thus we should eat and drink and clothe ourselves. And thus should we improve the conversation and enjoyment of friends.

And whatever business we are setting about, whatever design we are engaging in, we should inquire with ourselves, whether this business or undertaking will forward us in our way to heaven? And if not, we should quit our design. We ought to make use of worldly enjoyments, and pursue worldly business in such a degree and manner as shall have the best tendency to forward our journey heavenward and no otherwise.

I shall offer some reasons of the doctrine.

1. This world is not our abiding place.

Our continuance in this world is but very short. Our days on the earth are as a shadow. It was never designed by God this world should be our home. We were not born into this world for that end. Neither did God give us these temporal things that we are accommodated with for that end. If God has given us good estates, if we are settled in families, and God has given us children, or other friends that are very pleasant to us, 'is with no such view or design that we should be furnished and provided for here, as for a settled abode, but with a design that we should use them for the present, and then leave them again in a very little time.

If we are called to any secular business, or if we are charged with the care of a family, with the instruction and education of children, we are called to these things with a design that we shall be called from them again, and not to be our everlasting employment. So that if we improve our lives to any other purpose, than as a journey toward heaven, all our labor will be lost. If we spend our lives in the pursuit of a temporal happiness; if we set our hearts on riches, and seek happiness in them; if we seek to be happy in sensual pleasures; if we spend our lives in seeking the credit and esteem of men, the good-will and respect of others; if we let our hearts on our children, and look to be happy in the enjoyment of them, in seeing them well brought up, and well settled, etc.—all these things will be of little significance to us. Death will blow up all our hopes and expectations, and will put an end to our enjoyment of these things....

2. The future world was designed to be our settled and everlasting abode.

Here it was intended that we should be fixed and here alone is a lasting habitation, and a lasting inheritance and enjoyments to be had. We are designed for this future world. We are to be in two states, the one in this world, which is an imperfect state, the other in the world to come. The present state is short and transitory, but our state in the other world is everlasting. When we go into another world, there we must be to all eternity. And as we are there at first, so we must be without change. Our state in the future world therefore being eternal, is of so exceedingly greater importance than our state in this world that it is worthy that our state here, and all our concerns in this world, should be wholly subordinated to it.

3. Heaven is that place alone where our highest end, and highest good is to be obtained.

God has made us for himself. "Of God, and thro' God, and to God are all things." Therefore then do we attain to our highest end, when we are brought to God; but that is by being brought to heaven, for that is God's throne; that is the place of his special presence, and of his residence. There is but a very imperfect union with God to be had in this world, a very imperfect knowledge of God in the midst of abundance of darkness, a very imperfect conformity to God, mingled with abundance of enmity and estrangement. Here we can serve and glorify God, but in an exceeding imperfect manner, our service being mingled with much sin and dishonor to God.

But when we get to heaven (if ever that be), there we shall be brought to a perfect union with God. There we shall have the clear views of God. We shall see face-to-face, and know as we are known. There we shall be fully conformed to God, without any remainder of sin. We shall be like him, for we shall see him as he is. There we shall serve God perfectly. We shall glorify him in an exalted manner and to the utmost of the powers and capacity of our nature. Then we shall perfectly give up ourselves to God. Then will our hearts be pure and holy offerings to God, offered all in a flame of divine love. In heaven alone is the attainment of our highest good. God is the highest good of the reasonable creature. The enjoyment of him is our proper happiness and is the only happiness with which our souls can be satisfied. To go to heaven, fully to enjoy God, is infinitely better than the most pleasant accommodations here. Better than fathers and mothers, husbands, wives or children, or the company of any, or all earthly friends.

4. Our present state, and all that belongs to it, is designed by him that made all things, to be wholly in order to another world.

This world was made for a place of preparation for another world. Our mortal life was given us only here that we might here be prepared for his fixed state. And all that God has here given us is given to this purpose. The sun shines upon us; the rain falls upon us; the earth yields her increase to us; civil and ecclesiastical affairs; family affairs; and all our personal concerns are designed and ordered in a subordination to a future world, by the Maker and Disposer of all things. They ought therefore to be subordinated to this by us.

William Williams, "Guide me, O Thou great Jehovah"[5]

Guide me, O Thou great Jehovah,
  Pilgrim thro' this barren land;
I am weak, but Thou art mighty,
  Hold me with thy powrful hand:
    Bread of heaven! bread of heaven!
    Feed me now and evermore.

Open now the crystal fountain
   Whence the healing streams do flow;
Let the fiery cloudy pillar
   Lead me all my Journey through:
     Strong Deliv'rer! Strong Deliv'rer!
     Be Thou still my strength and shield.

When I tread the verge of Jordan,
   Bid my anxious fears subside;
Death of deaths, and hell's destruction,
   Land me safe on Canaan's side.
     Songs of praises, songs of praises,
     I will ever give to Thee.

Musing on my habitation,
   Musing on my heav'nly home,
Fills my soul with holy longing,
   Come, my Jesus, quickly come.
     Vanity is all I see,
     Lord, I long to be with Thee!

Augustus Toplady, "Happiness Found" (known today as "Object of My First Desire")[6]

Happiness, thou lovely name,
   Where's thy seat, O tell me, where?
Learning, pleasure, wealth, and fame,
   All cry out, "It is not here."
Not the wisdom of the wise
Can inform me where it lies,
Not the grandeur of the great
Can the bliss I seek create.

Object of my first desire,
   Jesus, crucified for me!
All to happiness aspire,
   Only to be found in thee;
Thee to please, and thee to know,

Constitute our bliss below;
Thee to see and thee to love,
Constitute our bliss above.

Lord, it is not life to live,
    If thy presence thou deny;
Lord, if thou thy presence give,
    'Tis no longer death to die;
Source and giver of repose,
Singly from thy smile it flows;
Peace and Happiness are thine;
Mine they are, if Thou art mine.

Whilst I feel thy love to me,
    Ev'ry object teems with joy,
Here, O may I walk with Thee,
    Then into thy presence die!
Let me but Thyself possess,
Total sum of happiness!
Real bliss I then shall prove;
Heav'n below, and heav'n above.

William Cowper, "Walking with God," Genesis 5:24[7]

O! for a closer walk with God,
    A calm and heav'nly frame;
A light to shine upon the road
    That leads me to the Lamb!

Where is the blessedness I knew
    When first I saw the Lord?
Where is the soul-refreshing view
    Of Jesus, and his word?

What peaceful hours I once enjoyed!
    How sweet their memory still!
But they have left an aching void,
    The world can never fill.

Return, O holy Dove, return,
    Sweet messenger of rest;
I hate the sins that made thee mourn,
    And drove thee from my breast.

The dearest idol I have known,
    Whate'er that idol be;
Help me to tear it from thy throne,
    And worship only thee.

So shall my walk be close with God,
    Calm and serene my frame;
So purer light shall mark the road
    That leads me to the Lamb.

William Cowper, "Light Shining out of Darkness"[8]

God moves in a mysterious way,
    His wonders to perform;
He plants his footsteps in the sea,
    And rides upon the storm.

Deep in unfathomable mines
    Of never failing skill
He treasures up his bright designs,
    And works his sovereign will.

Ye fearful saints fresh courage take,
    The clouds ye so much dread
Are big with mercy, and shall break
    In blessings on your head.

Judge not the Lord by feeble sense,
    But trust him for his grace;
Behind a frowning providence,
    He hides a smiling face.

His purposes will ripen fast,
    Unfolding every hour;

The bud may have a bitter taste,
But sweet will be the flow'r.

Blind unbelief is sure to err,
    And scan his work in vain;
God is his own interpreter,
    And he will make it plain.

Hester Ann Rogers, Letter 6, to Mr. Robert Roe, February 12, 1778[9]

Dear cousin, Macclesfield, February 12, 1778.

Since I wrote to you before, I have been, to appearance, on the borders of eternity. My body was indeed brought very low, but my soul full of heavenly vigor, and longing for immortality! O what heavenly transport filled my ravished breast when I thought I had done, for ever done with all below! And, as I then thought, in a few days, or weeks at most, I should leave my cumbrous clay to bask in the beams of uncreated beauty—should stand before the slaughtered Lamb, and see the wonders received for me! "Should fall at his feet, the story repeat, and the Lover of sinners adore." When I should be lost in Father, Son, and Spirit and overwhelmed and implunged in the fathomless abyss to all eternity. What I felt cannot be described; it was a real taste of joys immortal, it was a drop of heaven let down. But behold! I am yet spared. Infinite wisdom protracts my stay a little longer, and I bow my soul in resignation at his feet. I am not my own, but his, and O may my language ever be, not as I will, but as you will! I find I need not drop the body to enjoy the presence of my God. He dwells in my heart. In him I live. He surrounds, supports, sustains me. Wrapped in his being, I resound his praise! O the heartfelt communion my soul enjoys with him, the intimate converse, the sweet fellowship! My spirit is filled and yet enlarged. It often seems as if mortality could bear no more; and yet my desires are insatiable. I long to plunge deeper into God.

I rejoice to find by your last letter that you are cleaving to your Lord, and happy in his precious love. O that every day and hour you breathe, you may sink deeper into him! All, all you want is there. Let not your trials be any discouragement; no, rejoice and be exceeding glad, for great is your reward in heaven. Remember, every cross is a pledge of your crown, and all your sufferings will add to your eternal weight of glory. I hope you are all in earnest for the precious pearl of perfect love. O look up to a present and a faithful God! Ask, and you shall receive; all things in him are now ready. Be not faithless, but believing. He has said, I will circumcise your heart, and will he not do it? Sooner shall heaven and earth pass away than his promise fail, if you only embrace it by believing. O claim your privilege, the inheritance of the land of promise, the rest of holiness purchased for you by blood! Go up and possess it, fear not. Come now, just as you are empty, to be filled filthy, to be cleansed. "Sink into the purple flood, rise to all the life of God." Be assured I ever remember you at a throne of grace, and remain your friend and sister in Jesus, H. A. Roe.

Susanna Anthony, Excerpt from *The Life and Character of Miss Susanna Anthony*[10]

June 23rd, 1746. O my unbelieving heart! How long will you rise in secret dissatisfaction at God's disposals of me? As I appear recovering from my disorders, I would fain think it best; cheerfully embrace life, and bless my God for it. And yet I feel a reluctance, even while I am writing. I am almost impatient for that state and world where my will shall be entirely swallowed up in God's. I believe [that] for above two years, there has not been a day, if an hour or minute when awake, in which if death had come, I could have said it is come in a day or hour wherein I have not longed and panted for it. The vanity of this world has rendered it burdensome to me. I am sure the bewitching pleasures of it have more embittered it to me, than all its sorrows.

When I compare infinite with finite, eternal with temporal, boundless and unfathomable with shallow nothing, I find there is a boundless unfathomable, infinite, eternal disproportion between those immense, immortal delights above and those of time and sense. And is it a small disappointment when I hoped in a short time to have been in the full enjoyment of God and these glories, when I seemed to be on the confines of eternity, new glories appearing to my gazing, astonished soul, all bright, all serene, the happy haven. From these happy views, to be ordered back to earth, all dark and gloom; the cavern far from God, my life and my all in all; to grovel among the insects of this earth; the fear of a vain heart, that it will choose vanity? O, how shocking, how surprising the change! What finite spirit, though of a superior order, would feel no emotion, no reluctance at such a disappointment, I cannot conceive....I know, I know, there are soul-ravishing, soul-quickening, soul-humbling, soul-transforming discoveries of invisibilities. These have inflamed my soul for those yet unknown glories, and yet well known by anticipation, and prelibation. O for a fresh view while here. O my God, mitigate the darkness by intervening light.

June 26th. Yesterday I had a sweet morning. My meditations of God were composed and solemn. My heart was fixed and enlivened in prayer. But nature was much spent, so that I felt the effects all the day after. O, what a clog is this body! At night, after serious examination by my rules, I addressed the throne of grace with some little life. The blessed Spirit came and filled my soul with a sense of the glory and majesty of the great Jehovah, and of the repeated affronts and indignities I had offered to him. Of his astonishing patience and forbearance that I was not made a monument of divine wrath, a spectacle to angels and people and devils. That, after such incorrigibleness, under divine cultivation, both of the Spirit, providences, and ordinances, all the sweet sunbeams of overflowing, unbounded, infinite, ever-flowing love, I was not bound over to suffer the strange punishment assigned to the workers of iniquity; but that God was yet accessible, through the glorious Mediator; my infinite need of the Mediator; my ground of strong confidence in him; that he was a surety whom God the Father had appointed, and declared himself well pleased with. I saw myself a sinner, and dare not approach absolute perfection in any way but through a Mediator. The faithfulness of God afforded strong consolation....

O, if this body were no help to my devotion, yet if it would but keep pace with my nobler powers, I could bear it. But that it should drag down my immortal powers, I could not bear it from any hand but you wise, good, gracious, just, sovereign God and Father. It seems to me I should resent it with contempt, as an affront, should the greatest monarch on earth offer me a reprieve from those immortal joys which are in your presence. I receive life, and bless you for it, only as it is the will of my wise God. Not all the creatures on earth, nor the dearest relations here, would make me willing to stay a moment, had you not said, "Return and live." But now, welcome this body, and this (otherwise) my hated clog and continual burden. On these terms, the will and glory of God, whatever I receive from you, my God, I would choose and love, as I have chosen your will for mine, in all things....

July. Lord, I am yours; resolvedly so. It is my constant study: What shall I render to the Lord for all his benefits toward me? I look back with pleasure on all those engagements whereby I am bound to be the Lord's. O, never let me retract those solemn vows! It is you who have pitied my weakness, and pardoned my most unnatural rebellion. O, infinite mercy, free grace, unbounded love, unspeakable condescension!...O, I long to bathe myself in this infinite fountain, and let out all my soul in God. But ah, finite, narrow, depraved capacity, when shall you be enlarged, O when!...

Feb. 13, 1751. Last Monday, Feb. 11, at night, my soul was led to contemplate the being and perfections of the blessed God. Here I stood and gazed, until all my soul was fixed with unutterable attention. O, how did the glory of this divine, infinite, self-existing, self-sufficient Being raise my contemplation, and draw out the strength of my soul with vigor and ardor, to dive as far, and take in as much as a finite mortal being could contain! O, how glorious, how infinitely glorious, did the exalted, immense, immortal, incomprehensible Deity then appear to my enlarged, adoring soul! And while I gazed, my soul was filled with inexpressible astonishment at the many and great affronts and indignities I had offered to this divine, infinite Majesty. O, how did my soul shrink into nothing, and less than nothing, before

Jehovah, while I lay prostrate before him, and confessed my aggra-vated guilt with renewed application to the blood of Jesus Christ his Son! O, how mean did all the human race then appear! Infinitely unworthy of the least regard from God. I cried, Lord, what is man, that thou art mindful of him! Man, who is a worm of the dust, that he should be capable of contemplating and enjoying a Being who is his own infinite delight and happiness. O, all incomprehensible, unfath-omable Divinity, it is thou, and thou only, who canst trace, and fully reach these boundless depths. In vain my finite soul, clogged with earth, stretched after clear and full discoveries....

But here again, my soul, reaching after higher degrees of won-der, love, and delight, looked on fallen men and women who had slighted and despised this dignity, and, by his apostasy, was put out of all possibility of enjoying this God by any thing he could do. Here I beheld this God providing a Mediator, even his own Son that so all who believe in him might be brought to the full enjoyment of him, in glory. Now my soul was all engaged and inflamed, my desire intensely reaching after the open vision and full fruition of this all amiable and glorious Being. My soul even broke with longing after God, my only desirable felicity. My thoughts were very deep and fixed. I can scarce remember any season in which I was more immovably fixed and engaged. Nor could my thoughts be diverted after I came out of my chamber, but continued very fixed, though I felt my body greatly disordered and racked. Went to bed, but a vio-lent pain seized the nerves and sinews of my head, so that I got little or no sleep.

March 26th. On Saturday the 24th, it thundered, but I felt com-posed, and not terrified, as I have been sometimes. But when I retired, though the thunder and lightning was over, yet Satan was permitted to work very powerfully on my fear, even to amazement. Yet I kept on in duty, rolling myself on God through Christ, claim-ing God as my covenant God and father; adoring God for the suffi-cient security he had provided in Christ Jesus for all that do believe; appealing to God for the sincerity of my faith; of the free, full and unreserved dedication of myself to him and his service; and choice of him for my portion, Lord and king; not only when in great fear and terror, but in the most sedate and composed seasons I ever knew; as well in prosperity as adversity. A choice which flowed from a deep, found conviction of his infinite excellency; a choice entirely free. I asserted the faithfulness of God; triumphed in his infinite grace and love....

March 29th, 1751...O when shall my soul be free and active! When shall it no more be clogged with this burden of mortality! O when! My God, I long to get near thee. I long to reach a more noble and exalted height of life and fervor. I long to get above the sun, and sing among the heirs of glory, those birds of paradise. There, transported, I shall enjoy unbounded felicity, and seeing him I hope to see the God I love—see him, in the sight of whom I hope to be like him, conformed to his image. O blessed vision! O endless fruition! Then I shall not fear or faint any more. O come, my Redeemer, come away. Break through these intervening clouds, and set the prisoner free from every interruption. O, bring me, where I long to be, near my God and Savior. You are all my rest, delight and desire, while I remain here; and you shalt be infinitely more so, when I see you without this veil of mortality. What is there in life I count worth living for, but you? Does it not appear all vain, yes, burdensome, without you, my God? Verily I see nothing worth living for, but this God; nothing but glorifying and enjoying God. O then, why should mortality confine me here, under such languishments! May I not glorify and enjoy you more, when my soul is more refined, and satisfied with full vision and fruition? Lord, you know what is best. Yet I long. O come, Lord Jesus, come quickly. Amen.

Sarah Osborn, Excerpt from *Memoirs of the Life of Mrs. Sarah Osborn*[11]

Thursday, June 21, 1744. Yesterday very much overcome in God's house, at the solemn ordination of the Rev. Mr. Helyer. My heart was then filled with joy and praises, and God excited and enabled me to breathe out my soul in vehement cries to him for all needful grace, for his servant, and for his church. Rejoiced much to think I was once more to enjoy the glorious feast instituted by my dear Redeemer. I longed to render a tribute of praise, and even to be swallowed up with praises all my life long, because God had so graciously given me the desire of my heart. But, alas! How short lived are my praises. All this day, with bodily indisposition and my own declining heart, I have been as water heated, returning to my former coldness again. O! it makes eternity glorious, that praises shall never cease....

Sabbath noon, July 15. Bless the Lord, O my soul, and forget not all his benefits. I have been to the table of the Lord, and he brought me into his banqueting house, and his banner over me was love. I sat under his shadow with great delight, and his fruit was sweet to my taste. My soul said, it is good for me to be here. I was enabled, with all my powers engaged, to renew my dedication of myself to God, and rejoice in my choice of him. I was, in a measure, brought to behold his glory in the perfections of his nature. I was enabled to wrestle with him for victory over my sins, and to be made more holy....

In time of partaking of the element of bread, my heart seemed to be most broken for sin; when feeding upon his broken body, I was filled with astonishment, and made to cry out, "Lord, why me! Why hast thou given thyself for me!" His blood was sweet to me, as it was shed for the remission of sins. At last I broke out in a rapture, "I found the pearl of greatest price, my heart doth sing for joy." I longed to get still nearer, while I seemed to be resting and leaning on my beloved. Surely I did find him whom my soul loves. O astonishing, all-conquering grace! O happy earnest of more near and intimate communion! O what a feast is this! O blessed Savior, for appointing such an ordinance! O my soul, bless God, for bringing me to partake thereof. Thanks be to God for such gracious smiles upon his church today, that you have restored this former privilege. Thanks be to God, for his presence with his poor, helpless, necessitous worm. Thanks be to God, for Jesus Christ....

Saturday evening, April 19 [1755]. I have been these two days past in very poor, low frames, much bodily indisposition, headache, great cold, quite unfit for close application to preparatory work for the sacrament. The Lord pity and pardon for Jesus' sake, who has died, the just for the unjust. O may I, by his blood, be brought near unto God. Lord, deal not with me according to my sins, nor reward me according to mine iniquities, for if you do, I shall surely profane your holy table and come empty away; yes, expose myself to terrible judgments. Lord, appear for me, unworthy as I am, and prepare my unprepared heart. O stir up suitable desires, hunger and thirst after communion with yourself. Yes, draw forth every sacramental grace into lively exercise. O melt this frozen heart. Grant me evangelical repentance that I may look on him whom I have pierced, and mourn bitterly as for an only son. O humble me to the dust, and give me a sense of pardon, if it be your blessed will....I long to arise. Lord, draw me near to yourself by the influences of your blessed Spirit. O water me with the dew of heaven, refresh my soul with a plentiful shower, now in this dry and thirsty land, where no water is. O may the Sun of righteousness arise with healing in his wings, and shine into, and warm this cold heart. O let every property of the blood of Christ be applied to my poor, necessitous soul. Lord, hear, for his sake who shed his precious blood on the accursed tree, even for such as me. O may I, by this ordinance, be bound ten thousand times faster to yourself than ever. O you great Captain of my salvation, go before me, and conquer all my foes. Subdue my stubborn will; yes, subdue me wholly and forever to yourself. Come, Prince and Savior, come and reign in me, whose right it is; and, O Lord, hasten the time when I shall enjoy you, behold your glory, see you as you are, when all veils and walls of separation shall be forever broken down, and I shall gaze, adore and praise, as glorified saints and angels do....

April 22. Blessed be God, the Sabbath was a sweet day to me. It pleased God graciously to afford me the influences of his Spirit all the day, and in special at his table. My whole soul was engaged. I think repentance, faith, love, desire, and every sacramental grace was in lively exercise. Sin appeared hateful; its utter destruction was vehemently longed for, and the increase of grace thirsted for. Renewed solemn covenant, pleaded that I might renew my strength. That sin might now be nailed to the accursed tree. Longed for the full enjoyment of God; did believe God would keep me by his mighty power here, and at last bring me to glory. And he will, my soul, he will. O he is a faithful God. The snare is broken, and I am escaped; broken by a glorious Christ. O blessed be God, for Jesus Christ. I longed that every soul there might be indeed united to him, and enjoy communion with him....

Thursday morning, August 7 [1755]....O my God, I have lately seen what the agonies of death mean. A shocking sight, indeed, while the poor unprepared soul shrinks back and would lodge in its crazy cottage! But go it must, and appear before God. I had a deep sense of things while with my dying neighbor, and God enabled me to send up strong cries to him for the poor soul. My spirits were overwhelmed, and my whole frame crushed with the weight. But alas! time is fled and gone, and the state of the soul is unalterably fixed in boundless eternity. Whether in weal, or woe, God knows. I determine not. But this I know, that the will of a just and sovereign God is done, and he is glorified, yes and will be glorified....But come, Lord Jesus, come now and possess a soul that is yours. Come, Lord, and satisfy it with yourself. O let the perpetual voice be there: "Christ and his Spirit, Christ and his grace, none but Christ, none but Christ."

O you altogether lovely One, come and abide with me. Lord, either stay with me, or take me to yourself. O I cannot let you go. What is all this world to me? If you be absent, you know I cannot be comforted. No, by your grace, I never will. Nothing but mine own portion shall content me. O let the blessed union be more and more complete day by day. Grant me sensible communion with you. O manifest yourself to me as you do not to the world, for you have redeemed me by your precious blood, and you have by your Spirit applied the purchased redemption. Lord, you know I am not of the world, for you have called me out of the world. I have heard your voice and have followed you. Yes, and by the assistance of your grace (for without you I can do nothing) I am determined to follow you wherever you go.

Wednesday morning, August 27....O that I could take every backsliding child in the whole world by the hand, and lead them back to their heavenly Father, since I, who have been a backslider, an abuser of the richest grace and dearest love, am, notwithstanding all, restored. O grace! O truth and faithfulness! Surely there is no god like my God, forgiving iniquity, transgression and sin; yes, crimson and scarlet sins, big with the greatest ingratitude. O blush and be astonished you heavens over my head, you earth under my feet. For I have sinned against that light and endearing love, that many thousands now in hell never did. And yet O how does that precious blood plead for me! O how does it cleanse, pardon and sanctify. How does it overflow and cover the huge rocks and mountains sin has raised in my soul, and triumphs over all, and will speak peace and pardon. Will bring home the guilty runaway to her God and Father, and cause him to be reconciled and smile again. O precious blood! O precious Christ! O blessed union between Christ and my soul.

Ann Griffiths, "Earth cannot, with all its trinkets," Hymn no. 14[12]

Earth cannot, with all its trinkets,
Slake my longings at this hour;
They were captured, they were widened,
When my Jesus showed his power.
None but he can now content me,
He, the Incomprehensible;
O to gaze upon his person,
God in man made visible.

Let my days be wholly given
Jesus' blood to glorify,
Calm to rest beneath his shadow,
At his feet to live and die,
Love the cross, and bear it daily,
('Tis the cross my husband bore,)
Gaze with joy upon his person,
And unceasingly adore.

Sarah Jones, Letter to Jeremiah Minter, Minister of the Gospel, January 25, 1790[13]

Dear brother, Monday night, Jan. 25, 1790.

As a weaned child in the nursery of angels, in the arms of Jesus, hushed without a murmur, I softly whisper, "Thy will be done, O Lord." The seals of mysteries burst before me, while the golden pipe pour forth fresh oil and sparkling love and pleasure fill my cup. Submission threatens every thorn with fire, obedience burns them up, and courage blunts the sword of hell, and bids the devil flee.

The remembrance of late favors hath roused up gratitude, and called diligence and self-denial to practice. I rush through a crowd of entreaties; with daggers like the sun I cut my way, and settle on the mount with God; my vitals fasten on his breast, my soul will not let him move without a guard. I dropped my pen and fell on my face before him, in which soul humbling posture I remained a considerable time; it was near midnight.

May I now go back to the moment you left us? As you set off on horseback not knowing your path until they hailed you the other way, it poured in my mind. O the willing herald, faithful anointed ambassador, how cheerfully he rushes to do his master's will; it filled me with noble thoughts of my heroic friend, which pressed the rolling brine. I retired to your late room, sunk at the feet of Jesus, and talked with him, as it were, face-to-face, until a cloud of pointed spears of acute flaming agony fell down upon me, of strong, vehement desire to have as much religion as my provoking mortifier enjoyed. Now you may behold me at my wits end, all enflamed with ten thousand daggers in my soul, for more pure unmixed holiness. O Lord! Is it to be had? Where? How? In the valley; I will go. In self-denial; I will run. In watching and prayer; there will I live.

Before sunset, sometime, I withdrew with your journal to a silent wood, where I swallowed such pills of mortification at my shortcomings [that] I wish I may ever surmount it. I read and roared praise, until heaven blossomed with stars, and the modest moonshine overspread the fields with beauty. I came home in the flame and began my lines. Entering my chamber I found dear S. E., sister K. Jennet, and Mr. Jones all on fire. A storm of glory poured and we spent some hours in reading, praising and adoring the God of love, mixing much prayer, and frequent retirement for more religion. The narrow path to heaven drawn by you was well perused, and while I live, I expect, will be preaching to me.

It is now Tuesday night, 26th, in which I feel solemn as death almost, and seriously bent to prepare to meet God. I have moved my table and books in the upper room over the hall, where I have settled with great preparation to spend much of this winter, as there is wood and fire, candles, books, paper and a willing mind. I want to enter a new degree of religion, and more I must have if it is to be attained. I depend much on your prayers, as I believe you to be my faithful dear brother. I have spent great part of this day reading your heavenly lines. All my soul is reaching, my poor frame is trembling, my heart is gone out after more of God....

I have just arisen from prayer, about an hour of wrestling agony, according to our agreement. O, what I felt! It is unspeakable. You are with me. I opened the sacred word and wet it with tears, this passage, he hath borne our grief, and carried our sorrows (Isa 53:4). My brother, your letters are before me, my jewels, my treasure. My heart almost broke in reading those dated December 29, 30; and when I came to where you prayed we might never wound each other, what a hearty amen I could say! I verily feel as if I had rather my body should molder into ashes and my soul be banished into annihilation than wound my dear Jesus, his cause, or his servant; and what a pity would it be for my precious brother to wound me....

You don't know how little I feel while all your burning torches blaze around me, your letters on one hand and journal on the other. I have thought I had a great mind not to sleep tonight. When will yon flaming chariot fetch us home to rest without sorrow and live without danger? Reason, which seems the root of faith, says to bed, it is near one in the morning. Jesus is by me, and angels who patrol the midnight scenes watch my sincere agony; and now I try to see how near I can get to my blessed Jesus. O to worship the Lord in Spirit and in truth, my brother, is the fat of the sacrifice: it is the soul and quintessence of religion (the richest cordials are made of spirits). O Sovereign Elixir, full of healing balm.

Wednesday morning the 28th. I arose with some deep exercise not without some temptation, which drove me to close work, yet cheerful to those around me. I don't know how it may be with you; but with me, when the blaze of ecstasy slacks in my soul, there stands the devil with ten thousand darts but he gets nothing by it. I flew to God and his word, and got a search, and found the serpent's haunt, twisted him out, and he flew like lightning from me, and I was caught up into the third heaven, and was wrapt in such flames of dying love, I can by no means express it. This was while in my room at work, Mr. Jones and family by. Such seas of bursting glory came rolling from heaven, I screamed out, weakness overpowered my limbs, my dear companion smiled in pleasing wonder, and joy and pleasure filled my room. I grasped happiness, and gazed in admiration, and swam in the full rivers that issued from the throne of God. I strained up the steep of excellent, [*sic*] and sunk in the flames of love divine. My brother, Austin [i.e. Augustine] reckons up 288 opinions among the philosophers about happiness, but they all would come short, yes very short of telling what I this moment enjoy. My soul trembles as the needle beneath the loadstone. O, what is it? What is it, I say? It is joy, and gladness. What joy? Spiritual joy, a sweet delightful passion, arising from Heaven, to fence me in against troubles. As David said, thy comforts, O Lord, delight my soul! It is the joy that distills from the Lembec of the promises. This joy makes the martyr's death a bed of roses, when the sun shines in his face. God candies our wormwood with sugar; are not you glad? Michael is stronger than the dragon. O Galilean you have overcome! Brother, set God's power to work by faith and prayer, and I ask you if hell can conquer us? No, verily, no.

I will tell you my friend, I have proved the devil a liar. O Lucifer, your pomp and schemes are brought down to the grave. Only let God speak and stars fight in their courses against Sicera or stamp with his foot, and behold an army of angels presently in Batallia. Let us fear as well as love this mighty God. Let me tell you, God's furnace is in Zion; is it any injustice in God to put his gold in the fire to purify it, my dear brother? No, surely, no....

Bro. Minter, my heart is broke for more religion; your journal will it kill me with longing for holiness. I see it needs wisdom, skill, great care, virtue, prudence, and all prayer to take a degree of perfect holiness (see 2 Cor 7:1). How Satan hates it. When the Lord God would humble Adam, he used this expression. Out of the dust art thou taken, &c. O pride, how I fear it! My select brother, who can tell the thousandth part of the devil's deep schemes to undo the souls of the sanctified? I have wept in the face of Jehovah this day to save us, until he has heard my cries, and now I have nothing to do but to go forward. I fell down before God, and might have washed my face with tears. I thought I saw heaven opened, and the blaze of his glory who heard my cries shone upon me, and the Son of Man stood before me. O how I prayed for you; be of good courage, and the Lord will help you; he cares for you; and his life guard of angels are about you. He keeps the very bones of his saints. I can truly say I have spent this day with God, and he has as sensibly answered my prayers as I know I am alive. Ah, Lord, how easy should I go to hell was I to leave off watching and prayer! I wonder how some professors live with so little prayer. O what would I do could I persuade them to pray more? I am almost in glory. Lord Jesus, tell my brother how happy I am; from about three, to ten, at night, every power melted. I walked to and fro in the evening and felt as if I were in a strange land. O how I longed for home. I felt such a power in covenant prayer I never can express while mortal. I am now in my upper study. I just laid down your journal, in which I reap whole sheaves of blessings; my good Jesus sent it to me. I am stirred through and through. O, if I could but do without sleep! I have taken a fresh start for heaven. O how the essence of quarterly meeting pours on my soul; it is good to see diligent Christians.

Are not you tired? I am not till I pay my debt, but drop my pen tonight.

Thursday, 29. I am lost and swallowed up in God. My dear brother, I can hardly keep my paper from the floods of rolling brine! How tender my poor mean heart has got!

I just now thought all the preachers would pray for me that were with us, and I could but just live. Farewell world and flesh, and ease, and everybody that don't love Jesus. Come along my friend and let us go home, for till then there will be something wanting, and that is real possession of God and glory. O how I long to behold him! Where burns his throne? Where blazes his bright court? On which hand shall I bend to find where he is? I walked out in the evening, and if ever I was solemn, I was then. My thoughts were deep, deep, deep; rolling tears, a present God, and I am sensible you prayed for me.

I have good news to tell you: Christ has overcome the world, flesh, and devil; and I have searched my heart well of late, and I can truly say thy will be done, in all things. I will tell you now what I think. I think it a condescension in you to read my scrawl. I feel as mean as dust, and as I am here I wonder what St. Paul meant when he said, "No man ever hated his own flesh"; but glory to God my conscience is as calm as sunshine and hell and all it maneuvers can't overturn my soul, if Jesus holds me.

I am your sister, Sarah Jones.

6

LOVE FOR NEIGHBOR

INTRODUCTION

One of the primary descriptors of early evangelicals was activism. Since they had experienced conversion and the good news of Jesus Christ, they realized the importance of communicating that message to others. The broad selection of texts from this category includes hymns, letters, sermons, missionary treatises, personal narratives, and appeals directed to the upper class to recognize their responsibility for action. These texts also explore a wide range of concerns that needed this good news. The evils of slavery were debated on both sides of the Atlantic, although the British successfully abolished it decades before the American colonies did. Missionary efforts were encouraged and societies formed specifically to prepare and send men and women to countries that had not heard the gospel. Some of these writings sought to remove the excuses related to the danger, expense, and challenges of learning new languages and cultures. Other missionary writings reflect new philosophies to travel only where they were invited or where no one else had previously been. The importance of evangelism is demonstrated both in addressing a specific people group of their need to receive Jesus Christ as their Savior and also in the narrative of a single person as he attempts to live a consistent life of faith that honors Christ amid the conflicts of business and daily life. The wealthy and privileged were reminded that religion was more than external formalism and that selfishness was the greatest barrier to vital Christianity. Those who had experienced abundant resources were challenged to practice benevolence to those less fortunate. Likewise, sermons proclaimed the necessity of charity to the poor. Giving to others was both a direct biblical command of Jesus but also produced a significant benefit to those who gave. Finally, some leaders were bold in their correspondence, openly expressing their love of and devotion to their wives.

THE TEXTS

Isaac Watts, "Christ's Kingdom among the Gentiles" (Second Part Ps 72)[1]

Jesus shall reign where e'er the sun
Does his successive journeys run;
His kingdom stretch from shore to shore,
Till moons shall wax and wane no more.

Behold the islands with their kings,
And Europe her best tribute brings;
From north to south the princes meet
To pay their homage at his feet.

There Persia glorious to behold,
There India shines in eastern gold;
And barbarous nations at his word
Submit and bow and own their Lord.

From him shall endless pray'r be made,
And praises throng to crown his head;
His name like sweet perfume shall rise
With every morning sacrifice.

People and realms of every tongue
Dwell on his love with sweetest song;
And infant voices shall proclaim
Their early blessings on his name.

Blessings abound where e'er he reigns,
The prisoner leaps to lose his chains,
The weary find eternal rest,
And all the sons of want are blest.

Where he displays his healing power,
Death and the curse are known no more;
In him the tribes of Adam boast
More blessings than their father lost.

Let every creature rise and bring
Peculiar honors to our King;
Angels descend with songs again,
And earth repeat the long amen.

John Cennick, "Following Christ, the Sinners Way to God" ("Jesus, my all to heaven")[2]

Jesus, my all, to heav'n is gone;
He that I plac'd my hopes upon;
His track I see—and I'll pursue
The narrow way, 'till him I view.

The way the holy prophets went,
The road that leads from banishment,
The King's highway of holiness
I'll go; for all the paths are peace.

No stranger may proceed therein,
No lover of the world, and sin;
No Lion, no devouring care,
No ravenous tiger shall be there.

No; nothing may go up thereon
But traveling souls, and I am one;
Wayfaring men to Canaan bound,
Shall only in the way be found.

Nor fools, by carnal men esteem'd,
Shall err therein; but they redeem'd
In Jesu's blood, shall shew their right
To travel there, 'till heav'n's in sight.

This is the way I long have sought,
And mourn'd, because I found it not;
My grief, my burden, long have been,
Because I cou'd not cease from sin.

The more I strove against its pow'r,
I sinn'd and stumbled but the more;
'Till late I heard my Savior say,
Come hither, soul, for I'm the way.

Lo! glad I come, and thou, dear Lamb,
Shalt take me to thee, as I am;
Nothing but sin I thee can give,
Yet help me, and thy praise I'll live.

I'll tell to all poor sinners round,
What a dear Savior I have found;
I'll point to thy redeeming blood,
And say, Behold the way to God!

Joseph Hart, "At Dismission"[3]

Dismiss us with thy blessing, Lord.
Help us to feed upon thy Word.
All that has been amiss forgive:
And let thy truth within us live.

Tho' we are guilty, Thou art good.
Wash all our works in Jesu's blood.
Give ev'ry fetter'd soul release;
And bid us all depart in peace.

Hannah More, Chapter 5, ["Unfruitful Professors"][4]

But these unfruitful professors would do well to recollect that,
by a conduct so little worthy of their high calling, they not only violate

243

the law to which they have vowed obedience, but occasion many to disbelieve or to despise it; that they are thus in a great measure accountable for the infidelity of others, and of course will have to answer for more than their own personal offenses. For did they in any respect live up to the principles they profess; did they adorn the doctrines of Christianity by a life in any degree consonant to their faith; did they exhibit any thing of the "beauty of holiness" in their daily conversation; they would then give such a demonstrative proof, not only of the sincerity of their own obedience, but of the brightness of that divine light by which they profess to walk, that the most determined unbeliever would at last begin to think there must be something in a religion of which the effects were so visible and the fruits so amiable, and might in time be led to "glorify" not them, not the imperfect doers of these works, but "their Father which is in heaven." Whereas, as things are at present carried on, the obvious conclusion must be either that Christians do not believe in the religion they profess or that there is no truth in the religion itself.

For will he not naturally say that if its influences were so predominant, its consequences must be more evident? That if the prize held out were really so bright, those who truly believed so would surely do something, and sacrifice something, to obtain it?

This swells the amount of the actual mischief beyond calculation. And there is something terrible in the idea of this sort of indefinite evil, that the careless Christian can never know the extent of the contagion he spreads, nor the multiplied infection which they may communicate in their turn whom his disorders first corrupted.

And there is this farther aggravation of his offense: that he will not only be answerable for all the positive evil of which his example is the cause, but for the omission of all the probable good which might have been called forth in others, had his actions been consistent with his profession. What a strong, what an almost irresistible conviction would it carry to the hearts of unbelievers, if they beheld that characteristic difference in the manners of Christians which their profession gives one a right to expect! If they saw that disinterestedness, that humility, sober-mindedness, temperance, simplicity, and sincerity which are the unavoidable fruits of a genuine faith!

But while a person talks like a saint and yet lives like a sinner, while he professes to believe like an apostle and yet leads the life of a sensualist, talks of an ardent faith and yet exhibits a cold and low practice, boasts himself the disciple of a meek master and yet is as much a slave to his passions as they who acknowledge no such authority; while he appears the proud professor of an humble religion or the intemperate champion of a self-denying one, such a person brings Christianity into disrepute, confirms those in error who might have been awakened to conviction, strengthens doubt into disbelief, and hardens indifference into contempt....

But in these times of relaxed principle and frigid indifference, to see people so vigilantly on their guard against the imaginary mischiefs of enthusiasm, while they run headlong into the real opposite perils of a destructive licentiousness, puts one in mind of the one-eyed animal in the fable who, living on the banks of the ocean, never fancied he could be destroyed any way but by drowning; but, while he kept that one eye constantly fixed on the sea, on which side he concluded all the peril lay, he was devoured by an enemy on the dry land, from which quarter he never suspected any danger.

Are not the mischiefs of an enthusiastic piety insisted on with as much earnestness as if an extravagant devotion were the prevailing propensity? Is not the necessity of moderation as vehemently urged as if an intemperate zeal were the epidemic distemper of the great world? As if all our apparent danger and natural bias lay on the side of a too rigid austerity which required the discreet and constant counteraction of an opposite principle? Would not a stranger be almost tempted to imagine, from the frequent invectives against extreme strictness, that abstraction from the world, and a monastic rage for retreat, were the ruling temper; that we were in some danger in seeing our places of diversion abandoned and the enthusiastic scenes of the holy fathers of the desert acted over again by the frantic and uncontrollable devotion of our young persons of fashion?

It is seriously to be regretted, in an age like the present remarkable for indifference in religion and levity in manners, and which stands so much in need of lively patterns of firm and resolute piety, that many who really are Christians on the soberest conviction should not appear more openly and decidedly on the side they have espoused, that they assimilate so very much with the manners of those about them (which manners they yet scruple not to disapprove) and, instead of an avowed but prudent steadfastness which might draw over the others, appear evidently fearful of being thought precise and overscrupulous and actually seem to disavow their right principles by concessions and accommodations not strictly consistent with them. They often seem cautiously afraid of doing too much, and going too far; and the dangerous plea, the necessity of living like other people, of being like the rest of the world, and the propriety of not being particular, is brought as a reasonable apology for a too yielding and indiscriminate conformity....

Few indeed of the more orderly and decent have any objection to that degree of religion which is compatible with their general acceptance with others, or the full enjoyment of their own pleasures. For a formal and ceremonious exercise of the outward duties of Christianity may not only be kept up without exciting censure, but will even procure a certain respect and confidence, and is not quite irreconcilable with a voluptuous and dissipated life. So far many go, and so far "as godliness is profitable to the life that is," it passes without reproach.

But as soon as people begin to consider religious exercises not as a decency, but a duty; not as a commutation for a self-denying life, but as a means to promote a holy temper and a virtuous conduct; as soon as they feel disposed to carry the effect of their devotion into their daily life; as soon as their principles discover themselves by leading them to withdraw from those scenes and abstain from those actions in which the gay [i.e., carefree or cheerful] place their supreme happiness; as soon as something is to be done, and something is to be parted with, then the world begins to take offense and to stigmatize the activity of that piety which had been commended as long as it remained inoperative and had only evaporated in words.

But when religion, like the vital principle, takes its seat in the heart and sends out supplies of life and heat to every part, diffuses motion, soul, and vigor through the whole circulation, and informs and animates the whole person; when it operates on the practice, influences the conversation, breaks out into a lively zeal for the honor of God, and the best interests of people; then the sincerity or the understanding of that person will become questionable, and it must be owing to a very fortunate combination of circumstances indeed, if he can at once preserve the character of parts and piety.

William Williams,
"O'er those gloomy hills of darkness"[5]

1. O'er those gloomy hills of darkness
   Look my soul, be still and gaze,
All the promises do travel
   On a glorious day of grace,
      Blessed jubil, &c.
      Let thy glorious morning dawn.

2. Let the Indian, let the Negro,
   Let the rude barbarian see
That divine and glorious conquest
   Once obtain'd on Calvary;
      Let the gospel, &c.
      Word resound from pole to pole.

3. Kingdoms wide that sit in darkness,
   Let them have the glorious light,
And from eastern coast to western
   May the morning chase the night,
      And redemption, &c.
      Freely purchas'd win the day.

4. May the glorious days approaching,
   From eternal darkness dawn,
And the everlasting gospel
   Spread abroad thy holy name.
      Thousand years, &c.
      Soon appear, make no delay.

6. Fly abroad, eternal gospel,
   Win and conquer, never cease;
May thy eternal wide dominions
   Multiply, and still increase;
      May thy scepter, &c.
      Sway th'enlight'ned world around.

Samuel Hopkins, "A Dialogue [on Slavery]"[6]

Open thy mouth, judge righteously, and plead the cause of
the poor and needy. (Prov 31:9)

And as ye would that men should do to you, do ye also to
them likewise. (Luke 6:31)

A. All this seems to be little to the purpose, since it was granted
in the beginning of our conversation that the slave trade, as it has
been carried on, is not to be justified. But what is this to the question
we proposed to consider: which is whether it be wrong to hold the
blacks we have among us in a state of slavery or ought to set them
free without delay? To this you have said little or nothing as yet.

B. All I have said upon the slave trade, to show the unrighteousness, the cruelty, the murder, the opposition to Christianity and the
spread of the gospel among the Africans, the destruction of whole
nations and myriads of souls which are contained in this horrid
practice, has been principally with a view to a more clear and satisfactory determination of the question before us, which you have now
renewedly proposed. For I think the following proposition may be
advanced as undeniable, if the slave trade is unjustifiable and wrong:
then our holding the Africans and their children in bondage is
unjustifiable and wrong, and the latter is criminal in some proportion to the inexpressible baseness and criminality of the former. For,

First, if they have been brought into a state of slavery by
unrighteousness and violence, they having never forfeited their liberty or given any one a right to enslave and sell them, then purchas-
ing them of these piratical tyrants, and holding them in the same
state of bondage into which they, contrary to all right, have brought
them, is continuing the exercise of the same unrighteousness and
violence toward them....

Secondly, holding these blacks in a state of slavery is a practical
justification of the slave trade and so brings the guilt of that on the
head of him who so far partakes in this iniquity as to hold one of
these a slave who was unrighteously made so by these sons of violence. The old adage, "The partaker is as bad as the thief," carries such
a plain truth in it that every one must discern it; and it is certainly

applicable to this case....It is not therefore possible for any of our slave keepers to justify themselves in what they are doing, unless they can justify the slave trade. If they fail here, they bring on themselves an awful degree of the guilt of the whole.

Thirdly, by keeping these slaves and buying and selling them, they actually encourage and promote the slave trade. And therefore, in this view, keeping slaves and continuing to buy and sell them is to bring on us the guilt of the slave trade, which is hereby supported. For so long as slaves are bought and possessed and in demand, so long the African trade will be supported and encouraged.

A. But there is a stop put to the importation of slaves into the American colonies, as they have resolved no more shall be bought. This being the case, the keeping those we have among us in slavery is no encouragement to the slave trade.

B. I grant, if this resolution should be perpetual and extend to the West Indies, it would discourage the slave trade, so far as the Americans are concerned in it. But it would be more effectually discountenanced and condemned if slavery was wholly abolished, and it cannot be consistently done without this. For if it be wrong to import and buy them now, it was always wrong; and therefore they that are already slaves among us are injured and unjustly enslaved, and we have made them our slaves without the least right and ought to retract it and repair the injury done to them, so far as is in our power, by setting them free and compensating them otherwise, so far as we are able. There is therefore a palpable inconsistency in resolving to import and buy no more slaves and yet refusing to let those go out free which we have already enslaved, unless there be some insuperable impediment in the way....

A. This reasoning looks something plausible, I confess; but the Holy Scripture approves of making and keeping slaves, and this surely is sufficient to keep us in countenance.

B. I hope you will not appeal to the Holy Scripture in support of a practice which you and every one else must allow to be so inexpressibly unjust, inhumane and cruel as is the slave trade, and consequently so glaringly contrary to the whole tenor of divine revelation. And if the slave trade is such a gross violation of every divine precept, it is impossible to vindicate the slavery to which the Africans have been reduced by this trade from the Holy Scripture. Of this we have such a certainty a priori, that it would be a horrid reproach of divine revelation to pretend this practice can be supported by that, or even to look into it with any hope or expectation of finding any thing there in favor of it....However, I am willing to hear what you can produce from Scripture in favor of any kind of slavery.

A. You know that a curse was pronounced on the posterity of Ham for his wickedness in the following words: A servant of servants shall he be unto his brethren. He could not be a servant unto his brethren unless they made him so, or a least held him in servitude. The curse could not take place unless they executed it, and they seem to be by God appointed to do this. Therefore while we, the children of Japheth, are making such abject slaves of the blacks, the children of Ham, we are only executing the righteous curse denounced upon them, which is so far from being wrong in us that it would be a sin, even disobedience to the revealed will of God, to refuse to make slaves of them and attempt to set them at liberty.

B. Do you think, my good sir, it was the duty of Pharaoh to make the Israelites serve him and the Egyptians, and to afflict them, by ruling over them with rigor, and holding them in hard and cruel bondage because God had expressly foretold this and said it should be done? And was the Assyrian king blameless while he executed the judgments which God had threatened to inflict on his professing people? Did God's threatening them with those evils warrant this king to distress, captivate and destroy them, as he did? And will you say the Jews did right in crucifying our Lord, because by this they fulfilled the Scriptures, declaring that thus it must be? Your argument, if it is of any force, will assert and justify all this, and therefore, I hope, will be renounced by you, and by all who have the least regard to the Holy Scripture, with proper abhorrence.

But if this argument were not so fraught with absurdity and impiety as it really is, and it were granted to be forcible with respect to all upon whom the mentioned curse was denounced, yet it would not justify our enslaving the Africans, for they are not the posterity of Canaan, who was the only son of Ham that was doomed to be a servant of servants. The other sons of Ham and their posterity are no more affected with this curse than the other sons of Noah and their posterity. Therefore this prediction is as much of a warrant for the Africans enslaving us as it is for us to make slaves of them....

A. The people of Israel were allowed by God to buy and make slaves from the nations that were round about them and the strangers that lived among them, which could not have been the case if this was wrong and unjust. And why have not we an equal right to do the same?

B. And why have we not an equal right to invade any nation and land, as they did the land of Canaan, and destroy them all, men, women and children, and beasts, without saving so much as one alive? It was right for the Israelites to do this because they had a divine permission and direction to do it, as the God of Israel had a right to destroy the seven nations of Canaan in what way he thought best and to direct whom he pleased to do it. And it was right for them to make bondservants of the nations round them, they having an express permission to do it from him who has a right to dispose of all people as he pleases. God saw fit, for wise reasons, to allow the people of Israel thus to make and possess slaves; but is this a license to us to enslave any of our fellow humans, any more than their being allowed to kill the seven nations in Canaan is a warrant to us to kill any of our fellow humans whom we please and are able to destroy and take possession of their estates? This must be answered in the negative by every one who will allow himself a moment's reflection....And this law respecting bondage is suited to answer these ends. This distinction is now at an end, and all nations are put upon a level; and Christ, who has taken down the wall of separation, has taught us to look on all nations as our neighbors and brethren without any respect of persons, and to love all persons as ourselves, and do to others as we would they should treat us, by which he has most effectually abolished this permission given to the Jews, as well as many other institutions which were peculiar to them.

Besides, that this permission was not designed for all nations and ages will be very evident if we consider what such a supposition implies; for if this be so, then all other nations had a right to makes slaves of the Jews. The Egyptians had a right to buy and sell them and keep them all in bondage forever. And the nations round about Canaan had a right to bring them into bondage, as they sometimes did. And the Babylonians and Romans had a good warrant to reduce them to a state of captivity and servitude. And the Africans have a good right to make slaves of us and our children. The inhabitants of Great Britain may lawfully make slaves of all the Americans, and transport us to England, and buy and sell us in open market, as they do their cattle and horses, and perpetuate our bondage to the latest generation....If the blacks now among us should by some remarkable providence have the power in their hands to reduce us, they have a right to make us and our children their slaves, and we should have no reason to complain.

This would put people into such a state of perpetual war and confusion, and is so contrary to our loving our neighbor as ourselves, that he who has the least regard for his fellow humans, or the divine law, must reject it, and the principle from which it flows, with the greatest abhorrence. Let no Christian then, plead this permission to the Jews to make bondslaves of their neighbors as a warrant to hold the slaves he has made and consequently for universal slavery.

Jonathan Edwards, "The Duty of Charity to the Poor, Explained and Enforced" (Deut 15:7–12)[7]

Doctrine. It is a most absolute and indispensable duty to give bountifully and willingly for the supply of the wants of the needy.

I have already discussed this doctrine under three propositions and have also applied it in one use of self-examination, and shall now proceed,

To a use of exhortation to this duty. We are professors of Christianity, we pretend to be the followers of Jesus and to make the gospel our rule. We have the Bible in our houses. Let us not behave ourselves in this particular as if we had never seen the Bible, as if we were ignorant of Christianity and knew not what kind of religion it is. What will it signify to pretend to be Christians and at the same time to live in the neglect of the rules of Christianity which are mainly insisted on in it? But there are several things which I would here propose to your consideration.

1. Consider that what you have is not your own; i.e., you have no absolute right to it; you have only a subordinate right. Your goods are only lent to you of God to be improved by you in such ways as he directs you. You yourselves are not your own. "Ye are not your own,

for ye are bought with a price; your body and your spirit are God's" (1 Cor 6:19–20). And if you yourselves are not your own, so then neither are your possessions your own. You have many of you by covenant given up yourselves and all you have to God. You have disowned and renounced any right in yourselves or in any things that you have, and have given God all the absolute right; and if you be true Christians, you have done it from the heart.

Your money and your goods are not your own, they are only committed to you as stewards, to be used for him who committed them to you. "Use hospitality one to another without grudging. As every man hath received the gift, even so minister the same one to another, as good stewards of the manifold grace of God" (1 Pet 4:9–10). A steward has no business with his master's goods to use them any otherwise than for the benefit of his master and his family, or according to his master's direction. He hath no business to use them as if he were the proprietor of them; he has nothing to do with them, only as he is to use them for his master. He is to give every one of his master's family their portion of meat in due season....

2. Consider that God tells us that he shall look upon what is done in charity to our neighbors in want as done unto him, and what is denied unto them as denied unto him. "He that hath pity on the poor lendeth to the Lord" (Prov 19:17). God hath been pleased to make our needy neighbors his receivers. He in his infinite mercy hath so interested himself in their case that he looks upon what is given in charity to them as given to himself; and when we deny them what their circumstances require of us, he looks upon it that we therein rob him of his right.

So Christ teaches that we are to look upon our fellow Christians in this case as himself, and that our giving or withholding from them shall be taken as if we so behaved ourselves toward him (see Matt 25:40). There Christ says to the righteous on his right hand, who had supplied the wants of the needy, "In that ye have done it to one of the least of these my brethren, ye have done it unto me." In like manner he says to the wicked who had not shown mercy to the poor (v. 45), "In as much as ye did it not unto one of the least of these, ye did it not to me." Now what stronger enforcement of this duty can be conceived or is possible than this, that Jesus Christ looks upon our kind and bountiful, or unkind and uncharitable treatment of our needy neighbors as such a treatment of himself?...

3. Consider that there is an absolute necessity of our complying with the difficult duties of religion. To give to the poor in the manner and measure that the gospel prescribes is a difficult duty, i.e., it is very contrary to corrupt nature, to that covetousness and selfishness of which there is so much in the wicked heart of people. We are naturally governed only by a principle of self-love, and it is a difficult thing to corrupt nature, for people to deny themselves of their present interest, trusting in God to make it up to them hereafter.

But how often has Christ told us the necessity of doing difficult duties of religion if we will be his disciples, that we must sell all, take up our cross daily, deny ourselves, renounce our worldly profits and interests, etc. And if this duty seem hard and difficult to you, let not that be an objection with you against doing it, for you have taken up quite a wrong notion of things if you expect to go to heaven without performing difficult duties, if you expect any other than to find the way to life a narrow way.

4. The Scripture teaches us that this very particular duty is necessary...in three ways.

> (1) In that the Scripture teaches that God will deal with us as we deal with our fellow creatures in this particular, and that with what measure we mete to others in this respect, God will measure to us again. This the Scripture asserts both ways; it asserts that if we be of a merciful spirit, God will be merciful to us: "Blessed are the merciful, for they shall obtain mercy" (Matt 5:7). "With the merciful thou wilt show thyself merciful" (Ps 18:25). On the other hand it tells us that if we be not merciful, God will not be merciful to us, and that all our pretenses to faith and a work of conversion will not avail us to obtain mercy unless we be merciful to them that are in want. "For he shall have judgment without mercy, that hath showed no mercy. What doth it profit, my brethren, though a man say he hath faith, and have not works? Can faith save him? If a brother or sister be naked, and destitute of daily food; and one of you say

unto them, Depart in peace, be you warmed, and filled, notwithstanding ye give them not those things which are needful to the body; what doth it profit?" (Jas 2:13–16).

(2) This very thing is often mentioned in Scripture as an essential part of the character of a godly person: "The righteous showeth mercy, and giveth" (Ps 37:21), and again, in verse 26, "He is ever merciful, and lendeth." "A good man showeth favor, and lendeth" (Ps 112:5), and in verse 9, "He hath dispersed, and given to the poor." So, Proverbs 14:31: "He that honoreth God hath mercy on the poor." Again, Proverbs 21:26 and in Isaiah 57:1, a *righteous man*, and a *merciful man* are used as synonymous terms: "The righteous perisheth, and merciful men are taken away," etc....

(3) Another thing whereby the Scripture teaches us the necessity of this duty in order to salvation is that Christ teaches that judgment will be passed at the great day according to one's works in this respect. This is taught us by Christ in the account which he gives us of the day of judgment in Matthew 25, which is the most particular account of the proceedings of that day that we have in the whole Bible (see Matt 25:34, etc.). It is evident that Christ thus represented the proceedings and determinations of this great day as turning upon this one point: on purpose and on design to lead us into this notion and to fix it in us that a charitable spirit and practice toward our brethren is necessary to salvation.

5. Consider what abundant encouragement the word of God gives that you shall be no losers by your charity and bounty to them that are in want. As we have already observed, that there is scarce any duty prescribed in the word of God which is so much insisted on as this, so there is scarce any to which there are so many promises of reward made as to this duty. We could not desire more nor greater promises. This virtue especially has the promises of this life and that which is to come. If we may believe the Scriptures, when a person charitably gives to his neighbor in want, it is the giver that has the

greatest advantage by it, greater than the receiver: "I have showed you all things, how that so laboring ye ought to support the weak, and to remember the words of the Lord Jesus, how he said, It is more blessed to give than to receive" (Acts 20:35). He that gives bountifully is happier than he that receives bountifully and "he that hath mercy on the poor, happy is he" (Prov 14:21).

Many persons are ready to look upon what is bestowed for charitable uses as lost. But we ought not so to esteem it; we ought not to look upon it as lost, because it benefits those to whom it is given, whom we ought to love as ourselves....He that gives to the poor lends to the Lord; and God is not one of those who will not pay again what is lent to him. If you lend anything to God, you commit it into faithful hands. "He that hath pity on the poor lendeth to the Lord, and that which he hath given will he pay him again" (Prov 19:17). God will not only pay you again, but he will pay you with great increase: "Give and it shall be given you, good measure pressed down, and shaken together, and running over" (Luke 6:38).

People do not account that lost that is let out to use, but what is bestowed in charity is lent to the Lord, and he repays with great increase: "The liberal deviseth liberal things, and by liberal things shall he stand" (Isa 32:8). Here I would particularly observe,

(1) That if you give what you give with a spirit of true charity, you shall be rewarded in what is infinitely more valuable than what you give. For parting with a small part of your earthly substance, you shall be rewarded with eternal riches in heaven. "Whosoever shall give to drink unto one of these little ones, a cup of cold water only, in the name of a disciple; verily I say unto you, he shall in no wise lose his reward" (Matt 10:42)....

(2) If you give to the needy only in the exercise of moral virtue, you will not be in the way to lose by it, but greatly to gain in your temporal interest. They that give in the exercise of a gracious charity are in the way to be gainers both here and hereafter, and those that give in the exercise of a moral bounty and liberality have many

temporal promises made to them. We learn by the word of God that they are in the way to be prospered in their outward affairs. Ordinarily such do not lose by it, but such a blessing attends their concerns that they are paid doubly for it: "There is that scattereth, and yet increaseth; there is that withholdeth more than is meet, but it tendeth to poverty. The liberal soul shall be made fat, and he that watereth, shall be watered also himself" (Prov 11:24–25). And "He that giveth to the poor, shall not lack" (Prov 28:27)....

The husbandman does not look upon his seed which he sows in his field to be lost, but is glad that he has opportunity to sow it. It grieves him not that he has land to be sowed, but he rejoices in it. For the like reason should we not be grieved that we find needy people to bestow our charity upon, for this is as much an opportunity to obtain increase as the other....

God has told us that this is the way to have his blessing attending our affairs. Thus, in the text, verse 10: "Thou shalt surely give him, and thine heart shall not be grieved when thou givest unto him; because that for this thing the Lord thy God shall bless thee in all thy works, and in all that thou puttest thine hand unto"; and "He that hath a bountiful eye, shall be blessed" (Prov 22:9). It is a remarkable evidence how little many people realize the things of religion, whatever they pretend—either how little they realize that the Scripture is the word of God, or if it be, that he speaks true; that notwithstanding all the promises made in the Scripture to bounty to the poor, yet they are so backward to this duty and are so afraid to trust God with a little of their estates.

But observation may confirm the same thing which the word of God teaches on this head. It may be observed that God in his providence generally smiles upon and prospers those who are of a liberal, charitable, bountiful spirit. I propose at another time, if God give opportunity, to offer some other motives, to answer some objections that are commonly made against this duty.

Augustus G. Spangenberg, "Of the Occasion of the Brethren's Labor among the Heathen"[8]

§ 25.The congregation of the brethren undertook the service of the gospel among the heathen without having any very extensive views or intentions. They had heard of the laudable endeavors of the Reverend Mr. Egede to bring the natives of Greenland to the knowledge of Christ, but were informed at the same time that the difficulties arising partly from that undertaking itself, and partly from adventitious circumstances, might possibly defeat the purposes of the arduous labors of that worthy man. They were, about the same time, made acquainted with the desire of a negro who, having been baptized at Copenhagen, now ardently wished that his sister, a slave in St. Thomas, might also be instructed in the way of life. The then warden of the congregation at Herrnhut, who had, according to the grace of God given him already in his younger days, made a firm resolution to promote the missions among the heathen to the extent of his abilities, did not fail to recommend the above mentioned objects in the strongest terms.

Upon this God moved the hearts of two brethren to agree together before the Lord, that they would undertake a voyage to St. Thomas in order to acquaint the said slave how she might be saved through faith in Christ Jesus; the Lord likewise made two other brethren willing to go to Greenland. These brethren having, after mature deliberation and hearty prayers to God, obtained sufficient clearness in this matter, mentioned their design and purpose, by letters, to the congregation. However, a whole year elapsed before the congregation came to a resolution to permit these brethren to go to St. Thomas and to Greenland. And thus they had sufficient time to have changed their minds, but they kept to their first resolution. On their setting out, they were commended to the Lord and to the word of his grace, with the assurance that their brethren would thank God, if they should, by their walk and conversation, bring only one or another of their fellow creatures to Christ....

§ 28. Upon this, now one and then another nation of the heathen was recommended to the service of the brethren in the gospel. This called for their attention and made them resolve, on the one hand, never to go to any heathen without a call in which the hand of

God was evident to them, and on the other hand, never to refuse any call among the heathen in which they could perceive the finger of the Lord, though they should see beforehand that such a call might endanger their lives, and be otherwise connected with many things very difficult to human nature; and this is actually their intention to this very hour....

Often have I been astonished at the willingness and desire of the brethren for this service. Having once made known on a prayer day, at Bethlehem in North America, that five persons were departed this life in a very short time at St. Thomas, where the difficulties of our brethren were then very great, not less than eight brethren voluntarily offered themselves on that very day to go thither and replace them. We have certainly cause to thank the Lord our Redeemer alone for this, especially as the service of the gospel among the heathen is no easy matter. We lay it down, therefore, as a maxim, never to persuade, much less to urge anyone to go as a missionary among the heathen....

§ 31. The brethren observed, secondly, that the divisions of Christendom in so many parties made no favorable impression on the heathen. For if they hear one party affirm we are the true church, and whoever would be saved must join with us, and that the second, third and fourth parties maintain the same concerning themselves, then they say, how can we know or judge which party among you is in the right; do you agree first among yourselves. Thus it happened by the grace of our Lord Jesus Christ that the brethren firmly resolved to be neither for nor against this or the other party, but simply to preach Christ. And experience hath shown that our Lord and Savior graciously owned and blessed this method among the heathen.

§ 32. Another hindrance to the preaching of the gospel among the heathen arose in the European planters and merchants from a fear and concern lest it should hurt their commerce if the heathen were made wise and even learned to read and write. Not were the gentlemen in the West Indies without concern less their lives should be endangered, if the negroes, by dint of instruction, should get more understanding. Being once in St. Thomas, one of them said to me, Only consider whether that is proper. If we calculate the number of negroes in this island, we shall always find a hundred of them to one white person. Now if those are made wiser, how can we be safe?...This induced the brethren in their labor among the heathen to lay down the following invariable principles. Namely,

1. In our labor among the heathen, we will particularly endeavor that they become converted to Christ Jesus with all their hearts. This being the case, they not only become wiser but also better; then we shall have no need to fear that the same will occur which happens to people who take in something of the doctrine of Jesus with the head, but whose hearts remain void and destitute of that godliness which is in Christ Jesus; such are indeed bad people. Many years' experience has incontestably confirmed us in these ideas; and we are firmly persuaded that it is not our call to aim anywhere at national conversions or to introduce the Christian religion among whole nations.

2. We will consider it as our duty that our missionaries among the heathen are not to interfere with the commerce between them and the merchants, which ought never to be disturbed by us or any fault of ours. No, we will faithfully inculcate to the heathen who belong to us that they must in their dealings avoid all fraud and deceit (which are otherwise so peculiar to the heathen), and that they shall approve themselves honest and upright in all respects.

3. We will never omit diligently to set before the negro slaves the doctrines which the apostles preached to servants. Servants in those days were almost universally slaves. We will put them in mind that it is not by chance, but it is of God that one person is a master and another a slave, and that therefore they ought to acquiesce with the ways of God; no, that their service, if done with all faithfulness for the sake of Jesus, is looked upon as though they were serving our Lord Jesus Christ. This we have indeed done and, God be praised, with good effect.

4. We will frequently remind the heathen of what Paul said: "Let every soul be subject to the higher powers; for there is no power but of God; the powers that be, are ordained of God."...

§ 35. But what advice can be given the brethren who go among the heathen under such circumstances? The first thing is that they should not be so terrified by the inhuman wickedness prevailing among the heathen as to give up their hopes in laboring among them. For Christ has tasted death for all and he is the propitiation for our sins, and not for ours only, but also for the sins of the whole world. He has shed his blood for the heathen also; they are bought with a price. God spoke by the prophets already in the Old Testament, giving the most precious promises to the heathen, that they should be joint heirs of his kingdom....We ourselves have frequently seen in our days, according to the grace of God that was with us, some of the most impious heathen that were really an abomination become dear children of God. For the gospel is the power of God unto salvation to all them that believe. A witness of the truth, therefore, and of the gospel, who has been called by Jesus Christ to labor among the heathen, can, and should indeed, begin his work with pleasure; he surely will not labor in vain. For God will have all people to be saved, and to come unto the knowledge of the truth....

§ 37....For the conversion of the heathen is the work of God. He delivers them from the power of darkness and translates them into the kingdom of his dear Son. Wherever the brethren find an entrance with the gospel among the heathen, there they are by God's grace already prepared to receive it. Hence we have instances that heathen have prayed to God to send them one that might show them the way of life, and when a brother came and preached the gospel to them, they considered it as a proof that their prayers were heard, and became obedient to it with joy....

§ 39. As the brethren prefer going to those heathen who never before had any missionaries among them,...they consequently meet with more difficulties than usual in learning their language. For among those heathen who know nothing of reading or writing, one cannot meet with any books or writings which might help to make the learning of a language easy. They are obliged therefore to show this and the other thing to the heathen if they want to speak with them, to observe well the name that they hear and write it down and thus become acquainted with it. Reducing, in process of time, all this into alphabetical order, it forms a little dictionary. And when they have properly noted down the words which belong to the connection of speech, and which denote this or that action, they then form, perhaps, a little grammar of that language. By and by they perceive that the heathen want words to express this or the other thing with which they are either not acquainted or have never before thought of. They then furnish them with new words, or else the heathen perhaps invent some.

All this is a tedious affair, but not without its usefulness. As long as the brethren cannot yet speak, they teach by example. The heathen look at them while at work, and get an impression of them as of a good and outwardly useful people; whereas in general they have not the best impression of the Christians, which may perhaps be the fault of many people who trade with them.

Now the heathen, finding that the brethren seek not their own but the good of their souls, this removes an apprehension which easily arises in them when they have to do with Europeans. That the brethren occasionally yield them, according to Christian love, various little services, is so far right. Only they must beware of giving the smallest occasion to a surmise, as though they wanted to bring the heathen over to their way of thinking by dint of presents. For that would be attended with evil consequences. The time of waiting serves meanwhile this good purpose, that the brethren may watch in silence (which is very necessary) to see whether there be here or there a person whom God himself is preparing, by his grace, to hear and receive a word concerning Christ Jesus and of our salvation in him.

Olaudah Equiano, ["Challenge of Living a Consistent Christian Life"][9]

When our ship was got ready for sea again, I was entreated by the captain to go in her once more, but, as I felt myself now as happy as I could wish to be in this life, I for some time refused; however, the advice of my friends at last prevailed, and, in full resignation to the will of God, I again embarked for Cadiz in March 1775. We had a very good passage, without any material accident, until we arrived off the Bay of Cadiz, when one Sunday, just as we were going into the harbor, the ship struck against a rock and knocked off a garboard plank, which is the next to the keel. In an instant all hands were in the greatest confusion and began with loud cries to call on God to have mercy on them. Although I could not swim and saw no way of escaping death, I felt no dread in my then situation, having no desire to live. I even rejoiced in spirit, thinking this death would be sudden glory. But the fullness of time was not yet come. The people near to me were much astonished in seeing me thus calm and resigned, but I told them of the peace of God, which through sovereign grace I enjoyed....

At this time there were many large Spanish srukers (i.e., passage vessels) full of people crossing the channel who, seeing our condition, a number of them came alongside of us. As many hands as could be employed began to work, some at our three pumps and the rest unloading the ship as fast as possible. There being only a single rock called the Porpus on which we struck, we soon got off it, and providentially it was then high water; we therefore run the ship ashore at the nearest place to keep her from sinking. After many tides, with a great deal of care and industry, we got her repaired again. When we had dispatched our business at Cadiz, we went to Gibraltar and from thence to Malaga, a very pleasant and rich city where there is one of the finest cathedrals I had ever seen. It had been above fifty years in building, as I heard, though it was not then quite finished; great parts of the inside, however, was completed and highly decorated with the richest marble columns and many superb paintings; it was lighted occasionally by an amazing number of wax tapers of different sizes, some of which were as thick as a man's thigh; these, however, were only used on some of their grand festivals.

I was very much shocked at the custom of bull baiting, and other diversions which prevailed here on Sunday evenings, to the great scandal of Christianity and morals. I used to express my abhorrence of it to a priest whom I met with. I had frequent contests about religion with the reverend father, in which he took great pains to make a proselyte of me to his church, and I no less to convert him to mine. On these occasions I used to produce my Bible, and show him in what points his church erred. He then said he had been in England, and that every person there read the Bible, which was very wrong; but I answered him that Christ desired us to search the Scriptures. In his zeal for my conversion, he solicited me to go to one of the universities in Spain, and declared that I should have my education free; and told me, if I got myself made a priest, I might in time become even pope, and that Pope Benedict was a black man. As I was ever desirous of learning, I paused for some time upon this temptation, and thought by being crafty I might catch some with guile, but I began to think that it would be only hypocrisy in me to embrace his offer, as I could not in conscience conform to the opinions of his church. I was therefore enabled to regard the word of God, which says, "Come out from amongst them," and refused Father Vincent's offer. So we parted without conviction on either side.

Having taken at this place some fine wines, fruits, and money, we proceeded to Cadiz, where we took about two tons more of money, etc., and then sailed for England in the month of June. When we were about the north latitude 42, we had contrary wind for several days, and the ship did not make in that time above six or seven miles strait course. This made the captain exceeding fretful and peevish; and I was very sorry to hear God's most holy name often blasphemed by him. One day, as he was in that impious mood, a young gentleman on board, who was a passenger, reproached him, and said he acted wrong; for we ought to be thankful to God for all things, as we were not in want of anything on board; and though the wind was contrary for us, yet it was fair for some others, who, perhaps, stood in more need of it than we. I immediately seconded this young gentleman with some boldness, and said we had not the least cause to murmur, for that the Lord was better to us than we deserved, and that he had done all things well. I expected that the captain would be very angry with me for speaking, but he replied not a word. However, before that time on the following day, being the 21st of June, much to our great joy and astonishment, we saw the providential hand of our benign Creator, whose ways with his blind creatures are past finding out....

We embarked in the month of November 1776, on board of the sloop Morning Star, Captain David Miller, and sailed for Jamaica. In our passage, I took all the pains that I could to instruct the Indian prince in the doctrines of Christianity, of which he was entirely ignorant; and, to my great joy, he was quite attentive, and received with gladness the truths that the Lord enabled me to set forth to him. I taught him in the compass of eleven days all the letters, and he could put even two or three of them together and spell them. I had Fox's *Martyrology* with cuts, and he used to be very fond of looking into it, and would ask many questions about the papal cruelties he saw depicted there, which I explained to him. I made such progress with this youth, especially in religion, that when I used to go to bed at different hours of the night, if he was in his bed, he would get up on purpose to go to prayer with me, without any other clothes than his shirt; and before he would eat any of his meals amongst the gentlemen in the cabin, he would first come to me to pray as he called it. I was well pleased at this, and took great delight in him, and used much supplication to God for his conversion. I was in full hope of seeing daily every appearance of that change which I could wish, not knowing the devices of Satan, who had many of his emissaries to sow his tares as fast as I sowed the good seed, and pull down as fast as I built up. Thus we went on nearly four-fifths of our passage, when Satan at last got the upper hand. Some of his messengers, seeing this poor heathen much advanced in piety, began to ask him whether I had converted him to Christianity, laughed and made their jest at him, for which I rebuked them as much as I could; but this treatment caused the prince to halt between two opinions. Some of the true sons of Belial, who did not believe that there was any hereafter, told him never to fear the devil, for there was none existing; and if ever he came to the prince, they desired he might be sent to them. Thus they teased the poor innocent youth, so that he would not learn his book any more! He would not drink nor carouse with these ungodly actors, nor would he be with me, even at prayers. This grieved me very much. I endeavored to persuade him as well as I could, but he would not come; and entreated him very much to tell me his reasons for acting thus. At last he asked me, "How comes it that all the white men on board who can read and write, and observe the fun, and know all things, yet swear, lie, and get drunk, only excepting yourself?" I answered him, the reason was that they did not fear God, and that if any one of them died, so they could not go to or be happy with God. He replied that if these persons went to hell he would go to hell too. I was sorry to hear this, and as he sometimes had the toothache, and also some other persons in the ship at the same time, I asked him if their toothache made his easy; he said no. Then I told him if he and these people went to hell together, their pains would not make his any lighter. This answer had great weight with him; it depressed his spirits much, and he became ever after, during the passage, fond of being alone....On the fifth of January we made Antigua and Montserrat, and ran along the rest of the islands, and on the fourteenth we arrived at Jamaica. One Sunday while we were there I took the Musquito Prince George to church, where he saw the sacrament administered. When we came out we saw all kinds of people, almost from the church door for the space of half a mile down to the waterside, buying and selling all kinds of commodities, and these acts afforded me great matter of exhortation to this youth, who was much astonished. Our vessel being ready to sail for the Musquito shore, I went with the doctor on board, a Guinea man, to purchase some slaves to carry with us, and cultivate a plantation; and I chose them all my own countrymen. On the twelfth of February we sailed from Jamaica, and on the eighteenth arrived at the Musquito shore, at a place called Dupeupy. All our Indian guests now, after I had admonished them and a few cases of liquor given them by the doctor, took an affectionate leave of us, and went ashore, where they were met by the Musquito king, and we never saw one of them afterward. We then sailed to the southward of the shore, to a place called Cape Gracias a Dios, where there was a large lagoon or lake, which received the emptying of two or three very fine large rivers, and abounded much in fish and land tortoise. Some of the native Indians came on board of us here, and we used them well, and told them we were come to dwell amongst them, which they seemed pleased at. So the doctor and I, with some others, went with them ashore, and they took us to different places to view the land, in order to choose a place to make a plantation of. We fixed on a spot near a river's bank, in a rich soil, and having got our necessaries out of the sloop, we began to clear away the woods and plant different kinds of vegetables, which had a quick growth. While we were employed in this manner, our vessel went northward to Black River to trade....The women generally cultivate the ground, and the men are all fishermen and canoe makers. Upon the whole, I never met any nation that were so simple in their manners as these people, or had so little ornament in their houses. Neither had they, as I ever could learn, one word expressive of an oath. The worst word I ever heard amongst them when they were quarreling, was one that they had got from the English, which was "you rascal." I never saw any mode of worship among them, but in this they were not worse than their

European brethren or neighbors, for I am sorry to say that there was not one white person in our dwelling, nor anywhere else, that I saw, in different places I was at on the shore, that was better or more pious than those unenlightened Indians; but they either worked or slept on Sundays and, to my sorrow, working was too much Sunday's employment with ourselves, so much so that in some length of time we really did not know one day from another.

William Carey, "The Practicality of Something Being Done"[10]

The impediments in the way of carrying the gospel among the heathen must arise, I think, from one or other of the following things: either their distance from us, their barbarous and savage manner of living, the danger of being killed by them, the difficulty of procuring the necessaries of life, or the unintelligibleness of their languages.

First, as to their distance from us, whatever objections might have been made on that account before the invention of the mariner's compass, nothing can be alleged for it with any color of plausibility in the present age. People can now sail with as much certainty through the Great South Sea as they can through the Mediterranean, or any lesser sea. Yes, and providence seems in a manner to invite us to the trial, as there are to our knowledge trading companies whose commerce lies in many of the places where these barbarians dwell. At one time or other ships are sent to visit places of more recent discovery, and to explore parts the most unknown, and every fresh account of their ignorance, or cruelty, should call forth our pity, and excite us to concur with providence in seeking their eternal good. Scripture likewise seems to point out this method: "Surely the isles shall wait for me; the ships of Tarshish first, to bring my sons from far, their silver, and their gold with them, unto the name of the Lord, thy God" (Isa 60:9). This seems to imply that in the time of the glorious increase of the church, in the latter days (of which the whole chapter is undoubtedly a prophecy), commerce shall subserve the spread of the gospel. The ships of Tarshish were trading vessels which made voyages for traffic to various parts; thus much therefore must be meant by it, that navigation, especially that which is commercial, shall be one great mean of carrying on the work of God, and perhaps it may imply that there shall be a very considerable appropriation of wealth to that purpose.

Secondly, as to their uncivilized and barbarous way of living, this can be no objection to any, except those whose love of ease renders them unwilling to expose themselves to inconveniences for the good of others.

It was no objection to the apostles and their successors, who went among the barbarous Germans and Gauls, and still more barbarous Britons! They did not wait for the ancient inhabitants of these countries to be civilized before they could be Christianized, but went simply with the doctrine of the cross, and Tertullian could boast that "those parts of Britain which were proof against the Roman armies were conquered by the gospel of Christ." It was no objection to an Elliot, or a Brainerd,* in later times. They went forth, and encountered every difficulty of the kind, and found that a cordial reception of the gospel produced those happy effects which the longest intercourse with Europeans without it could never accomplish. It is no objection to commercial men. It only requires that we should have as much love to the souls of our fellow creatures, and fellow sinners, as they have for the profits arising from a few otter skins, and all these difficulties would be easily surmounted.

After all, the uncivilized state of the heathen, instead of affording an objection against preaching the gospel to them, ought to furnish an argument for it. Can we as people, or as Christians, hear that a great part of our fellow creatures, whose souls are as immortal as ours, and who are as capable as ourselves of adorning the gospel, and contributing by their preaching, writings, or practices to the glory of our Redeemer's name, and the good of his church, are enveloped in ignorance and barbarism? Can we hear that they are without the gospel, without government, without laws, and without arts, and sciences, and not exert ourselves to introduce amongst them the sentiments of people, and of Christians? Would not the spread of the gospel be the most effectual mean of their civilization? Would not that make them useful members of society? We know that such

---

*John Elliot (1604–1690) and David Brainerd (1718–1747) were missionaries to the Native Americans.

effects did in a measure follow the aforementioned efforts of Elliot, Brainerd, and others amongst the American Indians, and if similar attempts were made in other parts of the world, and succeeded with a divine blessing (which we have every reason to think they would), might we not expect to see able divines, or read well conducted treatises in defense of the truth, even amongst those who at present seem to be scarcely human?

Thirdly, in respect to the danger of being killed by them, it is true that whoever does go must put his life in his hand, and not consult with flesh and blood; but do not the goodness of the cause, the duties incumbent on us as the creatures of God, and Christians, and the perishing state of our fellow humans loudly call upon us to venture all, and use every warrantable exertion for their benefit? Paul and Barnabas, who hazarded their lives for the name of our Lord Jesus Christ, were not blamed as being rash, but commended for so doing, while John Mark, who through timidity of mind deserted them in their perilous undertaking, was branded with censure. After all, as has been already observed, I greatly question whether most of the barbarities practiced by the savages upon those who have visited them have not originated in some real or supposed affront, and were therefore, more properly, acts of self-defense than proofs of ferocious dispositions. No wonder if the imprudence of sailors should prompt them to offend the simple savage, and the offence be resented; but Elliot, Brainerd, and the Moravian missionaries have been very seldom molested. No, in general the heathen have showed a willingness to hear the word, and have principally expressed their hatred of Christianity on account of the vices of nominal Christians.

Fourthly, as to the difficulty of procuring the necessaries of life, this would not be so great as may appear at first sight, for though we could not procure European food, yet we might procure such as the natives of those countries which we visit subsist upon themselves. And this would only be passing through what we have virtually engaged in by entering on the ministerial office. A Christian minister is a person who in a peculiar sense is not his own; he is the servant of God, and therefore ought to be wholly devoted to him. By entering on that sacred office he solemnly undertakes to be always engaged, as much as possible, in the Lord's work, and not to choose his own pleasure, or employment, or pursue the ministry as a something that is to subserve his own ends, or interests, or as a kind of bye work. He engages to go where God pleases, and to do, or endure what he sees fit to command, or call him to, in the exercise of his function. He virtually bids farewell to friends, pleasures, and comforts, and stands in readiness to endure the greatest sufferings in the work of his Lord and Master....

Fifthly, as to learning their languages, the same means would be found necessary here as in trade between different nations. In some cases interpreters might be obtained who might be employed for a time, and where these were not to be found, the missionaries must have patience, and mingle with the people, till they have learned so much of their language as to be able to communicate their ideas to them in it. It is well-known to require no very extraordinary talents to learn, in the space of a year, or two at most, the language of any people upon earth, so much of it at least as to be able to convey any sentiments we wish to their understandings....

John Newton, Letter to a Wife, While Resident at Olney, May 20, 1770[11]

I have had a morning walk, in which I was favored with some liberty; at such seasons you are always remembered. While I would praise God that we have been so long and so comfortably spared to each other, I must not forget that an hour of separation must come, and that the time is uncertain. It must be so, and it is well. Surely we could not wish to live always here! Oh for a clearer view of our interest in the love and all-sufficiency of the Savior, that we may stay our souls upon him, and possess a stable, unshaken peace! It is He who has given us a desire to seek him, because He has purposed to be found of us (Jer 31:3). And though our desires are too faint, and disproportionate, to the greatness of their object, he will not despise the day of small things, nor quench the smoking flax.

I feel your absence, and long for your return, but I am not disconsolate. It was otherwise with me once. I can remember when the sun seemed to shine in vain, and the whole creation appeared as a blank if you were from me. Not that I love you less. The intercourse of many successive years has endeared you, more and more, to my heart. But I hope the Lord has weakened that idolatrous disposition for which I have so often deserved to lose you. I am astonished at his patience and forbearance, that when I presumptuously gave you that place in my heart which was only due to him, He did not tear my idol from me! To what dangers has my ill-conducted regard often exposed you! But he is God and not man. I hope it is now my desire to hold nothing in competition with him, and to entrust my all to his keeping and disposal. If we hold each other in a proper submission and subordination to him, he will bless us, and make us mutually comforts and helpmates. He will sanctify the bitter of life, and give the sweet a double sweetness. His blessing is the one thing needful; without it, there is neither security for what we possess, nor true satisfaction in the possession. We have no good in or of ourselves, or which we can impart to another. We may pity, but we cannot relieve each other, when in trouble. We cannot remove one pain, or give one moment's peace of mind, to those whom we best love.

Many prayers are and will be put up for you and Mrs. U while you are away. It is this [that] endears Olney to me. The Lord has a praying people here, and they pray for us. To be interested in the simple, affectionate, and earnest prayers of such a people is a privilege of more value than the wealth of kings. In answer to their prayers, the Lord has placed a hedge about all our concerns, blessed our going out and coming in, and preserved us and ours in health, when sickness or death have been in almost every house around us. And, doubtless, I am much indebted to their prayers, that with such a heart as mine, and such a frame of spirit as I frequently mourn under, I am still favored with some liberty, acceptance, and usefulness, in my ministry.

John Newton, Letter to a Wife, Clapham, July 2, 1772[12]

If it was not to my dearest M. I could not write so soon after dinner. But though my belly is full, and my head empty, I must tell you that I had very quiet, agreeable company in the coach, and a pleasant ride to Deptford, where I mounted a horse my dear Mr. T had sent for me, which said horse brought me safely hither. Thus the Lord graciously preserves me, from place to place.

I am always a little awkward without you, and every room where you are not present looks unfurnished. It is not a humble servant who says this, but a husband, and he says it, not in what is called the honeymoon, but in the twenty-third year after marriage. Nor do I speak it to my own praise, but to the praise of our good Lord, who, by his blessing, has endeared us to each other. Inconstancy and vanity are inherent in our fallen nature, and if left to ourselves, we might have been indifferent, weary, and disgusted, long ago. But he has united our hearts, and, I trust, the union shall subsist to eternity. May we possess, while here, the peace which passes understanding, and live under the abiding expectation of perfect happiness hereafter.

William Wilberforce, ["Vital Christianity Stresses the Importance of Morality"][13]

Thus also in the case before us society consists of a number of different circles of various magnitudes and uses, and that circumstance, wherein the principle of patriotism chiefly consists, whereby the duty of patriotism is best practiced, and the happiest effects to the general weal produced, is that it should be the desire and aim of every individual to fill well his own proper circle, as a part and member of the whole, with a view to the production of general happiness. This our Savior enjoined when he prescribed the duty of universal love, which is but another term for the most exalted patriotism. Benevolence, indeed, when not originating from religion, dispenses but from a scanty and precarious fund; and therefore, if it be liberal in the case of some objects, it is generally found to be contracted toward others. People who, acting from worldly principles, make the greatest stir about general philanthropy or zealous patriotism, are often very deficient in their conduct in domestic life, and very neglectful of the opportunities, fully within their reach, of promoting the comfort of those with whom they are immediately connected. But true Christian benevolence is always occupied in producing happiness to the utmost of its power, and according to the extent of its sphere, be it larger or more limited; it contracts itself to the measure of the smallest; it can expand itself to the amplitude of the largest. It resembles majestic rivers, which are poured from an unfailing and abundant source. Silent and peaceful in their outset, they begin with dispensing beauty and comfort to every cottage by which they pass. In their further progress they fertilize provinces and enrich kingdoms. At length they pour themselves into the ocean, where, changing their names but not their nature, they visit distant nations and other hemispheres, and spread throughout the world the expansive tide of their beneficence....

But, more than all this, it has not perhaps been enough remarked that true Christianity, from her essential nature, appears peculiarly and powerfully adapted to promote the preservation and healthfulness of political communities. What is in truth their grand malady? The answer is short: selfishness. This is that young disease received at the moment of their birth, "which grows with their growth, and strengthens with their strength," and through which they at length expire, if not cut off prematurely by some external shock or intestine convulsion.

The disease of selfishness, indeed, assumes different forms in the different classes of society. In the great and the wealthy, it displays itself in luxury, in pomp and parade, and in all the frivolities of a sickly and depraved imagination which seeks in vain its own gratification, and is dead to the generous and energetic pursuits of an enlarged heart. In the lower orders, when not motionless under the weight of a superincumbent despotism, it manifests itself in pride, and its natural offspring, insubordination in all its modes. But though the external effects may vary, the internal principle is the same: a disposition in each individual to make self the grand center and end of his desires and enjoyments; to overrate his own merits and importance, and of course to magnify his claims on others, and in return to under rate theirs on him; a disposition to undervalue the advantages, and overstate the disadvantages, of his condition in life. Thence spring rapacity and venality and sensuality. Thence imperious nobles, and factious leaders, and an unruly commonalty, bearing with difficulty the inconveniences of a lower station, and imputing to the nature or administration of their government the evils which necessarily flow from the very constitution of our species, or which perhaps are chiefly the result of their own vices and follies. The opposite to selfishness is public spirit, which may be termed, not unjustly, the grand principle of political vitality, the very life's breath of states, which tends to keep them active and vigorous, and to carry them to greatness and glory....

To provide, however, for the continuance of a state by the admission of internal dissensions, or even by the chilling influence of poverty, seems to be in some sort sacrificing the end to the means. Happiness is the end for which people unite in civil society, but in societies thus constituted, little happiness, comparatively speaking, is to be found. The expedient, again, of preserving a state by the spirit of conquest...is not to be tolerated for a moment, when considered on the principles of universal justice. Such a state lives, and grows, and thrives, by the misery of others, and becomes professedly the general enemy of its neighbors, and the scourge of the human race. All these devices are in truth but too much like the fabrications of people, when compared with the works of the Supreme Being: clumsy, yet weak in the execution of their purpose, and full of contradictory principles and jarring movements....Humility is one of the essential qualities which her precepts most directly and strongly enjoin, and which all her various doctrines tend to call forth and cultivate; and humility, as has been before suggested, lays the deepest and surest grounds for benevolence. In whatever class or order of society Christianity prevails, she sets herself to rectify the particular faults, or if we would speak more distinctly, to counteract the particular mode of selfishness to which that class is liable. Affluence she teaches to be liberal and beneficent; authority, to bear its faculties with meekness, and to consider the various cares and obligations belonging to its elevated station, as being conditions on which that station is conferred. Thus, softening the glare of wealth, and moderating the insolence of power, she renders the inequalities of the social state less galling to the lower orders, who also she instructs, in their turn, to be diligent, humble, patient, reminding them that their more lowly path has been allotted to them by the hand of God; that it is their part faithfully to discharge its duties, and contentedly to bear its inconveniences; that the present state of things is very short; that the objects about which worldly people conflict so eagerly are not worth the contest; that the peace of mind which religion offers to all ranks indiscriminately, affords more true satisfaction than all the expensive pleasures which are beyond the poor person's reach; that in this view, however, the poor have the advantage, and that if their superiors enjoy more abundant comforts, they are also exposed to many temptations from which the inferior classes are happily exempted; that "having food and raiment, they should be therewith content," for that their situation in life, with all its evils, is better than they have deserved at the hand of God; finally, that all human distinctions will soon be done away, and the true followers of Christ will all, as children of the same Father, be alike admitted to the possession of the same heavenly inheritance. Such are the blessed effects of Christianity on the temporal well-being of political communities.

But the Christianity which can produce effects like these must be real, not nominal; deep, not superficial. Such then is the religion we should cultivate, if we would realize these pleasing speculations, and arrest the progress of political decay. But in the present circumstances of this country, it is a farther reason for endeavoring to cultivate this vital Christianity, still considering its effects merely in a political view, that, according to all human appearance, we must either have this or none; unless the prevalence of this be in some degree restored, we are likely, not only to lose all the advantages which we might have derived from true Christianity, but to incur all the manifold evils which would result from the absence of all religion.

In the first place, let it be remarked that a weakly principle of religion, and even such an one in a political view, is productive of many advantages, though its existence may be prolonged if all external circumstances favor its continuance, can hardly be kept alive when the state of things is so unfavorable to vital religion as it must be confessed to be in our condition of society. Nor is it merely the ordinary effects of a state of wealth and prosperity to which we here allude. Much also may justly be apprehended from that change which has taken place in our general habits of thinking and feeling, concerning the systems and opinions of former times. At a less advanced period of society, indeed, the religion of the state will be generally accepted, though it be not felt in its vital power. It was the religion of our forefathers; with the bulk it is on that account entitled to reverence, and its authority is admitted without question. The establishment in which it subsists pleads the same prescription, and obtains the same respect. But in our days, things are very differently circumstanced. Not merely the blind prejudice in favor of former times, but even the proper respect for them, and the reasonable presumption in their favor, has abated. Still less will the idea be endured of any system being kept up, when the imposture is seen through by the higher orders, for the sake of retaining the common people in subjection. A system, if not supported by a real persuasion of its truth, will fall to the ground. Thus it not infrequently happens that in a more advanced state of society, a religious establishment must be indebted for its support to that very religion which in earlier times it fostered and protected, as the weakness of some aged mother is sustained, and her existence lengthened, by the tender assiduities of the child whom she had reared in the helplessness of infancy. So in the present instance, unless there be reinfused into the mass of our society something of that principle which animated our ecclesiastical system in its earlier days, it is vain for us to hope that the establishment will very long continue, for the anomaly will not much longer be borne of an establishment, the actual principles of the bulk of whose members, and even teachers, are so extremely different from those which it professes. But in proportion as vital Christianity can be revived, in that same proportion the church establishment is strengthened; for the revival of vital Christianity is the very reinfusion of which we have been speaking. This is the very Christianity on which our establishment is founded, and that which her articles, and homilies, and liturgy, teach throughout....

Let true Christians then, with becoming earnestness, strive in all things to recommend their profession, and to put to silence the vain scoffs of ignorant objectors. Let them boldly assert the cause of

Christ in an age when so many who bear the name of Christians, are ashamed of him; and let them consider as devolved on them the important duty of suspending for a while the fall of their country and, perhaps, of performing a still more extensive service to society at large, not by busy interference in politics, in which it cannot but be confessed there is much uncertainty, but rather by that sure and radical benefit of restoring the influence of religion, and of raising the standard of morality.

Samuel Pearce, Letter to the Lascars[14]

Lascars! [Late autumn, 1798]

You are far from home, and in a country of strangers. Most of the Europeans you have been accustomed to observe have perhaps discovered a desire for nothing but gain, or honor, or personal indulgence. But you know not all. In this strange land there are many who think of you, weep over you, and pray to the great Allah for you. Their hearts are filled with the most affectionate concern for your happiness. Some have observed, and others have inquired after your manner of life. And they are grieved to find that your bodies, and the pursuits of this world, engage all your attention. They consider that you have immortal souls within you, and they send you this paper to beseech you to consider it with seriousness. Consider that this life is the passage to another, and that while you are unconcerned about eternity, you cannot be prepared for it. You profess to believe that there is a God who made you and all things. God has not made all things alike. Some creatures have no capacity for attaining the knowledge of God, as the beasts, birds, and fishes. And as they cannot know God nor his will, so there is no good nor evil in their doings. But you who are made capable of this great attainment, you who must live forever, are accountable for all your actions. God hears everything you say and sees everything you do. God knows all your thoughts, and desires, and purposes, and he will call you to an account for all at the great day when he shall judge the world in righteousness.

Were you ever concerned to know what you must do to please God? Did you ever consider that, as he gives you your life and all its comforts, you ought therefore to praise him? That, as you are constantly dependent upon him for all things, you ought to pray to him; and that as he is altogether good and holy, you ought supremely to love him and delight in him. Surely, if you have never thought upon these things before, it is now high time to begin, lest you should die in your sins, and God at last should say, concerning each of you, "Here is a vile ungrateful Lascar, whom I made, and fed, and clothed, and preserved all the days of his life; but he never thought upon me, never praised me, never loved me. Cast him into hell forever!"…

What then will you do? O, dear Lascars! we send you glad tidings of great joy. The God whom we have offended has taken pity on us, and in his love and mercy, has raised up an all-sufficient Savior; a Savior fit for us, and fit for you; able to save us both to the uttermost; to restore us to the enjoyment of God, from whom we have wandered, to fill us with a sense of his love in life, to comfort us when we are sinking in death, and to raise us to the enjoyment of immortal blessedness.

In communicating these glad tidings to you, we do not deceive you with the words of human invention. We have the authority of the great God himself for what we say, and the experience of our own hearts assures us of its truth. Once indeed we were all like you, ignorant of our guilty and dangerous state. We thought only about being happy in this world. But the more we strove to be so, the more wretched we became. Till at length, it pleased God to teach us the danger of dying as we were, and the folly of delaying, for a single moment, to search if salvation might be obtained. Our hearts were filled with fear, and we put the same question to ourselves which we have now put to you. What must we do to be saved? Then we fell down before God, and confessed that we were rebellious sinners who had deserved his everlasting anger; and that, if he punished us forever, he would do us no wrong. We earnestly entreated him for his mercy, and besought him to show to us some way of salvation. Behold he was graciously entreated of us. He sent his word, and healed us. He made known to us the way of peace; and, dispelling fear from our hearts, filled them with consolation and joy....

Hear then, Lascars! the heavenly message. "God so loved the world, that he gave his only begotten Son, that whosoever believeth in him might not perish, but have everlasting life" (John 3:16). The great Gift of God to us, and for us, is Jesus Christ. You perhaps have been taught that this Jesus was only a prophet, like Moses, and could do no more for you. But you have been misled. The Jewish prophets who came before him most plainly foretold that he was to be a divine Savior, and his disciples, who were taught from his own lips, went about the world, declaring that they had found him of whom Moses in the law and the prophets had written, even Jesus of Nazareth, who they affirmed, as to his natural descent, came from the stock of Abraham, but who was also "God over all, blessed forever" (Rom 9:5). And all who heartily received their report found, as we also have, deliverance, and peace, and joy, by believing on his name.

You allow that Jesus was God's prophet. Now he said that he and the Father were one, so that they who honored the Son did honor the Father also. But the prophets of God do not lie, and therefore we adore him as the Son of God.

This blessed Savior, for the great love that he bore to us poor sinners, from before the foundation of the world, at length clothed himself in our nature, and became bone of our bone and flesh of our flesh. For he was born of a virgin, in whose womb he was formed by the power of God, on which account he was free from all sin in his nature. And when he grew up to manhood, although many who were his enemies, because he preached so faithfully against their wicked practices, continually watched him to find some evil of which they might accuse him, yet they could find none. For the first thirty years of his life, he lived mostly in obscurity, but at length he made a more public appearance. Twice did the Holy Father give notice of his dignity by proclaiming from heaven, "This is my beloved Son, in whom I am well pleased; hear ye him" (Matt 17:5; 3:17). Then he went forth in his omnipotent goodness. He raised people to life from death and the grave, and daily employed himself in healing all manner of sickness and diseases among the people, without a single failure. This he did in the sight of all ranks of people, for three years together. And when the fame of his miracles drew the people around him, his heart being filled with compassion and tender love to them, he faithfully told them of their sins, seriously warned them of their danger, exhorted them to repent, and affectionately invited them to come to him for salvation, promising them the remission of their sins, and the gift of everlasting life.

But the remission of our sins cost him most grievous sufferings, for nothing besides his precious blood was sufficient for our redemption. Yet so much was his heart set upon our salvation that he was content to undergo the severest torments and to die the most shameful and cruel death, rather than we should be lost forever.

This, Lascars, this is the blessed news! These are the glad tidings of great joy which must be preached to all people, and which the God of heaven, by our means, now sends to you. Jesus was crucified for us. He died that we may live. He suffered that we may be happy....

Jesus shed his blood for the Jews, and there were thousands of the posterity of Abraham who believed in his name, and loved him till they died. Jesus died for Gentiles too. He died for us, and since we knew his love, our hearts have been drawn to love him in return. Jesus died for Lascars! Jesus suffered unnumbered tortures for Lascars! O Lascars, have you no love to Jesus? Long indeed you have remained ignorant of our dear Savior; but now God has made sailors of you, and sent you to England, that you might no longer be unacquainted with Jesus. O, how great the privilege that you hear his blessed name, and are taught the truths of his great salvation before you die. Lascars! receive into your hearts this word of life. Give thanks to God that you are not suffered to perish for want of a Savior. Put your trust in the Almighty Jesus, and yield yourselves to him as living sacrifices. Then shall you have the witness in yourselves that he is the Son of God, for you will find such peace, such joy, such delight in God, such desires after purity, such love to our Savior and to all who love him too, of every country and of every color, as will assure your hearts more strongly than all the force of arguments that the religion of Jesus came from heaven, and that it leads thither every soul who sincerely embraces it.

Consider, dear Lascars! this Jesus, though he died, yet he arose again to life on the third day, after which he ascended up into heaven, to dwell with his Father, and to govern the world, until he shall come the second time to judge all people, and fix their states for ever, when it will be found that those who have believed on him, and owned him before all people, shall be eternally saved, but those who persist in disbelieving on his name shall be everlastingly condemned.

Lascars! believe in the Lord Jesus Christ, and you shall be saved!

NOTES

INTRODUCTION

1. For a helpful overview of the eighteenth-century context, see Mark A. Noll, *Rise of Evangelicalism: The Age of Edwards, Whitefield and the Wesleys* (Downers Grove, IL: InterVarsity Press, 2003), esp. 27–49; and David Hempton, *The Church in the Long Eighteenth Century* (London: I. B. Tauris, 2011), esp. 3–33; and W. R. Ward, *Early Evangelicalism: A Global Intellectual History, 1670–1789* (Cambridge: Cambridge University Press, 2006), esp. 6–23.

2. David W. Bebbington, *Evangelicalism in Modern Britain: A History from the 1730s to the 1980s* (London: Routledge, 1989), 5–17.

3. Timothy Larsen, "Defining Evangelicalism," in *Advent of Evangelicalism: Exploring Historical Continuities*, ed. Michael A. G. Haykin and Kenneth J. Stewart (Nashville: B & H Academic, 2008), 21–36; cf. Larsen, "Defining and Locating Evangelicalism," in *The Cambridge Companion to Evangelicalism*, ed. Timothy Larsen and Daniel J. Treier (New York: Cambridge University Press, 2007), 1–2.

4. See especially Haykin and Stewart, *The Advent of Evangelicalism*.

5. Ibid., 417–32.

6. See especially Noll, *Evangelicalism*, 50–75; and Mark Hutchinson and John Wolffe, *A Short History of Global Evangelicalism* (Cambridge: Cambridge University Press, 2012), 26–32.

7. W. R. Ward, *The Protestant Evangelical Awakening* (Cambridge: Cambridge University Press, 1992), esp. chaps. 2 and 4; cf. Ian Randall, "Methodists and Moravians: The Shaping of Evangelical Spirituality," in *The Path of Holiness*, ed. J. W. Cunningham and David Rainey (Lexington, KY: Emeth Press, 2014), 43–59.

8. Leigh Eric Schmidt, *Holy Fairs: Scottish Communions and American Revivals in the Early Modern Period* (Princeton: Princeton University Press, 1989).

9. Ted A. Campbell, *The Religion of the Heart* (Eugene, OR: Wipf & Stock, 2000), 102.

10. Ian Randall, *What a Friend We Have in Jesus: The Evangelical Tradition* (London: Darton, Longman and Todd, 2005), 183–84.

11. This reflects the structure that Newton followed in organizing book 3 of his *Olney Hymns* (1779).

12. For an overview of the history of the term *spirituality*, see Philip Sheldrake, *Spirituality and History*, rev. ed. (Maryknoll, NY: Orbis Books, 1995), 42–44; and Walter Principe, "Toward Defining Spirituality," *Studies in Religion* 12, no. 2 (Spring 1983): 127–41.

13. Nathan Bailey, *An Universal Etymological English Dictionary*, 25th ed. (London: J. F. and C. Rivington, 1790), n.p.; and Thomas Sheriden, *A Complete Dictionary of the English Language*, 5th ed. (Philadelphia: William Young, 1789), n.p.

14. George Whitefield, *A Select Collection of Letters of the Late Reverend George Whitefield*, vol. 3 (London: Edward and Charles Dilly, 1772), letter to Mr.——, no. 1041, April 12, 1755, p. 89.

15. Newton, *Works*, letter 5 to Miss D——, April 13, 1776, 3:241–42.

16. Francis Asbury, *An Extract from the Journal of Francis Asbury...From August 7, 1771, to December 29, 1778*, vol. 1 (Philadelphia: Joseph Crukshank, 1792), 159, 203, 188.

17. Joseph Bellamy, *True Religion Delineated; or Experimental Religion* (Boston: S. Kneeland, 1750), 145.

18. Jonathan Edwards, *Sermon Discourses, 1743–1758*, ed. Wilson H. Kimnach (New Haven, CT: Yale University Press, 2006), 25:359.

19. Jonathan Edwards, *Religious Affections*, ed. Paul Ramsey, Works of Jonathan Edwards Online, vol. 2 (1754), 100, 104; cf. 83, 85, 86, 93, 94, etc., for variations on the nature and importance of true religion, http://edwards.yale.edu/archive?path=aHR0cDovL2Vkd2FyZHMueWFsZS5lZH UvY2dpLWJpbi9uZXdwaGlsby9zZWxlY3QucGw/d2plby4x.

20. Mary Fletcher, *Jesus, Altogether Lovely: Or, a Letter to Some of The Single Women in the Methodist Society*, 2nd ed. (Bristol: n.p, 1766), 10.

21. William Wilberforce, *Practical View of the Prevailing Religious System*, 4th ed. (London: T. Cadell, Jun. and W. Davies, 1797), 487, 491.

22. Samuel Hopkins, *The Works of Samuel Hopkins*, 3 vols. (Boston: Doctrinal Tract and Book Society, 1852), 1:249; cf. Bellamy, *True Religion Delineated*, 9–10; and Jonathan Edwards, *An Account of the Life of the Late Reverend David Brainerd* (Boston: D. Henchman, 1749), 283, etc.

23. Newton, *Works*, letter 3 to the Rev. Mr. B, January 21, 1766, 3:112.

24. Newton, *Works*, letter 6 to the Rev. Mr P, 2:251; cf. *Works*, letter 2 to a Nobleman, 2:8; letter 3 to Mr——, 3:57; letter 3 to Miss D——, 3:236.

25. George Whitefield, *Law Gospelized; or, an Address to All*

Christians Concerning Holiness of Heart and Life, in *Works*, vol. 4 (London: Edward and Charles Dilly, 1771), 376.

26. Ibid., 394, 423.

27. Edwards, *Religious Affections*, 452; cf. 275, 303, 451 for variations on experimental knowledge and religion.

28. Anne Dutton, *A Discourse upon Walking with God* (London: E. Gardner, 1735), 44, 89–90.

29. George Whitefield, *Sermons by the Late Rev. George Whitefield; Walking with God* (Glasgow: n.p.,1740), 8, 16–17.

30. Dieter Meyer, *Der Christozentrismus des späten Zinzendorf: Eine Studie zu dem Begriff 'Täglicher Umgang mit dem Heiland'* (Bern: Peter Lang, 1973).

31. John Fletcher, *Posthumous Pieces of the Reverend John William de la Flechere*, ed. Melville Horne (Philadelphia: Parry Hall, 1793), 267; cf. Asbury, *Journal*, 153.

32. Hester Ann Rogers, *A Short Account and Experience of Mrs. Hester Ann Rogers* (New York: John Totten, 1804), 105.

33. Asbury, *Journal*, 210; cf. 180, cf. 224, 238, 240, where Asbury speaks of "sweet communion" with God.

34. Ibid., 37; cf. 39, 85, 150 for variations on this theme.

35. Dutton, *Walking with God*, 13; cf. 100.

36. Newton, "On Communion with God," in *Works*, 1:274.

37. Samuel Hopkins, *Memoirs of the Life of Mrs. Sarah Osborn* (Worcester: Leonard Worcester, 1799), 33; cf. 29, 46, 126, 270, 279, etc.

38. Samuel Hopkins, *The Life and Character of the Late Reverend Jonathan Edwards* (Boston: S. Kneeland, 1765), 29.

39. Joann Ford Watson, ed., *Selected Spiritual Writings of Anne Dutton: Eighteenth-Century, British-Baptist, Woman Theologian*, vol. 1 (Macon, GA: Mercer University Press, 2003), 34.

40. Hempton, *The Church in the Long Eighteenth Century*, 148.

41. Personal communication with the author, January 31, 2015.

42. Richard W. Evans, "The Relations of George Whitefield and Howell Harris, Fathers of Calvinistic Methodism," *Church History* 30, no. 2 (June 1961): 179.

43. D. Bruce Hindmarsh, *John Newton and the English Evangelical Tradition* (Grand Rapids: Eerdmans, 1996, 2001), 250.

44. Watson, *Selected Spiritual Writings of Anne Dutton*, 1:xix. See p. 403 for the reproduction of her tombstone.

45. D. Bruce Hindmarsh, "Evangelical Epistolarity: Spiritual Experience in the Familiar Letters of the Early English Evangelicals," unpublished conference paper delivered at Regent College, Vancouver, July

2005, p. 7. I am most grateful to Hindmarsh for sharing his paper, and some of what follows is adapted from him. An expanded version of this paper will appear as D. Bruce Hindmarsh, "Evangelical Epistolarity: Spiritual Experience in the Familiar Letters of the Early Evangelicals," in *Studies in the Cultural History of Letter Writing*, ed. Linda C. Mitchell and Susan Green (San Marino, CA: Huntington Library Press, 2015).

46. Vicki T. Burton, *Spiritual Literacy in John Wesley's Methodism: Reading, Writing, and Speaking to Believe* (Waco, TX: Baylor University Press, 2008), esp. 175–196.

47. Watson, *Selected Spiritual Writings of Anne Dutton*, 3:254–55.

48. Ibid., 1:xxi.

49. Susan O'Brien, "A Transatlantic Community of Saints: The Great Awakening and the First Evangelical Network," *The American Historical Review* 91, no. 4 (Oct 1986): 825–26. For the Moravian letter days, see Colin Podmore, *The Moravian Church in England, 1728–1760* (Oxford: Clarendon, 1998), 44, 76, 82, 89, 123–244, 136.

50. Hindmarsh, "Evangelical Epistolarity," 9.

51. Susan M. Fitzmaurice, *The Familiar Letter in Early Modern English: A Pragmatic Approach* (Amsterdam: John Benjamins Publishing, 2002), 18. The definition is Erasmus's citation from Turpilius.

52. Hindmarsh, *John Newton and the English Evangelical Tradition*, 244, 245.

53. Elizabeth West Hopkins, ed., *Familiar Letters, Written By Mrs. Sarah Osborn, and Miss Susanna Anthony* (Newport, RI: Newport Mercury, 1807).

54. D. Bruce Hindmarsh, *The Evangelical Conversion Narrative: Spiritual Autobiography in Early Modern England* (Oxford: Oxford University Press, 2005), esp. 130–31.

55. G. R. Balleine, *A History of the Evangelical Party in the Church of England*, new ed. (London: Church Book Room Press, 1951), 84.

56. Susan O'Brien, "Eighteenth Century Publishing Networks in the First Years of Transatlantic Evangelicalism," in *Evangelicalism: Comparative Studies of Popular Protestantism in North America, the British Isles, and Beyond, 1700–1990*, ed. Mark A. Noll, David W. Bebbington, and George A. Rawlyk (New York: Oxford University Press, 1994), 46–47.

57. George M. Marsden, *Jonathan Edwards: A Life* (New Haven, CT: Yale University Press, 2003), 553n12.

58. My development resembles Marshall and Todd, who assert that hymns both explained biblical doctrine and cultivate "devotional sensibility." Madeleine Forell Marshall and Janet Todd, *English Congregational Hymns in the Eighteenth Century* (Lexington, KY: University Press of

Kentucky, 1982), 151–52; cf. J. R. Watson, *English Hymn: A Critical and Historical Study* (Oxford: Clarendon Press, 1997, 1999), 16.

59. John D. Witvliet, *Worship Seeking Understanding: Windows into Christian Practice* (Grand Rapids: Baker Academic, 2003), 231.

60. D. Bruce Hindmarsh, "'Amazing Grace': The History of a Hymn and a Cultural Icon," in *Sing Them Over Again to Me: Hymns and Hymnbooks in America*, ed. Mark A. Noll and Edith L. Blumhofer (Tuscaloosa, AL: University of Alabama Press, 2006), 5.

61. Witvliet, *Worship Seeking Understanding*, 232. For the importance of the actual singing of hymns and the use of tunes, see Mark A. Noll, "The Defining Role of Hymns in Early Evangelicalism," in *Wonderful Words of Life: Hymns in American Protestant History and Theology*, ed. Richard J. Mouw and Mark A. Noll (Grand Rapids: Eerdmans, 2004), 4–6.

62. See Witvliet, *Worship Seeking Understanding*, 231–49; Susan Tara Brown, *Singing and Imagination of Devotion: Vocal Aesthetics in Early English Protestant Culture* (Milton Keynes: Paternoster, 2008); and Candy Gunther Brown, "Singing Pilgrims: Hymn Narratives of a Pilgrim Community's Progress from This World to That Which Is to Come, 1830–1890," in Noll and Blumhofer, *Sing Them Over Again to Me*, 194–213. On the hermeneutics of hymnody, see Tom Schwanda, "'The Spirit Breathes upon the Word': The Formative Use of Scripture in the Hymns of William Cowper," *Journal of Spiritual Formation and Soul Care* 5 (Spring 2012): 86–87.

63. Stephen Marini, "Hymnody and Development of American Evangelism, 1737–1970," in *Singing the Lord's Song in a Strange Land: Hymnody in the History of North American Protestantism*, ed. Edith L. Blumhofer and Mark A. Noll (Tuscaloosa: University of Alabama Press, 2004), 11; cf. 14. While Marini's focus is on North American hymnody, the majority of hymns used by Americans in the eighteenth century were of British composition. Noll affirms the same concentration of hymn themes. Mark A. Noll, "The Defining Role of Hymns in Early Evangelicalism," 7–8.

64. Marini, "Hymnody and Development of American Evangelism," 10–17; cf. Marini, "Hymnody as History: Early Evangelical Hymns and the Recovery of American Popular Religion," *Church History* 71, no. 2 (June 2002): 273–306.

65. Mark Noll, "George Whitefield, Hymnody and Evangelical Spirituality," in *George Whitefield: Life, Context and Legacy*, David Ceri Jones and Geordan Hammond (Oxford: Oxford University Press, 2016), forthcoming.

66. Noll, "The Defining Role of Hymns in Early Evangelicalism," 4, 11–12.

67. Noll, *Evangelicalism*, 295–99.

68. Frank Whaling, *John and Charles Wesley: Selected Writings and Hymns* (New York: Paulist Press, 1981).

THE AUTHORS IN THIS VOLUME

1. See *BDEB; ODNB*; L. E. Elliott-Binns, *The Early Evangelicals: A Religious and Social Study* (London: Lutterworth Press, 1953); and G. C. B. Davies, *The Early Cornish Evangelicals 1735–1760* (London: SPCK, 1951).

2. See *ANB; BDE; BDEB*; Richard S. Newman, *Freedom's Prophet: Bishop Richard Allen, the AME Church, and the Black Founding Fathers* (New York: New York University Press, 2008); and Carol V. R. George, *Segregated Sabbaths: Richard Allen and the Emergence of Independent Black Churches 1760–1840* (New York: Oxford University Press, 1973).

3. See *ANB; BDE; BDEB*; D. G. Bell, *Henry Alline and Maritime Religion* (Ottawa: Canadian Historical Association, 1999); and George A. Rawlyk, ed., *Henry Alline: Selected Writings* (Mahwah, NJ: Paulist Press, 1987).

4. See Catherine A. Brekus, *Sarah Osborn's World: The Rise of Evangelical Christianity in Early America* (New Haven, CT: Yale University Press, 2013); and Ellen Butler Donovan, "Susanna Anthony," in *American Women Prose Writers to 1820*, ed. Carla Mulford (Detroit: Gale Research, 1999), 28–33.

5. See *ANB; BDE; BDEB*; John Wigger, *American Saint: Francis Asbury and the Methodists* (New York: Oxford University Press, 2009); and John H. Wigger, "Francis Asbury and American Methodism," in *The Oxford Handbook on Methodist Studies*, ed. William J. Abraham and James E. Kirby (New York: Oxford University Press, 2009), 51–66.

6. See *ANB; BDE; BDEB*; Stanley Grenz, *Isaac Backus: Puritan and Baptist* (Macon, GA: Mercer University Press, 1983); and William G. McLoughlin, *Isaac Backus and the American Pietistic Tradition* (Boston: Little, Brown and Company, 1967).

7. See *ANB; BDE; BDEB*; Oliver D. Crisp and Douglas A. Sweeney, eds., *After Jonathan Edwards: The Courses of the New England Theology* (Oxford: Oxford University Press, 2012); and Mark Valeri, *Law & Providence in Joseph Bellamy's New England* (New York: Oxford University Press, 1994).

8. See *BDE; BDEB; ODNB*; Brian Stanley, *The History of the Baptist Missionary Society 1792–1992* (London: T & T Clark, 1992); and Timothy

George, *Faithful Witness: The Life and Mission of William Carey* (Birmingham, AL: New Hope Publishing, 1991).

9. See *BDEB*; *ODNB*; Tom Schwanda, "Gazing at the Wounds: The Blood of the Lamb in the Hymns of John Cennick," in *Heart Religion: Evangelical Piety in England and Ireland, 1690–1850*, ed. John Coffey (Oxford: Oxford University Press, 2016); and Vernon Couillard, *The Theology of John Cennick* (Nazareth, PA: Moravian Historical Society, 1957).

10. See *BDE*; *BDEB*; *ODNB*; John Cromarty, "Grace in Affliction: William Cowper, Poet of Olney," part 1, *Reformed Theological Review* 58, no. 2 (August 1999): 65–79; and James King, *William Cowper: A Biography* (Durham, NC: Duke University Press, 1986).

11. See *ANB*; *BDE*; *BDEB*; Iain H. Murray, "Samuel Davies and the Meaning of 'Revival,'" in *Revival & Revivalism: The Making and Marring of American Evangelism 1750–1858* (Edinburgh: Banner of Truth, 1994), 3–31; and George W. Pilcher, *Samuel Davies: Apostle of Dissent in Colonial Virginia* (Knoxville, TN: University of Tennessee Press, 1971).

12. See *BDE*; *BDEB*; *ODNB*; Robert Strivens, "The Thought of Philip Doddridge in the Context of Early Eighteenth-Century Dissent," PhD diss., University of Stirling, 2011, dspace.stir.ac.uk/bitstream/1893/3636/1/PhD%20thesis%20-%20R.%20Strivens%20-%20Nov.%202011.pdf; Malcolm Deacon, *Philip Doddridge of Northampton 1702–1751* (Northampton: Northamptonshire Libraries, 1980); and Geoffrey Nuttall, ed., *Philip Doddridge 1702–1751: His Contribution to English Religion* (London: Independent Press, 1951).

13. See *BDEB*; *ODNB*; Michael Sciretti, "'Feed My Lambs': The Spiritual Direction Ministry of Calvinistic British Anne Dutton during the Early Years of the Evangelical Revival," PhD diss., Baylor University, 2009; https://beardocs.baylor.edu/xmlui/handle/2104/5535; and Joann Ford Watson, *Selected Spiritual Writings of Anne Dutton: Eighteenth-Century, British-Baptist, Woman Theologian*, vol. 1 (Macon, GA: Mercer University Press, 2003).

14. See *ANB*; *BDE*; *BDEB*; Kyle Strobel, *Formed for the Glory of God: Learning from the Spiritual Practices of Jonathan Edwards* (Downers Grove, IL: InterVarsity Press, 2013); George M. Marsden, *A Short Life of Jonathan Edwards* (Grand Rapids: Eedrmans, 2008); and George M. Marsden, *Jonathan Edwards: A Life* (New Haven, CT: Yale University Press, 2003).

15. See *ANB*; *BDEB*; *ODNB*; Vincent Carretta, *Equiano the African: Biography of a Self-Made Man* (Athens, GA: University of Georgia Press, 2005); and James Walvin, *An African's Life: The Life and Times of Olaudah Equiano, 1745–1797* (London: Cassell, 1998).

16. See *BDE*; *BDEB*; *ODNB*; George Lawton, *Shropshire Saint: A Study in the Ministry and Spirituality of Fletcher of Madeley* (Eugene, OR: Pickwick, 1960, 2014); Geordan Hammond and Peter S. Forsaith, eds., *Religion, Gender, and Industry: Exploring Church and Methodism in a Local Setting* (Eugene, OR: Pickwick, 2011); and Peter Streiff, *Reluctant Saint? A Theological Biography of Fletcher of Madeley*, trans. G. W. S. Knowles (Peterborough, UK: Epworth Press, 2001).

17. See *BDEB*; *ODNB*; Phyllis Mack, *Heart Religion in the British Enlightenment: Gender and Emotion in Early Methodism* (Cambridge: Cambridge University Press, 2008); and Candy G. Brown, "Prophetic Daughter: Mary Fletcher's Narrative and Women's Religious and Social Experiences in Eighteenth-Century British Methodism," in *Eighteenth-Century Women: Studies in Their Lives, Work, and Culture*, ed. Linda Troost, vol. 3 (New York: AMS Press, 2003), 77–98.

18. See *BDE*; *BDEB*; *ODNB*; Peter J. Morden, *The Life and Thought of Andrew Fuller* (Waynesboro, GA: Paternoster, 2015); and Michael A. G. Haykin, *The Armies of the Lamb: The Spirituality of Andrew Fuller* (Dundee, Ontario: Joshua Press, 2001).

19. See *BDEB*; *ODNB*; E. Wyn James, "Introduction to the Life and Works of Ann Griffiths," http://www.anngriffiths.cf.ac.uk/introduction.html; Dorian Llywelyn, "'The Fiery, Blessed Ann': Experience and Doctrine in the Spirituality of Ann Griffiths," *Spiritus* 9, no. 2 (Fall 2009): 217–40; and A. M. Allchin, *Songs to Her God: Spirituality of Ann Griffiths* (Cambridge, MA: Cowley Publications, 1987).

20. See *BDE*; *BDEB*; *ODNB*; Geraint Tudur, *Howell Harris: From Conversion to Separation 1735–1750* (Cardiff: University of Wales Press, 2000); and Geoffrey F. Nuttall, *Howel Harris 1714–1773: The Last Enthusiast* (Cardiff: University of Wales Press, 1965).

21. See *BDEB*; *ODNB*; Brian G. Najapfour, "The Piety of Joseph Hart as Reflected in His Life, Ministry, and Hymns," *Puritan Reformed Journal* 4, no. 1 (Jan 2012): 201–22; and Peter C. Rae, "Joseph Hart and His Hymns," *Scottish Bulletin of Evangelical Theology* 6, no. 1 (Spring 1988): 20–39.

22. See *BDE*; *BDEB*; *ODNB*; Edwin Welch, *Spiritual Pilgrim: A Reassessment of the Life of the Countess of Huntingdon* (Cardiff: University of Wales Press, 2013); and Boyd Stanley Schlenther, *Queen of the Methodists: The Countess of Huntingdon and the Eighteenth-Century Crisis of Faith and Society* (Durham, UK: Durham Academic Press, 1997).

23. See *ANB*; *BDE*; *BDEB*; Peter Jauhiainen, "Samuel Hopkins and Hopkinsianism," in Crisp and Sweeney, *After Jonathan Edwards*, 107–17, 279–82; and Joseph A. Conforti, *Samuel Hopkins & the New Divinity Movement* (Grand Rapids: Christian University Press, 1981).

24. See *ANB*; *BDEB*; Thomas S. Kidd, "Devereux Jarratt (1733– 1801)," *Encyclopedia Virginia* (Virginia Foundation for the Humanities, March 23, 2014), http://www.encyclopediavirginia.org/Jarratt_Devereux_1733-1801# start_entry; and Devereux Jarratt, *The Life of the Reverend Devereux Jarratt*, foreword by David L. Holmes (Cleveland: Pilgrim Press, 1995).

25. See Rhonda D. Hartweg, "All in Raptures: The Spirituality of Sarah Anderson Jones," *Methodist History* 45, no. 3 (April 2007): 166–79; and Cynthia Lynn Lyerly, *Methodism and the Southern Mind, 1770–1810* (New York: Oxford University Press, 1998).

26. Lyerly, *Methodism and the Southern Mind, 1770–1810*, 96–97.

27. See *BDEB*; *ODNB*; Keith E. Beebe, ed., *The McCulloch Examinations of the Cambuslang Revival (1742)*, vol. 1 (Woodbridge, Suffolk, UK: Boydell Press, 2013), esp. xi–lx; and Arthur Fawcett, *The Cambuslang Revival: The Scottish Evangelical Revival of the Eighteenth Century* (London: Banner of Truth, 1971).

28. See *BDE*; *BDEB*; *ODNB*; Karen Swallow Prior, *Fierce Convictions: The Extraordinary Life of Hannah More* (Nashville: Thomas Nelson, 2014); and Anne Stott, *Hannah More: The First Victorian* (New York: Oxford University Press, 2004).

29. See *BDE*; *BDEB*; *ODNB*; Jonathan Atkins, *John Newton: From Disgrace to Amazing Grace* (Wheaton, IL: Crossway, 2007); D. Bruce Hindmarsh, *John Newton and the English Evangelical Tradition* (Grand Rapids: Eerdmans, 1996, 2001); and John Pollock, *Amazing Grace: John Newton's Story* (San Francisco: Harper & Row, 1981).

30. See *ANB*; *BDEB*; Joanna Brooks, ed., *The Collected Writings of Samson Occom, Mohegan* (New York: Oxford University Press, 2006); and Margaret C. Szasz, "Samson Occom: Mohegan as Spiritual Intermediary," in *Between Indian and White Worlds: The Cultural Broker*, ed. Margaret C. Szasz (Norman and London: University of Oklahoma Press, 1994), 61–78, 312–14.

31. See *ANB*; Catherine A. Brekus, *Sarah Osborn's World: The Rise of Evangelical Christianity in Early America* (New Haven, CT: Yale University Press, 2013); and Charles Hambrick-Stowe, "The Spiritual Pilgrimage of Sarah Osborn (1714–1796)," *Church History* 61, no. 4 (Dec 1992): 408–21.

32. See *BDEB*; *ODNB*; Michael A. G. Haykin, *Joy Unspeakable and Full of Glory: The Piety of Samuel and Sarah Pearce* (Kitchener, Ontario: Joshua Press, 2012); and S. Pearce Carey, *Samuel Pearce: The Baptist Brainerd*, 3rd. ed. (London: Carey Press, n.d.).

33. See *BDEB*; *ODNB*; Phyllis Mack, *Heart Religion in the British Enlightenment* (Cambridge: Cambridge University Press, 2008); and Vicki

Tolar Burton, *Spiritual Literacy in John Wesley's Methodism* (Waco, TX: Baylor University Press, 2008).

34. See *BDEB*; *ODNB*; Tim Shenton, *An Iron Pillar: The Life and Times of William Romaine* (Darlington, UK: Evangelical Press, 2004); and William Romaine, *The Life, Walk and Triumph of Faith* (Cambridge & London: James Clarke, 1970), v–xxiv.

35. See *BDE*; *BDEB*; *ODNB*; Arthur Pollard, "Angelical Evangelical Views of the Bible, 1800–1850," *Churchman* 74 (September 1960): 166–74; and A. C. Downer, *Thomas Scott the Commentator* (London: Chas. J. Thynne, 1906).

36. See *ANB*; *BDEB*; Craig D. Atwood, "Spangenberg: A Radical Pietist in Colonial America," *Journal of Moravian History* 4 (2008): 7–27; and David A. Schattschneider, "The Missionary Theologies of Zinzendorf and Spangenberg," *Transaction of the Moravian Historical Society* 22, no. 3 (1775): 213–33.

37. See *BDEB*; *ODNB*; Julia B. Griffin, ed., *Nonconformist Women Writers, 1720–1840*, vol. 2 (London: Pickering & Chatto, 2011), esp. 1–29; and Cynthia Y. Aalders, *To Express the Ineffable: The Hymns and Spirituality of Anne Steele* (Milton Keynes: Paternoster, 2008).

38. See *ANB*; *BDE*; *BDEB*; C. N. Wilborn, "Gilbert Tennent: Pietist, Preacher, and Presbyterian," in *Colonial Presbyterianism: Old Faith in a New Land*, ed. S. Don Fortson III (Eugene, OR: Pickwick, 2007), 135–55; and Milton J. Coalter Jr., *Gilbert Tennent, Son of Thunder* (Westport, CT: Greenwood Press, 1986).

39. See *BDEB*; *ODNB*; George Lawton, *Within the Rock of Ages: The Life and Work of Augustus Montague Toplady* (Cambridge: J. Clarke & Co., 1983); and Paul E. G. Cook, *Augustus Toplady: The Saintly Sinner* (London: Evangelical Library, 1978).

40. See *BDE*; *BDEB*; *ODNB*; Bill Reimer, "The Spirituality of Henry Venn," *Churchman* 114, no. 4 (2000): 300–15; and Wilbert R. Schenk, "'T'owd Trumpet': Venn of Huddersfield and Yelling," *Churchman* 93, no. 1 (1979): 39–54.

41. See *BDEB*; Mack, *Heart Religion in the British Enlightenment*; and Richard Green, *Thomas Walsh: Wesley's Typical Helper* (London: Charles H. Kelly, 1906).

42. See *BDE*; *ODNB*; J. R. Watson, "The Hymns of Isaac Watts and the Tradition of Dissent," in *Dissenting Praise: Religious Dissent and the Hymns in England and Wales*, ed. Isabel Rivers and David L. Wykes (Oxford: Oxford University Press, 2011), 33–67; and Harry Escott, *Isaac Watts, Hymnographer* (London: Independent Press, 1962).

43. See *ANB*; *BDEB*; *ODNB*; Vincent Carretta, *Phillis Wheatley: Biography of a Genius in Bondage* (Athens and London, GA: University of Georgia Press, 2011); and Elizabeth J. West, *African Spirituality in Black Women's Fiction* (Lanham, MD: Lexington Books, 2011), esp. 27–42.

44. See *ANB*; *BDE*; *BDEB*; *ODNB*; Thomas S. Kidd, *George Whitefield: America's Founding Spiritual Father* (New Haven, CT: Yale University Press, 2014); Michael A. G. Haykin, *The Revived Puritan: The Spirituality of George Whitefield* (Dundas, Ontario: Joshua Press, 2000); and Frank Lambert, *"Pedlar in Divinity": George Whitefield and the Transatlantic Revivals 1737–1770* (Princeton: Princeton University Press, 1994).

45. See *BDE*; *BDEB*; *ODNB*; Stephen Tompkins, *William Wilberforce: A Biography* (Grand Rapids: Eerdmans, 2007); and Murray A. Pura, *Vital Christianity: The Life and Spirituality of William Wilberforce* (Fearn, Tain, Ross-shire, Scotland: Christian Focus, 2004).

46. See *BDE*; *BDEB*; *ODNB*; Eifion Evans, *Bread of Heaven: The Life and Work of William Williams, Pantycelyn* (Bryntirion, Wales: Bryntirion Press, 2010); and Bruce Hindmarsh, "'End of Faith as Its Beginning': Models of Spiritual Progress in Early Evangelical Devotional Hymns," *Spiritus* 10, no. 1 (spring 2010): 1–21.

47. See *ANB*; *BDEB*; L. Gordon Tait, *The Piety of John Witherspoon: Pew, Pulpit, and Public Forum* (Louisville: Geneva Press, 2001); Richard B. Sher, "Witherspoon's *Dominion of Providence* and the Scottish Jeremiad Tradition," in *Scotland & America in the Age of the Enlightenment*, ed. Richard B. Sher and Jeffrey R. Smitten (Princeton: Princeton University Press, 1990), 46–64.

48. See *ANB*; *BDE*; *BDEB*; Peter Vogt, "'Honor to the Side': The Adoration of the Side Wound of Jesus in Eighteenth-Century Moravian Piety," *Journal of Moravian History* 7 (2009): 83–106; and Craig D. Atwood, *Community of the Cross: Moravian Piety in Colonial Bethlehem* (University Park, PA: Pennsylvania State University Press, 2004).

Part 1

1. From Isaac Watts, *Hymns and Spiritual Songs* (London: J. Humfreys, 1707), book 3, hymn 7, p. 189.

2. From Gilbert Tennent, *The Danger of an Unconverted Ministry* (Philadelphia: B. Franklin, 1740), 3–16, 18–19, 21–22.

3. From J[ohn] C[ennick], *Sacred Hymns for the Children of God* (London: John Lewis, 1742), hymn 55, pp. 66–67.

4. From Craig D. Atwood, *Community of the Cross: Moravian Piety in Colonial Bethlehem*, trans. Craig D. Atwood (University Park, PA: Pennsylvania State University Press, 2004), 253–56. Used by permission.

5. From Joseph Hart, *Hymns Composed on Various Subjects* (London: J. Everingham, 1759), hymn 100, pp. 133–34.

6. From Mary Fletcher, *Jesus, Altogether Lovely: Or, a Letter to Some of the Single Women in the Methodist Society*, 2nd ed. (Bristol: n.p, 1766), 2–7, 9–10, 12.

7. From Rev. Samson Occom, an Indian Minister, *Extracts of Several Sermons Preached Extempore...* (Bristol: n.p, 1766), 15–18.

8. From Occom, *Extracts of Several Sermons*, 25–28.

9. From Thomas Gibbons, *Hymns Adapted to Divine Worship* (London: J. Buckland, J. Johnson, and J. Payne, 1769), book 1, hymn 59, pp. 67–68.

10. From Augustus Toplady, *Psalms and Hymns for Public and Private Worship* (London: E. and C. Dilly, 1776), hymn 337, pp. 308–9.

11. From John Newton, *Olney Hymns* (London: W. Oliver, 1779), book 1, hymn 41, p. 47.

12. From Theodosia [Anne Steele], *Poems on Subjects Chiefly Devotional*, new ed., (Bristol: W. Pine, 1780), vol. 1, pp. 17–18.

13. From Henry Alline, *The Life and Journal of the Rev. Mr. Henry Alline* (Boston: Gilbert & Dean, 1806), 31–37.

14. From Richard Allen, *The Life, Experiences, and Gospel Labours of the Rt. Rev. Richard Allen* (Philadelphia: Martin & Boden, 1833), 5–10. Permission from The Library Company of Philadelphia to use this selection is gratefully acknowledged.

15. From Aaron C. H. Seymour, ed., *The Life and Times of Selina Countess of Huntingdon*, vol. 2 (London: William Edward Painter, 1839), 407–9.

Part 2

1. From Isaac Watts, *Sermons on Various Subjects, Divine and Moral with a Sacred Hymn Suited to Each Subject*, vol. 3 (London: E. Matthews, 1729), 463–64.

2. From George Whitefield, *Discourses on the Following Subjects...* (London: Charles Whitefield, 1739), sermon no. 12 (pagination begins with each sermon), 3–11, 15–16, 18–19, 21–26.

3. From Jonathan Edwards, *An Account of the Life of the Late Reverend Mr. David Brainerd* (Boston: D. Henchman, 1749), 276–79, 281–87.

4. From William Williams, *Hosannah to the Son of David; or Hymns of Praise to God for Our Glorious Redemption by Christ* (Bristol: John Grabham, 1759), hymn 27, p. 24.

5. From Samuel Davies, *Sermons on the Most Useful and Important Subjects, Adapted to the Family and Closet*, vol. 1 (London: J. Buckland and J. Payne, 1766), sermon no. 9, pp. 270–83.

6. From William Cowper in John Newton, *Olney Hymns* (London: W. Oliver, 1779), book 2, hymn 62.

7. From Theodosia [Anne Steele], *Poems on Subjects Chiefly Devotional*, new ed., (Bristol: W. Pine, 1780), vol. 1, pp. 144–46.

8. From Howell Harris, *A Brief Account of His Life* (Trevecka: n.p, 1791), 120–22.

9. Ibid., 188–89.

10. From William Romaine, *Triumph Faith Romaine*, 2nd ed. (London: T. Bensley, 1795), 254–64, 266–67, 270–85.

11. From John Newton, "Divine Guidance," letter 28, in *Letters and Sermons*, vol. 1. (Edinburgh, 1798) 288–95.

12. From Ann Griffiths, *Homage to Ann Griffiths*, ed. James Coutts (Penarth: Church in Wales Publications, 1976; orig. composed c. 1802–1804), hymn 7, www.anngriffiths.cardiff.ac.uk (used with permission).

13. From Devereux Jarratt, *The Life of the Reverend Devereux Jarratt* (Baltimore: Warner & Hanna, 1806), 217–21.

Part 3

1. From George Whitefield, *Discourses on the Following Subjects...* (London: Charles Whitefield, 1739), sermon 8, pp. 3–19 (each sermon is numbered individually).

2. From James Morgan, ed., *The Life and Death of Mr. Thomas Walsh* (London: H. Cock, 1762), 213–21.

3. From Henry Venn, *The Complete Duty of Man: Or a System of Doctrinal & Practical Christianity* (London: J. Newberry, 1763), 486–95, 499.

4. From Phillis Wheatley, *Poems on Various Subjects, Religious and Moral* (London: A. Bell, 1773), 22–24.

5. From Augustus Toplady, *Gospel Magazine* (October 1774), 449–50.

6. From Theodosia [Anne Steele], *Poems on Subjects Chiefly Devotional*, new ed., vol. 1 (Bristol: W. Pine, 1780), 58–60.

7. From Thomas Scott, *The Holy Bible Containing the Old and New Testaments with Original Notes and Practical Observations*, vol. 4 (London: Bellamy and Robarts, 1792), unpaginated.

8. From Samuel Hopkins, *The System of Doctrines, Contained in Divine Revelation, Explained and Defended*, 2 vols. (Boston: Isaiah Thomas and Ebenezer T. Andrews, 1793), 1:43–52.

9. From Thomas Adam, *Private Thoughts on Religion*, 2nd ed. (York: G. Peacock, 1795), 41–49.

10. From John Newton to the Rev. Mr. B——, Oct. 1778 in *Works*, 3:273–75.

11. From John Ryland Jr., *The Work of Faith, the Labour of Love, and the Patience of Hope Illustrated in the Life and Death of the Rev. Andrew Fuller*, 2nd ed. (London: Button and Son, 1818), 129–30.

Part 4

1. From John Cennick, *Sacred Hymns for the Children of God*, 2nd ed. (London: B. Milles, 1741), hymns 130 and 131, p. 198.

2. From Anne Dutton, *Thoughts on the Lord's Supper: Written at the Request of a Friend, and Address'd by Letter to the Tender Lambs of Christ* (London: J. Hart, 1748), 25–34, 36.

3. From Philip Doddridge's *Rise and Progress of the Soul*, 6th ed. (Boston: Rogers and Fowle, 1749), 149–60.

4. From Samuel Hopkins, *The Life and Character of the Late Reverend Mr. Jonathan Edwards* (Boston: S. Kneeland, 1765), 25–32, 34–38.

5. From Joseph Hart, *Hymns Composed on Various Subjects*, 5th ed. (London: M. Lewis, 1765), hymn 76, p. 214.

6. From Isaac Backus, *Family Prayer Not to Be Neglected* (Newport, RI: Samuel Hall, 1766), 2, 20–26.

7. From John Witherspoon, *Dominion of Providence over the Passions of Men* (Philadelphia: R. Aitken, 1776), 29–36, 39–42.

8. From Phillis Wheatley, *Poems on Various Subjects, Religious and Moral* (London: A. Bell, 1773), 90–91.

9. From James Robe, *Narratives of the Extraordinary Work of the Spirit of God at Cambuslang, Kilsyth, etc. Begun in 1742* (Glasgow: David Niven, 1790), 33–38.

10. From Francis Asbury, *An Extract from the Journal of Francis Asbury*, vol. 1 (Philadelphia: Joseph Crukshank, 1792), August 7, 1771, to December 29, 1778, pp. 33–38, 225–28.

11. From Melvill Horne, ed., *Posthumous Pieces of the Reverend John William de la Flechere* [i.e., Fletcher] (Philadelphia: Parry Hall, 1793), 118–21.

12. From ibid., 339–45.

Part 5

1. From Anne Dutton, *Letters on Spiritual Subjects, and Diverse Occasions; Sent to Relations and Friends* (London: J. Hart, 1748), 101–3.

2. From George Whitefield, sermon 1, "Christ the Believer's Husband," in *Five Sermons* (Philadelphia: B. Franklin, 1746), 1–2, 5–21.

3. From Joseph Bellamy, *True Religion Delineated; or Experimental Religion* (Boston: S. Kneeland, 1750), 7–14.

4. From Jonathan Edwards, sermon 17, Sept. 1733, "A True Christian's Life, a Journey towards Heaven," in *The Life and Character of Jonathan Edwards*, ed. Samuel Hopkins (Boston: S. Kneeland, 1765), 253–66.

5. From William Williams, *Gloria in Excelsis: or Hymns of Praise to God and the Lamb*, printed with *Hosannah to the Son of David* (Carmarthen, Wales: John Ross, 1772), hymn 72, p. 73.

6. From Augustus Toplady, *The Gospel Magazine* (October 1774): 449.

7. From John Newton, *Olney Hymns* (London: W. Oliver, 1779), book 1, hymn 3, p. 7.

8. From ibid., book 3, hymn 15, p. 269.

9. From Mrs. H. A. Rogers, *Spiritual Letters* (Bristol, UK: R. Edwards, 1796), 13–14.

10. From Samuel Hopkins, ed., *The Life and Character of Miss Susanna Anthony* (Worcester: Leonard Worcester, 1796), 77–80, 95–99.

11. From Samuel Hopkins, ed., *Memoirs of the Life of Mrs. Sarah Osborn* (Worcester: Leonard Worcester, 1799), 84–87, 156–58, 165–67.

12. From *Homage to Ann Griffiths*, ed. James Coutts (Penarth: Church in Wales Publications, 1976; originally composed c. 1802–4), hymn 14, http://www.anngriffiths.cardiff.ac.uk/hymns.html#vi (used with permission).

13. From Jeremiah Minter, ed., *Devout Letters: Or, Letters Spiritual and Friendly* (Alexandria, VA: Samuel Snowden, 1804), 4–14.

Part 6

1. From Isaac Watts, *The Psalms of David* (London: J. Clark, 1719), 186–87.

2. From John Cennick, *Sacred Hymns for the Use of Religious Societies*, part 2 (Bristol, UK: Felix Farley, 1743), hymn 64, pp. 81–83.

3. From Joseph Hart, *Hymns Composed on Various Subjects*, 5th ed. (London: M. Lewis, 1765), hymn 78, pp. 216–17 (supplement).

4. From Hannah More, *An Estimate of the Religion of the Fashionable World*, 3rd ed. (Dublin: P. Wogan, etc., 1791), 179–97.

5. From William Williams, *Gloria in Excelsis or Hymns of Praise to God and the Lamb* (Carmarthen: John Ross, 1772), hymn 37, pp. 33–34.

6. From Samuel Hopkins, *A Dialogue, Concerning the Slavery of the Africans; Showing it to be the Duty and Interest of the American Colonies to emancipate all their African Slaves* (Norwich, UK: Judah P. Spooner, 1776), 14–22.

7. From Jonathan Edwards, *Practical Sermons*, sermon 30 (Edinburgh: M. Gray, 1788), 353–62.

8. From August G. Spangenberg, *An Account of the Manner in Which the…United Brethren Preach the Gospel, and Carry on Their Missions among the Heathen* (London: H. Trapp, 1788), 33–34, 36–38, 40–42, 45–46, 48, 50–51.

9. From Olaudah Equiano, *The Interesting Narrative of the Life of Olaudah Equiano, or Gustavus Vassa, the African*, vol. 2, 2nd ed. (London: T. Wilkins, 1789), 168–75, 180–87, 190–91.

10. From William Carey, *An Enquiry into the Obligations of Christians, to Use Means for the Conversion of the Heathens* (Leicester, UK: Ann Ireland, 1792), 67–72, 74–75.

11. From John Newton, *Letters to a Wife*, vol. 2 (London: J. Johnson, 1793), 133–36.

12. From ibid., 138–39.

13. From William Wilberforce, *A Practical View of the Prevailing Religious System of Professed Christians in the Higher and Middle Classes in this Country Contrasted with Real Christianity*, 4th ed. (London: T. Cadell, 1797), 396–400, 402–9, 485–86.

14. From John Rippon, ed., *Baptist Annual Register*, vol. 3 (London: n.p., 1798–1801), 433–38.

General Bibliography

This bibliography does not repeat sources listed previously in the book except for the most significant items. For sources on the authors of this volume, please consult the chapter on the authors. For information on letter writing and hymns, see the introduction.

Abraham, William J., and James E. Kirby, eds. *The Oxford Handbook of Methodist Studies*. Oxford: Oxford University Press, 2009.

Bebbington, David W. *Evangelicalism in Modern Britain: A History from 1730s to the 1980s*. London: Unwin Hyman, 1989.

Brown, Stewart, and Timothy Tackett, eds. *Enlightenment, Reawakening and Revolution 1660–1815*. Vol. 7 of *The Cambridge History of Christianity*. Cambridge: Cambridge University Press, 2006.

Crawford, Michael J. *Seasons of Grace: Colonial New England's Revival Tradition in Its British Context*. New York: Oxford University Press, 1991.

Gibson, William, Peter Forsaith, and Martin Wellings, eds. *The Ashgate Research Companion to World Methodism*. Farnham, UK: Ashgate, 2013.

Hempton, David. *The Church in the Long Eighteenth Century*. London: I. B. Tauris, 2013.

Hindmarsh, D. Bruce. *The Evangelical Conversion Narrative: Spiritual Autobiography in Early Modern England*. Oxford: Oxford University Press, 2005.

Jeffrey, David Lyle. *A Burning and Shining Light: English Spirituality in the Age of Wesley*. Grand Rapids: Eerdmans, 1987.

Jones, David Ceri, Boyd Stanley Schlenther, and Eryn Many White. *The Elect Methodists: Calvinistic Methodism in England and Wales 1735–1811*. Cardiff: University of Wales Press, 2012.

Kidd, Thomas S. *The Great Awakening: The Roots of Evangelical Christianity in Colonial America*. New Haven, CT: Yale University Press, 2009.

Mack, Phyllis. *Heart Religion in the British Enlightenment: Gender and Emotion in Early Methodism*. New York: Cambridge University Press, 2008.

Noll, Mark A. *The Rise of Evangelicalism: The Age of Edwards, Whitefield and the Wesleys*. Downers Grove, IL: InterVarsity Press, 2003.

Rack, Henry D. *Reasonable Enthusiast: John Wesley and the Rise of Methodism*, 3rd ed. Peterborough, UK: Epworth Press, 2002.

Randall, Ian. *What a Friend We Have in Jesus: The Evangelical Tradition*. London: Darton, Longman and Todd, 2005.

Sweeney, Douglas A. *The American Evangelical Story: A History of the Movement*. Grand Rapids: Baker Academic, 2005.

Ward, R. W. *Early Evangelicalism: A Global Intellectual History, 1670–1789*. Cambridge: Cambridge University Press, 2006.

———. *The Protestant Evangelical Awakening*. Cambridge: Cambridge University Press, 1992.

Wolffe, John. *The Expansion of Evangelicalism: The Age of Wilberforce, More, Chalmers and Finney*. Downers Grove, IL: InterVarsity Press, 2007.

Yeager, Jonathan M. *Early Evangelicalism: A Reader*. New York: Oxford University Press, 2013.

INDEX

Advance Praise for

Emergence of Evangelical Spirituality
In the Age of Edwards, Newton, and Whitefield

"Until recently there has been a relatively small standard corpus of evangelical texts available for those interested in the Christian tradition of evangelicalism, and the depth and richness of evangelical writing has been largely unknown. This new reader in the classic age of evangelical witness, the eighteenth century, is therefore very welcome indeed. With a wide range of texts and incisive introductions, Tom Schwanda has provided a tremendous resource for both new students of this movement and established scholars. Ideal for classroom usage as a textbook, it could also be profitably used as a personal devotional. Highly recommended!"

—Michael A. G. Haykin, professor of
Church History and Biblical Spirituality,
The Southern Baptist Theological Seminary

"This compelling collection of evangelical writings showcases an intensely personal piety inspired by a vision of God's grace shown to humanity in the person of Jesus Christ. These selections show the lyrical beauty of many evangelical contributions and the pervasive influence of scriptural images, themes, and phrases. This volume is an exceptionally instructive resource for evangelical Christians eager to understand their heritage, and for others who seek to understand evangelical Christianity empathetically."

—John D. Witvliet, Calvin College and
Calvin Theological Seminary

Advance Praise for

Emergence of Evangelical Spirituality
In the Age of Edwards, Newton, and Whitefield

"In displaying the richness, variety, and deep texture of the evangelical movement's beginnings, *The Emergence of Evangelical Spirituality* is as interesting and delightful as the age it examines. The volume's selection of primary texts, both major and minor, along with Schwanda's insightful organization and contextualization of the writers and their works, is a gift to church history and evangelical scholarship."

—Karen Swallow Prior, Liberty University, author of
Fierce Convictions: The Extraordinary Life of
Hannah More: Poet, Reformer, Abolitionist

"This is a wonderful collection of crucial primary sources from a diverse cross-section of eighteenth-century evangelicals. Judiciously selected and reliably introduced, it offers the best introduction to early evangelical piety that has ever been produced—must reading for anyone interested in the history of Christianity."

—Douglas A. Sweeney, Trinity Evangelical
Divinity School